PENGUIN CLASSICS

THE COMEDIES

ADVISORY EDITOR: BETTY RADICE

TERENCE (c. 186–159 B.C.) was born at Carthage of Libyan parentage, and was brought to Rome as a young slave. According to Roman tradition his talents and good looks won him an education, manumission, and entry to a patrician literary circle, with whose encouragement he wrote six Latin plays, modelled on Greek New Comedy, all of which survive. Only one, *The Eunuch*, was a popular success in his lifetime, but he was read and admired in Roman times and throughout the Middle Ages, and became the main influence on Renaissance comedy.

BETTY RADICE read classics at Oxford, then married and, in the intervals of bringing up a family, tutored in classics, philosophy and English. She became joint editor of the Penguin Classics in 1964. As well as editing the translation of Livy's *The War with Hannibal* she translated Livy's *Rome and Italy*, Pliny's Letters, *The Letters of Abelard and Heloise* and Erasmus's *Praise of Folly*, and also wrote the introduction to Horace's *Complete Odes and Epodes*, all for the Penguin Classics. She also edited Edward Gibbon's *Memoirs of My Life* for the Penguin English Library, and edited and annotated her translation of the younger Pliny's works for the Loeb Library of Classics and translated from Renaissance Latin, Greek and Italian for the Officina Bodoni of Verona. She collaborated as a translator in the Collected Works of Erasmus, and was the author of the Penguin Reference Book *Who's Who in the Ancient World*. Betty Radice was an honorary fellow of St Hilda's College, Oxford, and a vice-president of the Classical Association. Betty Radice died in 1985.

TERENCE

THE COMEDIES

TRANSLATED WITH AN INTRODUCTION
BY BETTY RADICE

PENGUIN BOOKS

PENGUIN BOOKS

Published by the Penguin Group
27 Wrights Lane, London w8 5tz, England
Viking Penguin Inc., 40 West 23rd Street, New York, New York 10010, USA
Penguin Books Australia Ltd, Ringwood, Victoria, Australia
Penguin Books Canada Ltd, 2801 John Street, Markham, Ontario, Canada l3r 1b4
Penguin Books (NZ) Ltd, 182 190 Wairau Road, Auckland 10, New Zealand

Penguin Books Ltd, Registered Offices: Harmondsworth, Middlesex, England

The Brothers and Other Plays first published in Penguin Classics 1965
Phormio and Other Plays first published in Penguin Classics 1967
First published together in this edition 1976
Reprinted 1979, 1982, 1984, 1986, 1987, 1988

Translation copyright © Betty Radice, 1965, 1967, 1976
All rights reserved

Application for permission to perform these plays should be
made to the League of Dramatists, 84 Drayton Gardens,
London sw10 9sd

Made and printed in Great Britain by
Richard Clay Ltd, Bungay, Suffolk
Set in Monotype Bembo

CONTENTS

C'est une tâche bien hardie que la traduction de Térence: tout ce que la langue latine a de délicatesse est dans ce poète.

DIDEROT

PREFACE AND ACKNOWLEDGEMENTS

THIS translation, first published by Penguin Books in 1965 and 1967, is based on the Oxford Classical Text of B. Kauer and W. M. Lindsay (1958 edition) and aided by the French Budé text of J. Marouzeau (1947–9) and the special editions and publications on Terence listed in the bibliography. I should like to thank Professor G. P. Goold, Dr J. G. Landels and Professor O. Skutsch for advice from which this revised edition has greatly benefited, and to say again how much I owe to Mr E. F. Watling, whose expertise as a translator of Plautus and practical experience of stage production were always made available when I needed help. I am also grateful to all the people who actively pleaded for the return of Terence to the Penguin Classics, and so helped to make a reissue possible.

November 1975   B.R.

INTRODUCTION

COMEDY is a more intellectual and sophisticated art than tragedy, and on the stage it depends for its effects on verbal exchange. Its characters must be wholly articulate, and if it is to succeed it needs an equally articulate, civilized audience, who can respond not with hilarity so much as with a delighted amusement. Audiences of this kind evidently existed for comedy to flourish in fifth-century Athens, in Hellenistic Greece, in Elizabethan and Restoration England, in the Paris of Louis XIV, eighteenth-century Venice, and in Edwardian London, but Rome of the second century B.C. gave small encouragement to a young man who had all the requisites to make him a great writer of comedy. Terence died young, and could be judged a failure in his own day, but the originality he showed in his treatment of his Greek models had a lasting influence on the history of western drama. The six plays of Terence are his complete works and were preserved in a single corpus from an early date. Attached to each play is an authentic author's prologue, a personal apologia of unique literary interest, and several of the medieval MSS. are headed by a production notice giving the date of the play's composition and details of the first production. There is also a Life of Terence[1] ascribed to Suetonius with an addition by the grammarian Aelius Donatus, preserved with Donatus's very full commentaries on the plays. It would seem that a lot is known about Terence and his work and no early author was more quoted by poets and prose-writers alike; yet he remains one of the most problematic of ancient authors, and there were conflicting accounts of him within a century of his death.

1. See Appendix A, p. 389.

Tradition says that Publius Terentius Afer was born in Carthage in 185 B.C. (some say 195) and came to Rome as the slave of the senator Terentius Lucanus, who gave him a good education and his freedom. He was slight, dark, and good looking, and his abilities won him entry into the 'Scipionic circle' – the group of young intellectuals and philhellenes gathered round Scipio Aemilianus. He made a good impression on the elderly dramatist Caecilius, to whom he read his first play, and so he embarked on his own stormy career. Though he won instant success with *The Eunuch*, *The Mother-in-Law* failed twice and only succeeded at the third attempt through the loyal efforts of his actor–producer, Lucius Ambivius Turpio. His association with the Scipios led to slanderous rumours that his noble friends had helped him, or even written his plays for him, and he was frequently accused by an old playwright, Luscius Lanuvinus, of plagiarizing earlier Latin plays and tampering with the Greek models he professed to be translating. Soon after 160, in his twenty-fifth year, he left Italy in search of more Greek comedies for adaptation, met with some accident in Greece or Asia Minor, and never returned. By the time Suetonius wrote his *Life* at the end of the first century A.D. there were at least four versions of his death and no agreement on whether he died rich or poor.

Amid so many conflicting views it is not surprising that some modern scholars have argued that the *Life* is no more than invention based on the few facts that emerge from the plays themselves, the prologues, and the production notices. For example, the connection with the Scipio circle could have been conjectured simply from the statement in the production notice to *The Brothers* that it was first performed at the funeral games of Aemilius Paullus, Scipio's father before adoption. Even the surname Afer is no proof that Terence was of north African origin; witness the distinguished orator, Gnaeus

Domitius Afer. Terence has been conjectured to be a Semitic Carthaginian, a Berber, or the son of one of Hannibal's captives from South Italy, and so racially either Greek or Italian. What is clear from the multiplicity of opinion quoted by Suetonius is that the Romans themselves were always puzzled by Terence's brief career and sudden end.

There is no doubt that Terence did have 'noble friends', for they are mentioned in the prologues, where he glories in his association with 'men whose services in war, in peace, and in your private affairs are given at the right moment, without ostentation, to be available for each one of you' (*The Brothers*, 19–21). The suggestion that they helped him with his plays lingered on, to be referred to by Cicero in a letter to Atticus (7.3.10) and much later by Quintilian, though with reserve (*Institutio Oratoris*, 10.1.99). But if Scipio or any of his friends wrote the plays, it is surprising that no more of the same type were written after Terence's early death. Internal evidence from the plays themselves points to more indirect influence. The lively farcical element, the colourful word-play, the earthy vulgarity, the song and dance which made Plautus deservedly popular have gone; instead Terence offers subtlety of plot, development and interplay of character, and economy of dialogue. He needs an attentive, educated audience ready to appreciate the finer points of a Hellenistic comedy presented in the most lucid and elegantly simple Latin which had yet been written. *The Mother-in-Law* is not a play likely to succeed on a large open-air stage before a crowd expecting the rollicking gaiety of Plautus, and consequently only too ready to slip off to see the gladiators and tight-rope walkers; but is it too fanciful to imagine its being performed in the house of a cultivated aristocrat to an invited audience of his friends?

Publius Cornelius Scipio Aemilianus Africanus Numantinus Minor was the son of Lucius Aemilius Paullus Macedonicus,

the victor over the Greeks at the battle of Pydna which ended
the Third Macedonian War. As part of the spoils of war Paullus took the Greek library of King Perseus of Macedon and
sent it home to Rome. Scipio had fought at Pydna and toured
Greece with his father; his early education on Greek lines is
described by Plutarch in his Life of Aemilius Paullus. Before
168 he was adopted by his cousin, the elder son of Scipio Africanus Major, himself a writer and philhellene, and in Rome he
headed a group of young men with literary and philosophic
interests, notably Lucius Furius Philus, Gaius Lucilius, the
satirist admired by Horace, and Gaius Laelius, surnamed
Sapiens for his Stoic inclinations. The philosopher Panaetius
of Rhodes (after he came to Rome about 145) and the Greek
historian Polybius were among their friends. Laelius and
Scipio both appear in Cicero's *de Senectute*, and his *de Amicitia*
commemorates their friendship. Furius Philus joins them in
the discussion which forms the framework of *de Republica*, and
this takes place in Scipio's garden in the winter sunshine. In *de
Oratore* (2.6.22) there is the well-known account of Laelius and
Scipio on a carefree holiday, picking up shells on the seashore,
and Horace writes of Scipio, Laelius, and Lucilius 'fooling
about till the cabbage was boiled' (*Satires*, 2.1.71); the scholiast
caps this with a tale of how Laelius surprised Lucilius chasing
Scipio round the dining-room with a knotted napkin. One
can imagine these young men more ready to make a friend of
someone of different race and social class than the 'men of
consular rank' whom the grammarian Santra believed to have
been Terence's patrons. And it seems from the plays that
Terence was more in sympathy with the civilizing influence of
the new Hellenism than with the strict discipline and con-
servatism preached by the elder Cato, or the robust
humour of Italian rural life. This is what makes the difference
between Terence and Plautus more than one of generation;

the great gap which was never again to be bridged over had been made between the mass of the people and a small educated class.

Plautus is said by Cicero to have died in 186 B.C., so that all his plays were first written in the years of austerity at the end of the second Carthaginian war and in the changed social conditions produced by the rapid increase of an urban and slave population. They were all taken from Greek New Comedy of Menander and his contemporaries, and military service must have brought many Romans in contact for the first time with the more sophisticated Greek cities of South Italy and Sicily; but Roman society was still parochial and puritanical, based on the close ties of family life. There was nothing in it to correspond with the *jeunesse dorée* of the Hellenistic world, young men in debt to pimps and mistresses, their elders worldly-wise, and their servants as pert and resourceful as a Figaro or Scapin. Plautus took the stock characters of comedy, 'a running slave, virtuous wives and dishonest courtesans, greedy spongers and braggart soldiers' (*The Eunuch*, 36–8), but he could not risk outraging Roman morality by humanizing them. Sometimes the result is caricature, but at his best Plautus created something more vigorous and exuberant than his original, mixing Roman with Greek elements and developing the comic potentiality of a scene in whatever way his sense of theatre suggested. As well as being a master of *vis comica* he has a gift for verbal extravaganza and metrical technique like that of Aristophanes; and the high spots of his plays are often his musical *cantica*.

Some twenty years after Plautus's death Terence brought out his *Andria*, and from the opening conversation between an Athenian gentleman and his trusted freedman it is immediately apparent that his aims are quite different. There is no formal prologue to describe the plot, and the use of dialogue to explain the situation is Terence's improvement on his Greek model. The tone is light but sympathetic towards young love, the language is direct and natural, and the whole scene has been beloved and quoted by literary critics from Cicero down to Sainte-Beuve, who compares some of its phrases with Andromache's smiling through her tears. Terence is consistent throughout his six plays in avoiding what is too Greek or too Roman, and this gives them their timeless quality. He creates a beautifully simple, fluid style of Latin to match the lucidity of Hellenistic Greek. He can handle genuine problems with perception and show people as much the same then as now – mixed in their motives, muddled in their intentions, but, like the young men in *The Brothers*, good at heart. In 'translating' Greek comedy into a different world, Terence's achievement was to take over the typical irascible father, irresponsible youth, courtesan and slave-dealer, and present them as individuals caught up in a complex plot which sets them at cross-purposes and has many comic possibilities when no one is in full possession of the truth until the final *dénouement*; in the meantime much is revealed about the persons involved by means of their reactions to the confusion. At the same time Terence's tolerant attitude to his characters is moral and serious. A young man seduces a girl, but 'there were excuses... it is human nature'. Yet he is not allowed to shirk the consequences and leave her in the lurch. A strict father believes he is doing the best thing for his son; but if he makes no allowances for youth he lives in a fool's paradise. A woman can be scorned by her neighbours as a professional courtesan and later show real generosity and an almost maternal affection to her former lover. It is easy to see why his words *homo sum: humani nil a me alienum puto* (*The Self-Tormentor* 77) have been so often quoted out of context with application to Terence himself.

It is also understandable that he has never had wide popular appeal, especially for those unwilling to accept the conventions of formal comedy, where the situations are always relatively stereotyped so as to provide a recognizable framework in which wit can sparkle and intrigue unfold. Some of his double plots and counterplots make great demands upon the concentration of a reader, let alone a theatre audience, and even as early as Cicero and Horace he was more quoted for his humanity and style than for his stagecraft. And in his concern for writing Latin which combines elegance with conversational ease, he makes no attempt to vary it for his different characters. Slaves speak as impeccably as their masters, and only Phormio is allowed more colourful phrases. In his own day he met with instant criticism from his older rivals, and in comparison with Plautus he was judged to be a half-size Menander lacking vigour.[1]

Four of Terence's plays were modelled on Menander's, two (*Phormio* and *The Mother-in-Law*) on plays by Apollodorus of Carystus. (Only three of the twenty-one extant plays of Plautus can be certainly said to follow Menander.) Opinions differ widely on the question how much in a play by Terence is original and how much directly due to the Greek model: T. B. L. Webster in *Studies in Menander* quotes Terence as evidence for the content of lost plays, while Gilbert Norwood in *The Art of Terence* is unwilling to allow anything to Menander at all. The larger surviving fragments of Menander are sufficient to show that his high reputation in antiquity was well deserved; he was a master of plot, of dialogue, of metre, and a creator of characters who are more than mere types. His tolerance and humanity are such as we find in Terence, and both authors are quotable for their observations on life and its problems. What they say may not be strikingly original but it always gives pleasure because it rings true.

It is certain that Terence was never a *translator* of Greek

1. By Caesar, quoted in Suetonius's *Life*, p. 393.

comedies; he has sharp words to say in his prologues about people who were. Moreover, Donatus says more than once in his commentaries that he has read the Greek original, for the purpose of comparison, and in the case of *Andria* that he has studied both the plays cited in the prologue in order to estimate how Terence had used them. He sometimes quotes a line in Greek to show that Terence took it over word for word, but the very fact that he singles out these passages shows that they were comparatively rare. Elsewhere he remarks on Terence's improvement on his original – the opening scene, in dialogue, of *Andria*, for instance. From the six remarkable prologues to the plays in which Terence answers his critics, it is possible to see what he set out to do. He was accused of writing thin dialogue, of stealing characters and scenes from earlier Latin plays, of accepting unacknowledged help from his noble patrons, and of tampering with his Greek originals by picking and choosing from more than one for each of his plays, thus rendering them useless to other translators. Instead of formally refuting the charges, Terence counter-attacks. His critic, he says, is a competent translator with no stage sense, whose fidelity to the text only turns a good Greek play into a bad Latin one. The question of plagiarism in his own work does not arise; he has only made use of stock situations and characters and ignored the plays of his Roman predecessors. 'Nothing in fact is ever said which has not been said before.' He is proud of his 'noble friends', and dismisses the charge that they helped him with his plays as no more than a 'spiteful accusation'. He has no intention of courting popularity by noisy crowd scenes or animals on the stage; all he asks for is an attentive audience. And if 'spoiling' plays (*contaminare*) means selecting what he wants from any source he likes, that is precisely what the great Plautus did and what Terence proposes to do.

Much has been written about the precise meaning of *contaminatio*.[1] The general meaning of the verb is 'pollute' or 'soil', and in its specialized sense it appears twice in Terence's prologues and nowhere else. Luscius Lanuvinus is quoted as protesting that this upstart young dramatist is 'soiling' or 'spoiling' Greek plays, and again as charging Terence with 'spoiling' Greek plays for others by using more than one to make a single Latin play. It seems very unlikely that so strong a word used pejoratively could mean no more than 'combine'. Luscius surely means that Terence makes a Greek play useless to a straight translator if he picks bits out to incorporate in another play. Terence's reply is that he intends to revert to the freedom and inventiveness of the earlier dramatists, seeing that pedantic accuracy in translation can never create a living Roman play.

The portrait of Terence which emerges from the prologues is one of a conscious artist, impatient of criticism which he feels to be malicious, and confident (as gifted young men must be) that he has it in him to do good work. He is self-assured and intolerant of the second-rate, but he is as sensitive and eager for appreciation as one of his own young men. He says more than once that his main concern is to give pleasure, and he knows very well that a play can never come to life without the support of its audience. Hence his repeated pleas for a fair hearing to enable a young man to make his way in the world, and his tone of hurt surprise in reference to the repeated failure of *The Mother-in-Law*. (No doubt he was well aware that in many ways it was his best-constructed play.) He certainly thought he was bringing something new to the stage, and it must be allowed that he did. Whatever Terence owed to Greek New Comedy, and however confused and contradictory were the traditional accounts of his life collected by

1. See W. Beare, *The Roman Stage*, pp. 96 ff. and Appendix K.

Suetonius, it remains a matter of astonishment to his latter-day admirers, as it was to their Roman predecessors, that six plays of such assurance and maturity could be written in as many years at that point in Rome's history by a young man who was apparently an obscure foreign immigrant, but had the power and personality to win the support of the leading actor-producer and be recognized as a dangerous rival by established older playwrights.

His chief original contribution was the double plot, and this enabled him to enlarge on his major interest, the effect of plot on character, and the contrasted reactions of different types of character to the same situation. He could then draw carefully diversified portraits of closely connected persons, the two young men and the two old fathers in *The Brothers*, the two neighbours in *The Self-Tormentor*, the three young men in *The Eunuch*, and end his plays with two resolutions of plot, each acting as a foil to the other: one young man enjoys a socially acceptable and legal marriage when the true identity of his bride is known, while the other is allowed only a temporary liaison with a *meretrix*, less romantic and less seriously taken by his elders. He created a Latin style which was an admirable counterpart to the natural rhythms of Hellenistic Greek, less rhetorical and dense, simpler and purer than anything written before. As Sainte-Beuve puts it, ' *C'est le secret des âges polis. Térence est le premier chez les Romains qui "D'un mot mis en sa place enseigne le pouvoir"*.'[1] He settled comedy more firmly in the real world by removing the formal expository prologue (which Plautus kept) and dispensing with divine intervention, thus retaining an element of suspense and making his plays more logical. He moved away from caricature in his minor characters, and was more sympathetic towards old people – the father is never a mere dupe nor the mother a figure of fun –

1. *Nouveaux Lundis*, 10 August 1863.

and more interested in women as persons. *The Mother-in-Law* is essentially a woman's play. He was the creator of serious or problem comedy, and became a major influence on European drama from the earliest days of the Renaissance.

A few names of other writers of *fabulae palliatae* (adaptations of Hellenistic comedies played in Greek dress) are known, the last being that of Turpilius who died as a very old man in 103 B.C. Only titles of plays survive; perhaps no one could handle material with Terence's inventiveness. *Fabulae togatae* using Italian themes lasted longer and left about six hundred quoted lines and seventy titles. There are three known writers, Titinius, L. Afranius, and T. Quinctius Atta, who is said to have died in 77 B.C. But as mimes, burlesques and sophisticated versions of the native Atelline farce took over the stage from true comedy, what was written under the Empire was intended for reading aloud to an invited audience. Juvenal starts his first Satire with a protest against the tedium of such readings, and Pliny writes enthusiastically of a young friend's gifts as a playwright without any suggestion that his plays might be staged. It is significant that when Quintilian wishes to illustrate a comment on the acting of comedy he quotes from Terence's *Eunuch* and nothing later.[2]

Terence continued to be studied and quoted for his humanity and purity of style down to the last days of the Empire, and when scholarship took refuge in the monasteries, he was one of the authors whose works were carefully preserved complete. The Codex Bembinus of the fourth or fifth century is still the best manuscript we have; in it only most of *Andria* and parts of *Hecyra* and *Adelphoe* are missing. Donatus's commentary is preserved in a sixth-century compilation, intact but for *Heauton Timorumenos*. The archetype of all the later MSS. of Terence is dated to the fifth century, and the extant versions

2. *Letters* 6.25; *Inst. Orat.* 11.3.178–82.

range from the ninth to the twelfth centuries, some of the earliest being illustrated by miniature drawings.[1] All this goes to show the loving care bestowed on Terence, whose Latin served as a model of clarity and style. As his plays had long since left the stage, they escaped the censure of the Fathers of the Church who attacked the brutality and indecency of the mime and stage spectacles of the later Empire. That Terence was read and enjoyed we know from St Augustine and Ammianus Marcellinus,[2] and from St Jerome who complained that the ancient comedies could distract the devout from their bibles. In the tenth century, an aristocratic Saxon nun, Hrotsvitha of Gandersheim, even wrote plays on sacred subjects in the manner of Terence, in an attempt to purge him of his worldliness; the resultant literary curiosity proves how well she knew her model, though she believed he wrote prose.

With the coming of the Renaissance, the popular pageants and morality plays encouraged by the western Church gradually yielded to the discipline of classical tragedy and comedy, with Seneca, Plautus, and Terence as the greatest influence on European drama. In Italy the movement started with learned works in classical style like the *Philodoxius* of Alberti; then came actual performances of such plays, such as those sponsored in the Rome of Sixtus IV by the antiquarian Pomponius Laetus. Finally, the ancient dramatists reached a wider public through direct translation, with some of the great principalities of North Italy leading the way. In 1496 we find the Marquis of Mantua writing to his father-in-law, Hercules I of Ferrara, for copies of the plays of Plautus and Terence translated and played at Ferrara, and there are performances also recorded at Milan under Lodovico Il Moro. Ariosto is known

1. See Bieber, pp. 153–4 and Duckworth, Plates 1–8.
2. *Eunuch* 585 and note; A. Marcellinus, 28.4.27, referring to Micio in *Adelphoe*.

to have translated *Andria* and *The Eunuch*. The presses of Venice produced both verse and prose translations of Terence and selections from Plautus; then original comedy began to be written in Italian, and by the mid sixteenth century the movement was spreading over western Europe. Spain provides one of the earliest examples of classical comedy in de Rojas' dramatized novel, *La Celestina*, and later in the plays of Lope de Vega and his contemporaries. The first English comedy, *Ralph Roister Doister*, written by Nicholas Udall about 1553, is directly modelled on Plautus's *Braggart Soldier* and Terence's *Eunuch*. In 1598 the first English translation, that of Richard Bernard, was published in Cambridge; accurate, lively, and free from verbal conceits, it is still one of the most readable. But the best of the Elizabethan comedies have an element of fantasy which is a distinguishing mark of English comedy at its best and something quite alien to the Latin–Italian style. Shakespeare realizes his powers in comedy when he moves away from the formal pattern of *The Two Gentlemen of Verona* and *The Comedy of Errors* towards the greater poetic depth and freedom of *As You Like It* and *Twelfth Night*. With the post-Restoration dramatists, Wycherley, Vanbrugh, and, above all, Congreve, there is a return to true classic comedy in a somewhat coarsened form; to be followed in the next century by Goldsmith and Sheridan writing with more polish in the same style. The greatest of these plays, *The Way of the World*, is prefaced by Congreve's personal tribute to Terence. But as Diderot pointed out, the characters in English classic comedy tend to become caricatures; in his opinion there have been only two comic dramatists with the gift of drawing characters in depth, with sympathy and without exaggeration, placing them in situations designed to reveal both their individuality and their timelessness: Terence and Molière. The great writers of English comedy have not written for the stage – they are among the poets, essay-writers, and novelists, Chaucer, Addison, Fielding, and Jane Austen.

Terence has had his most sympathetic admirers since the seventeenth century in France, where his humanism and his sense of style had greatest influence. This is apparent from the tributes of critics such as Montaigne, Diderot, and Sainte-Beuve, but his true spiritual descendant is of course Molière. In Molière we find the true humanistic approach – sanity and common sense, freedom from cant and exaggerated sentiment, an understanding of the sufficiency of the world and man's part in it. He can use comedy as a medium for a sustained social commentary, and his essential seriousness can lift it to its highest level so that under the impact of laughter we are made to feel the truth of his judgement on us all. Terence may be limited by the convention that he must 'translate' light Greek comedy into a different world of thought and sentiment, but he is as much the creator of Aeschinus, Demea, and Bacchis as Molière is of M. Jourdain and Célimène.

For those whose interests were wider and deeper than the study of dramatic comedy Terence had great appeal, especially for the Renaissance humanists in their aim to reconcile the best of pagan learning with the Christian ideal. He was read and quoted by Petrarch, by Politian, who studied the Bembine codex, by Boccaccio, and later by Colet, founder of St Paul's School as the realization of his theories of a Christian education on a classical basis. Erasmus worked on his *Adages* through the years in order to discuss the wisdom of antiquity transmitted through its proverbs and to show that its moral aspirations were not in conflict with the Christian ethic. He had learned the plays by heart in youth, and quoted from them repeatedly, both in his letters and in his published writings; there are more than 250 references and quotations in the *Adages* alone.

Terence was used as a teaching manual of Latin composition

until comparatively recent times, and in the early days of the English grammar schools the scholars gave regular performances of Roman comedies. The foundation statute of 1561 for Westminster School said that it should present a play every Christmas, and the second headmaster 'brought in the reading of Terence for the better learning the pure Roman style'. Bernard's translation was printed with the Latin text, with extensive notes on points of grammar and interpretation for the guidance of the children to whom he was tutor. It is our loss that nineteenth-century educationists thought that Terence's urbanity would corrupt schoolboys, and laid down a curriculum of Roman history and oratory and Augustan poetry, to the neglect of the apposite words, free-moving syntax and nimble repartee of colloquial classical Latin. It does not need a very profound knowledge of Latin to enjoy an exchange like that of *Adelphoe* 413 ff. (*The Brothers*, p. 358).

> DEMEA fit sedulo;
> nil praetermitto; consuefacio; denique
> inspicere, tamquam in speculum, in vitas omnium
> iubeo atque ex aliis sumere exemplum sibi:
> 'hoc facito.' SYRUS recte sane. DE. 'hoc fugito.' SY. callide.
> DÉ. 'hoc laudist.' SY. istaec res est. DE. 'hoc vitio datur.'
> SY. probissime. DE. porro autem . . . SY. non hercle otiumst
> nunc mi auscultandi. piscis ex sententia
> nactus sum: i mihi ne currumpantur cautiost.

Roman comedy took over its stage conventions from Greek New Comedy. The back of the stage showed the doors of two or three houses, and the side exits led to the country on the spectators' left and the town centre or market place (the forum) on the right. Whether the harbour should be thought of as on the right or left is disputed; the ancient evidence is not clear about Greek practice nor do we know how far Roman playwrights would follow it. All stage action took place in the open street, and though characters talk to people in the houses through the open door, nothing was allowed to be seen of the interior. The greater breadth of stage made it easier to accept the convention that characters only saw and heard what the author intended. The style of acting was declamatory, with formalized gestures, costume was stereotyped, and actors were probably masked in the Greek fashion to indicate typical characters: 'running slave, angry old man, greedy sponger, shameless impostor and rapacious slave-dealer' (*The Self-Tormentor* 37–9). Though Terence made little use of the sung aria in which Plautus had excelled, his spoken dialogue of six-foot iambics alternate with longer lines of mixed iambics and trochaics, which were rhythmically recited to the musical accompaniment of the pipe player. These passages are called by Donatus *mutatis modis cantica*. Perhaps Terence had no gift for writing lyric metre, or he may have considered it unsuitable for his more serious comedy.

The music for the plays was composed by a slave, Flaccus, named with his master Claudius in the production notices (*didascaliae*). The instrument was the *tibia* (Greek *aulos*), an oboe-style reed instrument (not a flute), translated as 'pipe'. Such pipes were played in pairs, held in the mouth of the player by a band passing over his head. *Tibiae pares*, of equal length, were evidently played in unison; those which were unequal were apparently tuned to play in harmony, one playing the melody, the other an accompaniment. It is generally thought that the longer (curved) one of lower pitch supplied the melody and the shorter (straight) one a kind of descant. It is not certain whether the longer pipe was held in the right or left hand: probably in the right. Usually the same combination was used throughout a play, but *The Self-Tormentor* starts with unequal pipes and changes to equal pipes at l. 410 – perhaps to mark the lapse of time and change of mood in the play. The true arias are thought to have been mimed by the actor while sung by a professional singer standing by the *tibicen*; he is probably to be identified with the *cantor* who invites the audience to applaud at the end of each play.

Modern editors, following the manuscripts, divide the plays into five acts and each act into several scenes. The scene-divisions date from the earliest manuscripts and are no more than headings which list the characters on the stage whenever a new character enters, and sometimes when he leaves the stage as well. Neither scene- nor act-divisions were the work of the playwright, as Donatus and the early commentators knew; Donatus remarks that *The Eunuch* was played continuously for fear that bored members of the audience might leave their seats, and Plautus in his short preface to *Pseudolus* indicates that a long non-stop performance was about to begin. Elsewhere Donatus seems to think it desirable to divide a play by Terence into five acts, doubtless thinking that Horace's ruling (in *Ars Poetica* 189) that a play must have five acts to be successful should be applied to the *fabula palliata*. This was to become the rigid five-act law of Renaissance drama. Greek plays were of course divided into sections by choral passages, though the chorus declined from its position of dramatic importance. New Comedy seems generally to have been divided into five acts by non-dramatic choral interludes, marked in the MSS. only by the word 'chorus'. As Terence made no use of a chorus, it was left to the grammarians to decide how to divide up his plays into five acts – with often very unsatisfactory results.

This translation has dropped all act-divisions, and indicates entries and exits of characters by conventional stage directions. Some guiding directions and notes have been added, and a few liberties taken in the interests of those who may want to act the plays. Slaves, for example, have been made to address their masters by a courtesy title, and a proper name used once only has been dropped. Prose has been used throughout, as the most satisfactory medium for the comic *genre*, but with the inevitable loss of most of Terence's delicate word-play and his enjoyment of alliteration, assonance and vivid asyndeton. The exact nuance of meaning in some of Terence's commonest expressions is very difficult to convey; an interpolation such as *quid ais* has no single equivalent, and exclamations like *perii* and *occidi* can be a simple expletive or, apparently, express a variety of emotions, alarm, dismay or uncertainty, and have been variously translated. Madame Dacier, in the Preface to her translation of Terence of 1706, says she would have despaired of conveying '*cette politesse, cette noblesse et cette simplicité*' but for her love of her own language and her conviction that French could be a medium with its own grace and beauty. An English translator today needs her dedication, and has no easier task if he is to offer neither clumsy modernization nor the 'dry and literal interpretation of the author's text' which was such a disappointment to Gibbon during his short stay at Oxford – 'the fourteen months the most idle and unprofitable of my whole life'.[1]

There is something elusive about comedy which makes it difficult to define, and that part of the *Art of Poetry* is lost where Aristotle gave it full treatment. He left only a provisional distinction between tragedy and comedy, the one dealing with the fate of an individual and stirring the emotions, and the other depicting social groups and aiming at a sense of the ridiculous. The writer of comedy may point his finger at wrong ideas, as Shaw did, or at social pretensions and sentimental notions, like Congreve and Sheridan. He can be as brilliant as Wilde, as romantic as Synge, or as caustic as Maugham; his interest may be primarily in character, as

1. Edward Gibbon, *Autobiography*, 1789.

Jonson in *Volpone*, or in intrigue of plot as in *Figaro*. But if he is not to write satire his handling of characters must be kindly, he must know people as they really are to avoid burlesque, and retain a sense of proportion to keep free of exaggeration and farce. He needs a natural optimism if his purpose is not sick comedy; as Meredith put it, 'To love Comedy you must know the real world, and know men and women well enough not to expect too much of them, though you may still hope for good.'[1] In his famous essay *On Books*, Montaigne wrote: 'As for Terence, who personifies the charm and grace of the Latin tongue, I am astounded by the lifelike way in which he depicts ways of thought and states of manners which are true of us today; at every turn our actions send me back to him.' This is still true, for, though the six plays are short and un-developed by modern standards, each one expresses in a differ-ent way Terence's own most quoted line: *Homo sum: humani nil a me alienum puto*. 'I am human myself, so I think every human affair is my concern.'

1. *An Essay on Comedy*, 1877.

THE GIRL FROM ANDROS

[ANDRIA]

INTRODUCTORY NOTE

It is generally agreed that *The Girl from Andros* is Terence's first play yet the Prologue is aimed at answering his critics, so either it was written for a later performance, or the play must have been known to his rivals even earlier (perhaps at a rehearsal similar to the one described in the Author's Prologue to *The Eunuch*). Terence's sympathetic treatment of the conventional theme of a young man in love with a girl he cannot legally marry makes this the first truly romantic comedy, and the first scene has been admired and quoted by critics from Cicero onwards. The commentator Donatus also says explicitly that Terence replaced a less dramatic monologue in the opening scene of Menander's *The Girl from Samos* by the conversation between Simo and his freedman as we have it, taking the idea from *The Girl from Perinthos*.

The alternative ending may have been an acting variation on Terence's original or a literary effort on the part of someone dissatisfied with what at first sight seems rather an abrupt settlement of the fortunes of the second young couple, Charinus and Philumena; but Terence is surely dramatically right in refusing to repeat a betrothal scene on-stage, and he solves the problem neatly by Davos's final words. This is, moreover, his practice elsewhere – in *The Self-Tormentor* Clinia disappears from the scene some time before the end of the play, so that interest can be concentrated on Clitipho.

The Prologue makes it clear that the double plot is also Terence's innovation, and he is thus enabled to draw the contrast between the two young men, the histrionic Charinus and Pamphilus, who is more fully realized as an ardently romantic young man, with something of his father Simo's forceful character. This is one of Terence's liveliest plays, allowing full scope for the ingenuity of the resourceful Davos. It was translated into Italian by Ariosto and by Machiavelli, and was the first of his plays to be translated into English, about 1530. It was also the play for which the young Dürer drew illustrations in 1492; these are preserved on the uncut woodblocks in the Künstmuseum in Basel.

PRODUCTION NOTICE[1]

Here begins THE GIRL FROM ANDROS by Terence:
performed at the Megalensian Games[2] during the curule
aedileship of Marcus Fulvius and Manius (Acilius) Glabrio.

Produced by Lucius Ambivius Turpio.

Music composed by Flaccus, slave of Claudius, the whole
for equal pipes.[3]

Greek original by Menander.

The author's first play, written during the consulship of
Marcus (Claudius) Marcellus and Gaius Sulpicius (Gallus).[4]

---

1. The *didascalia* is missing from the MSS. This is a translation
of the reconstruction by K. Dziatzko (1884) of the confused
paraphrase in the commentary of Donatus.

2. Celebrated annually in April in honour of the Great
Mother, the goddess Cybele.

3. See Introduction, p. 26.

4. In 166 B.C.

SYNOPSIS[1]

Glycerium, who is wrongly supposed to be the sister of a courtesan from Andros, is seduced and made pregnant by Pamphilus. He then promises to marry her, but his father, Simo, has already arranged another marriage for him with the daughter of Chremes. On hearing of Pamphilus's affair Simo pretends that the other wedding will still take place, hoping thereby to discover his son's real feelings. On the advice of his slave Davos Pamphilus raises no objections, but when Glycerium's child is born and Chremes sees it, he breaks off the marriage between Pamphilus and his daughter. Afterwards, he discovers to his surprise that Glycerium is really his daughter, so he marries her to Pamphilus and his other daughter to Charinus.

1. All Terence's plays have synopses written in the mid second century A.D. by Gaius Sulpicius Apollinaris of Carthage.

CHARACTERS[1]

SIMO	*an Athenian gentleman*
SOSIA	*his elderly freedman*
PAMPHILUS	*his son, in love with Glycerium*
CHREMES	*a neighbour*
CHARINUS	*a friend of Pamphilus, in love with Chremes'* *daughter Philumena*
CRITO	*a visitor from Andros, cousin to Chrysis*
DAVOS	*a slave of Simo, attendant on Pamphilus*
DROMO	*a slave of Simo*
BYRRIA	*a slave of Charinus*
MYSIS	*a maidservant of Glycerium*
LESBIA	*a midwife*
CANTHARA	*her assistant*

(Chrysis, a courtesan from Andros, has died before the play opens. Glycerium, 'the girl from Andros', and Chremes' daughter Philumena do not appear)

*

The scene is laid in a suburb of Athens in front of the houses of Simo and Glycerium. To the audience's right the street leads to the centre of the town, to their left to the harbour and the house of Chremes

1. There are no lists of characters in any of the MSS of Plautus and Terence, but they can be compiled from the scene headings which name speakers in each 'scene' and their rôles.

AUTHOR'S PROLOGUE TO
THE GIRL FROM ANDROS

WHEN the author first turned his thoughts to writing, he supposed that his sole concern was to write plays which would give pleasure to his audience. He has since learned how different things are in practice; for he now spends his time writing prologues, not to explain the plot of a play but to answer the slanderous attacks of a malevolent old playwright.[1]

Now please note the charge he faces today. Menander wrote two plays, *The Girl from Andros* and *The Girl from Perinthos*; know one and you know them both, for the plots are much the same, though there are differences in dialogue and style. The author admits that he has transferred anything suitable from the latter play to his adaptation of the former and made free use of it. This is the practice attacked by his critics, who argue that by so doing he is 'spoiling'[2] the original plays. Surely they miss the point here, for all their cleverness. In attacking the present author they are really attacking Naevius, Plautus and Ennius, whom he takes for his models and whose 'carelessness' he would far rather imitate than his critics' dreary accuracy. I therefore bid them hold their peace in future, and stop making these insinuations; or else they may find their own failings exposed.

Now pay attention, give us your support and a fair hearing; then you may determine what hope there is for the future – whether the author's coming plays merit a showing or deserve to be driven off the stage unseen.

1. Named by Donatus as Luscius Lanuvinus, Terence's rival and critic, about whom little else is known.
2. See Introduction, p. 19.

[SIMO, *a gentleman in late middle age, and his elderly freed slave* SOSIA *come on right with servants carrying food and drink for a party.*]

SIMO: Take those things in, you boys; hurry up. Sosia, wait a minute, I want a word with you.

[*The servants go into his house.*]

SOSIA: No need to say it, sir. I expect you want me to take charge of all that.

SIMO: No, it's something else.

SOSIA: But what better use can you make of my skill?

SIMO: I don't need your skill for what I'm planning at the moment; this demands the qualities I have always observed in you – loyalty and secrecy.

SOSIA: I'm at your service, sir.

SIMO: You know that ever since I bought you for my slave as a boy you have found me a just and considerate master. I gave you your freedom because you served me in a free spirit, and that was the highest reward at my disposal.

SOSIA: I don't forget it, sir.

SIMO: And I don't regret it.

SOSIA: I'm only too glad if anything I've done or do pleases you, sir, and I'm grateful for your gracious approval. But I'm a bit worried about the way you're reminding me about the circumstances – it looks like a reproach for ingratitude. Please tell me briefly what you want of me.

SIMO: I will. Let me start by saying that you're wrong about these preparations. There isn't going to be a real wedding.

SOSIA: Then why pretend there is?

SIMO: I'll tell you the whole story, then you'll know all about my son's conduct, my own plans and the part I want you to play in the matter. As soon as Pamphilus was grown up and free to live his own life – for no one could have known the truth or guessed his disposition as long as he was restrained by youth, timidity and his tutor –

SOSIA: That's true.

SIMO: The usual things young men do, their crazes for keeping horses or hounds or dabbling in philosophy, all took up his time to a certain extent, but he hadn't any special enthusiasms. I was pleased.

SOSIA: And rightly, sir. 'Nothing too much' is the best rule in life, I think.

SIMO: Let me tell you the sort of life he lived: he was patient and tolerant with all his friends, fell in with the wishes of any of them and joined in all their pursuits, never contradicting nor putting himself first. That's the best way to steer clear of jealousy, win a reputation and make friends.

SOSIA: A well-planned life! Agree with everything nowadays, if you want friends; truthfulness only makes you unpopular.

SIMO: Meanwhile a woman came here from Andros three years ago and settled down in the neighbourhood, the victim of poverty and the indifference of her relatives: a beautiful girl, in the flower of her youth.

SOSIA: Oh dear; I suspect she brings trouble with her.

SIMO: At first she led a modest life, thrifty and hard-working, trying to make a living out of spinning and weaving. Then lovers began to come offering payment, first one and then another; human nature takes to pleasure all too easily after a spell of hardship, and so she accepted their offers and soon afterwards set up as a professional. One day her current lovers happened to take my son there to dinner. 'Now he's caught,' I said to myself at once; 'she's got him.' I used to watch his friends' servant-boys coming and going every morning and call to them: 'You there! Can you tell me who was in favour with Chrysis yesterday?' (That was the woman's name.)

SOSIA: I see.

SIMO: They said it was Phaedrus or Clinias or Niceratus, for these three shared her at the time. 'What about Pamphilus?' 'Oh, he only stayed to dinner and paid his share.' I was delighted. I made the same inquiry another day, and found nothing at all to implicate Pamphilus. Naturally I concluded that he was a model of continence, tried and tested, for if a man's will has come up against characters like theirs and remained unmoved, you may feel sure of his self-control in his own way of life. To add to my satisfaction, everyone spoke well of him with one voice and congratulated me on my good fortune in having a son blessed with such character. Well, to cut a long story short, my neighbour Chremes was persuaded by what he'd heard to approach me of his own accord and offer his only daughter with a substantial dowry to my son in marriage. I approved and accepted the match, and today is the day fixed for the wedding.

SOSIA: What's stopping it then?

SIMO: You'll hear. A few days after we made the agreement our neighbour Chrysis died.

SOSIA: Good, I'm glad to hear it. Dear me, she made me nervous for Pamphilus.

SIMO: At the time my son was always at the house with the lovers of Chrysis, helping them with the funeral. He was often depressed and sometimes wept bitterly. I was quite pleased at the time, for if he took this woman's death so much to heart, I thought, when they were only slightly acquainted, what would he feel if he had been really in love? And how will he take it when death comes to me, his father? I assumed that everything was prompted by his sensitive nature and sympathetic disposition. In short, I went to the funeral myself to please him, still with no suspicion that anything was wrong.

SOSIA: What are you getting at, sir?

SIMO: I'll tell you. The body was brought out and we followed. Presently among the women who were there I caught sight of a young girl whose beauty was –

SOSIA: Not bad, perhaps.

SIMO: And her expression, Sosia, was so modest and lovely – nothing could be more so. Her grief seemed to me to exceed that of the other women, just as she outshone them all in the grace and refinement of her bearing, so I went up to the attendants and asked them who she was. They told me she was the sister of Chrysis. Then the truth came home to me. Why, that was it – the reason for his tears and tenderheartedness.

SOSIA: I dread to think what's coming next!

SIMO: Meanwhile the procession moved off, we joined it and came to the cemetery. The body was laid on the pyre. Everyone wept. Then the sister I spoke of, careless of what she did, went dangerously near the flames. Thereupon Pamphilus, in his terror, let out the secret of his well-hidden love. He ran up and caught her round the waist. 'Glycerium, my darling,' he cried, 'what are you doing? You'll kill yourself.' Then you could easily see that they had long been lovers; she fell back into his arms and wept, so confidingly...

SOSIA: Did she indeed!

SIMO: I returned home angry and disappointed in him, but I had no real grounds for reproving him. I could imagine his answer: 'What have I done, father? What's wrong? A girl tried to throw herself on the fire, and I held her back and saved her life. What harm have I done?' Proper enough.

SOSIA: You're right, sir. If you start blaming folk for saving lives, what will you do with those who do real harm or damage?

SIMO: Next day Chremes came to me full of complaints. He'd discovered that Pamphilus regarded this foreigner as his wife – a shocking affair! I hotly denied it. He insisted it was true. When we eventually parted he made it quite clear that he was withdrawing his consent to his daughter's marriage.

SOSIA: And your son, sir? Didn't you –

SIMO: No. I still hadn't good enough reason for reproving him.

SOSIA: Why? Please explain.

SIMO: Again, he'd have his answer: 'You've named the date yourself for this to stop, father. I shall have to adapt myself to another person's ways soon enough; meanwhile you might let me live my own life.'

SOSIA: Then what grounds have you left for reproving him?

SIMO: Well, he may refuse to marry at all on account of this love-affair; that would be a real act of insolence, and I couldn't let it pass. I'm now trying to find a genuine reason for rebuking him by this pretence of wedding preparations, that is, if he refuses to take part. At the same time, if that scoundrel Davos has some trap in hand I hope to make him spring it now while his tricks can do no harm. I fancy he'll fight tooth and nail for anything he's set on, and more to annoy me than to please my son.

SOSIA: Why, sir?

SIMO: Oh, you know: evil mind, evil heart. If I catch him – Well, that'll do. But if it turns out as I'd like and Pamphilus makes no difficulties, then I've only got Chremes to bring round, and I've hopes of succeeding there. Now it's your job for the moment to make a good show of this wedding, intimidate Davos, keep an eye on my son's doings and see if the two of them are plotting anything.

SOSIA: Right, sir. I'll see to that.

SIMO: Let's go in then. You go ahead, I'll follow.

[SOSIA *goes into* SIMO'*s house, but* SIMO *is prevented by the arrival of his smart young servant,* DAVOS.]

I feel pretty sure that Pamphilus *will* refuse to marry, for I could see that Davos was alarmed when he heard there was to be a wedding. But here he comes.

[DAVOS *comes on right.*]

DAVOS: I always was surprised that we could get away with it like that – the master took the news so calmly but all along I dreaded how it would end. Ever since he heard his son's wedding was off he's never seemed upset nor said a word to any of us.

SIMO [*aside*]: But he'll say one now – as you'll know to your cost.

DAVOS: Maybe he intended to lead us on with false rejoicing, off our guard as we were, full of hope, suspecting nothing, and then catch us unawares before we'd a chance to think of putting a stop to the wedding: the artful beggar!

SIMO: What's the rascal saying?

DAVOS: It's the master! I didn't see him.

SIMO: Davos!

DAVOS: What is it, sir?

SIMO: Turn round and look at me.

DAVOS [*not doing so*]: *Now* what does he want?

SIMO: What are you saying?

DAVOS: What about?

SIMO: Don't be silly. [DAVOS *reluctantly faces him.*] There's gossip – that my son's having an affair.

DAVOS [*cynically*]: Oh yes, the public's very interested; of course.

SIMO: Are you listening to me?

DAVOS: Of course I am.

SIMO: I don't intend to go into that any further. I'm not an unreasonable parent, and his past conduct is none of my concern. As long as circumstances permitted I left him free to do as he liked, but today must mark the beginning of a new life and demands a change in his ways. From now on I'm telling you, and I might even go so far as to beg you, Davos, to lead him back to the right path. Let me explain. Any man with a mistress dislikes having to take a wife –

DAVOS: So they say.

SIMO: Then if he comes under a bad influence concerning these matters, it directs his mind, lovesick as it is, towards the worse decision.

DAVOS: Sorry, sir, I can't understand a word you're saying.

SIMO: Nonsense!

DAVOS: I'm no good at riddles, sir; my name's Davos, not Oedipus.

SIMO: Then I suppose you prefer plain words? I haven't finished yet.

DAVOS: Yes, please, sir.

SIMO: If I catch you up to any of your tricks today to prevent this marriage or trying to show off your cleverness in this matter, I warn you, Davos, I'll have you beaten senseless and sent to the mill, with my solemn assurance that if I let you out I shall go there and grind in your place. Is that quite clear? Or is there something you still can't understand?

DAVOS: I understand all right, sir. You spoke nice and plain this time, no roundabout way at all.

SIMO: This is the one thing where I simply will not put up with any of your swindles.

DAVOS: Hush, hush, sir.

SIMO: You're laughing at me, I can see. But I'm telling you

this, Davos: don't do anything rash, and don't say you
haven't been warned. Be careful.

[*He goes off, right.*]

DAVOS: Well, Davos, if I took in what the old man was saying
just now about a wedding, this is no time for slackness and
go-slow methods. I must look out *and* look sharp or it'll be
the death of me and my young master. I'm not quite sure
what to do, help Pamphilus or listen to *him*. If I abandon
Pamphilus I'm afraid for his life, and if I help him there's the
old chap's threats, and he's not easy to deceive. In the first
place he's found out about the affair, and he's watching
me like the menace he is to see I don't trick him over the
wedding. If he finds me out, damn it, or if the whim takes
him, he'll find a reason, right or wrong, to pack me off to
the mill. And then I've another problem: this girl from
Andros, whether she's wife or mistress, is having a baby,
and Pamphilus is the father. You ought to hear their crazy
plans – they act more like lunatics than lovers. They're
determined to acknowledge the child, boy or girl, and now
they're concocting a silly story that the mother is Athenian
born. There was a man once, they say, a merchant who was
shipwrecked off Andros and lost his life. His child was
washed ashore and Chrysis' father took the poor little
orphan in. Nonsense I call it, a most unlikely tale, but
they're pleased with their fabrication. [*The door of* GLYCE-
RIUM's *house opens and her servant,* MYSIS, *comes out.*] Now
here's Mysis coming out of her mistress's house. I'll slip off
into town and find Pamphilus. I don't want his father to
spring this on him unawares.

[*He goes off, right.*]

MYSIS [*talking to the housekeeper indoors*]: All right, Archylis, I
heard you long ago; you want Lesbia fetched. I tell you, the
woman drinks and she's careless, quite unsuitable in fact to

be entrusted with a first confinement. Shall I fetch her all the same? [*To the audience*] Look at the obstinacy of the old fool – all because the two of them enjoy a drop together! I pray heaven that my mistress will have an easy delivery and the midwife do one of her bungled jobs elsewhere. [*Looking right down the street*] Why, I do believe that's Pamphilus, and what a state he's in! I'm afraid something's wrong. I'll just wait to see if this means trouble for us.

[PAMPHILUS *rushes on, in a state of agitation; evidently he has missed* DAVOS *but seen his father.*]

PAMPHILUS [*not seeing* MYSIS]: Oh, what a thing to do! The very idea! It's inhuman. Is this what you expect from a father?

MYSIS: Whatever's this?

PAMPHILUS: My God, if this isn't an outrage, what is? He'd made up his mind to marry me off today. Shouldn't I have had notice? Couldn't he have told me before?

MYSIS: Mercy me, what's this I hear!

PAMPHILUS: And what about Chremes? He'd refused once to trust me with his daughter; has he changed his mind – because he sees I haven't changed mine? Is he absolutely set on tearing me away from Glycerium and ruining my happiness? If he succeeds ... it'll kill me. Oh, is any man so crossed in love and cursed by fortune as I am! Heaven and earth, can't there be some way of escape from Chremes and this marriage? See how I'm mocked and scorned – and now everything's fixed and settled – how I'm refused and then recalled – what's the reason for it? Maybe my suspicions are right and they're harbouring a freak that they can't palm off on anyone else – so they pick on me.

MYSIS: Oh dear, dear, I'm frightened to death.

PAMPHILUS: As for my father, words fail me. How *could* he treat something so serious in this off-hand way? He passed me in the street just now. 'You're to be married today, Pamphilus,' was all he said: 'go home at once and get ready.' To me it sounded like 'Clear off and hang yourself.' I was staggered, couldn't get a word out, or any excuse, however false or silly or inept – struck dumb in fact. If I'd known of it before and anyone asked me now what I'd do – I'd do *something*, if only not to be doing this. . . . As it is, what can I set about first? So many worries block my path, pull me opposite ways: my love and pity for Glycerium, anxiety over this wedding, respect for my father who has been so indulgent up till now and let me do anything I liked. How can I think of going against him? Oh, it's terrible! What can I do? I just don't know.

MYSIS: That sounds bad; I don't like the sound of 'don't know' at all. But the main thing now is for him to talk to my mistress or for me to have a word with him about her. It doesn't take much to tip the balance either way when a man's in two minds.

PAMPHILUS [*waking up to her presence*]: Who's that talking? Oh, hullo, Mysis.

MYSIS: Good morning, sir.

PAMPHILUS: How are things going?

MYSIS: You should know. She's racked with labour pains and torn by anxiety, poor soul, when she remembers that this was the day fixed for your wedding. She's terrified too that you'll abandon her.

PAMPHILUS [*indignantly*]: How could I think of doing such a thing? Shall I let this poor girl be deceived on my account, after she had trusted me with her heart, nay, her very life, and I had treated her as the darling of my heart as if she were my wife? She was formed and fashioned in purity and virtue; should I allow her whole character to be changed through pressure of poverty? Of course not!

MYSIS: I shouldn't worry if it all rested with you, sir, but suppose they use force – can you stand up to it?

PAMPHILUS: Do you really think me so spiritless and unfeeling, so cruel and unnatural? Could I remain unmoved when thoughts of our love and association and my sense of honour all prompt me to keep my word?

MYSIS: One thing I do know, sir; she has earned the right to be remembered by you.

PAMPHILUS: *Remembered?* Oh, Mysis, Mysis, the words Chrysis used of her are forever written in my heart. Almost with her last breath she called me to her side; I drew near, and you all withdrew; we were alone. Then she began: 'My dear Pamphilus, you see this girl's youth and beauty, and you are well aware how little use these are to her today to protect her honour and property. Wherefore, by this right hand and your own better self, in the name of your pledged word and her own lonely state, I implore you not to put her from you nor abandon her. As surely as I have loved you like my own brother, and she has set you above all others and sought to please you in everything, I give you to her as husband and friend, guardian and parent; I bequeath you all our property here, and entrust it to your safe-keeping.' So she gave Glycerium into my care, and death took her at once. I accepted the charge; it is one I shall not lay down.

MYSIS: I hope not, sir.

[*She starts to go.*]

PAMPHILUS: Why are you leaving her now?

MYSIS: I'm fetching the midwife.

PAMPHILUS: Be quick then, and listen – not a word about this wedding. In her present condition it could –

MYSIS: I understand.

[*She goes off right, and* PAMPHILUS *moves to the other side of the stage, absorbed in his troubles, so that he does not notice the entry, right, of his friend* CHARINUS, *accompanied by his servant,* BYRRIA.]

CHARINUS: What's that, Byrria? Did you say Philumena was to be married to Pamphilus today?

BYRRIA: That's right.

CHARINUS: How do you know?

BYRRIA: I met Davos in town just now, and he told me.

CHARINUS: Oh, it's terrible! Up to now I've been torn between hope and fear – now all hope's lost and I'm left with a mind numbed by anxiety, worn out and exhausted.

BYRRIA: Good heavens, sir, if you can't have what you want, do try to want what you can have.

CHARINUS [*despondently*]: I don't want anything but Philumena.

BYRRIA: You'd do far better to make an effort to rid yourself of this passion, instead of saying things which only add fuel to the fire and do no good.

CHARINUS: It's easy for us all when we're healthy to give good advice to a sick man. If you were in my place you'd think differently.

BYRRIA: All right, have it your own way.

CHARINUS: Look, there's Pamphilus. I must try everything before I accept defeat.

BYRRIA [*aside*]: What's he up to?

CHARINUS: I'll appeal to him in person, fall at his knees, tell him of my love – I believe that'll persuade him at least to postpone the wedding for a few days. Meanwhile something'll turn up – I hope.

BYRRIA [*aside*]: 'Something'? Nothing, more like.

CHARINUS: What do you think, Byrria; shall I go up to him?

BYRRIA: You might as well; at least you'll succeed in giving him the idea that you're all set to be his wife's lover, if he marries her.

CHARINUS: Oh go to hell, you and your insinuations, you rascal!

PAMPHILUS [*waking up to their presence*]: Why, here's Charinus. Hullo.

CHARINUS: Hullo, Pamphilus. I come to you in search of hope, salvation, help and counsel.

PAMPHILUS: I'm in no position to give counsel, and I've no means of helping you. But what's the matter?

CHARINUS: Are you getting married today?

PAMPHILUS: So they say.

CHARINUS [*dramatically*]: Pamphilus, if you do so, this is the last time you will set eyes on me.

PAMPHILUS [*genuinely surprised*]: Why on earth?

CHARINUS: Alas, I dare not say. Byrria, you tell him.

BYRRIA: All right.

PAMPHILUS: Then what is it?

BYRRIA: He's in love – with the girl you're to marry.

PAMPHILUS: Well then, our tastes differ . . . [*Hopefully*] Now tell me, Charinus, has there been anything more between you?

CHARINUS: No, Pamphilus, nothing at all.

PAMPHILUS: If only there had!

CHARINUS: In the name of our friendship and my love for Philumena, I beseech you: don't marry her. That would be best.

PAMPHILUS: I'll certainly *try* not to.

CHARINUS: But if that proves impossible, or your heart is set on this marriage –

PAMPHILUS: *Set* on it!

CHARINUS: – do at least postpone it for a few days so that I can go away somewhere and not see it.

PAMPHILUS: Now listen to me, Charinus. I don't want credit when none is deserved. I don't think any gentleman should expect it. And in the case of this marriage – I'm much more anxious to get out of it than you are to take it on.

CHARINUS: Oh, I can breathe again!

PAMPHILUS: Now you and Byrria here do all you can, plot and plan and devise some means of getting the girl for yourself. On my side I'll do my best not to have her.

CHARINUS: I'm willing.

PAMPHILUS [*looking along the street*]: Splendid, I can see Davos. I can count on him for some good suggestions.

CHARINUS [*to* BYRRIA]: While you, damn you, are no good at all except to provide useless information. You can go.

BYRRIA [*rudely*]: That suits me!

    [*He goes off left as* DAVOS *hurries on right, too excited to see the young men.*]

DAVOS: Good heavens, good news! Now where's Pamphilus? I'll rid him of his fears and fill his heart with joy!

CHARINUS [*dubiously*]: Something's made him happy.

PAMPHILUS: Nothing in it. He hasn't heard our present troubles.

DAVOS [*still to himself*]: If he's heard by now there's a wedding prepared for him I expect he's –

CHARINUS: There, did you hear him?

DAVOS: – hunting wildly for me all over the town. Where can he be? Where shall I look first?

CHARINUS: Quick, speak to him.

DAVOS [*beginning to move off*]: I know –

PAMPHILUS: Davos, here, stop!

DAVOS: Who's that? Oh sir, the very man I want! And Charinus, hurrah! The two of you, how splendid! I need you both.

PAMPHILUS: Davos, I'm lost.

DAVOS: Just you listen to this –

CHARINUS: I'm finished.

DAVOS [*to* CHARINUS]: I know what you're afraid of.

PAMPHILUS: My life hangs in the balance.

DAVOS [*to* PAMPHILUS]: And you too: I know.

PAMPHILUS: That wedding for me –

DAVOS: I know.

PAMPHILUS: – today –

DAVOS: Why go on and on when I keep telling you I *know*? [*To* PAMPHILUS] You're afraid you'll have to marry the girl. [*To* CHARINUS] And you're afraid you can't.

CHARINUS: You've got it.

PAMPHILUS: Absolutely.

DAVOS: And there's absolutely no danger. Trust me.

PAMPHILUS: I implore you, free me quickly from my wretched fears.

DAVOS: All right, I'm freeing you. Chremes isn't giving you his daughter now.

PAMPHILUS: How do you know?

DAVOS: I know all right. Your father stopped me just now, told me you were to be married today, and a whole lot more things I haven't time to repeat now. I ran off at once into town to tell you. When I couldn't find you anywhere I climbed up a hill and looked all round – no sign of you. Then I caught sight of your friend's man Byrria and asked him. He said he hadn't seen you. I was worried and wondered what to do. On my way back I had a sudden suspicion: 'Why, there was very little bought for dinner, the master was in a bad temper, and the wedding was all very sudden: it doesn't make sense.'

PAMPHILUS: What are you getting at?

DAVOS: I went straight along to Chremes'. Not a soul outside the house when I got there. I was delighted.

CHARINUS [*eagerly*]: You're right.

PAMPHILUS: Go on.

DAVOS: I waited. During this time I saw no one go in, no one come out. There were no married women about the house, no preparations, no excitement. I went up and peeped in –

PAMPHILUS: I see. That's good proof.

DAVOS [*triumphantly*]: Does this look like a wedding?

PAMPHILUS: No, I don't think it does.

DAVOS: Only '*think*', sir? You can't have understood me. It's certain. What's more, as I came away I ran into Chremes' boy, and all he was carrying was a penn'orth of greens and a few scraps of fish for the old man's supper.

CHARINUS: I'm saved too, Davos, thanks to you.

DAVOS: Indeed you're not!

CHARINUS: Why not? He isn't marrying her to *him* [*indicating* PAMPHILUS] after all.

DAVOS: Don't be so silly. It doesn't follow that *you*'ll marry her if Pamphilus doesn't. You'll have to watch out, go round and canvass the old man's friends.

CHARINUS: You're right. I'll go, though heaven knows my hopes have come to nothing more often than not. Good-bye. [*He goes off, left.*]

PAMPHILUS: What does my father mean by this play-acting?

DAVOS: I can tell you. If he shows annoyance now at Chremes' refusing to give you his daughter, before he finds out your attitude to the match, he thinks he'll put himself in the wrong – and rightly. But if you're the one who refuses to marry the girl, he can shift the blame on to you – and then there'll be the usual scene.

PAMPHILUS: I can face anything.

DAVOS: But he's your father, sir, that's the problem; and besides, your lady hasn't anyone to stand up for her. He'll find a pretext to throw her out of the town, no sooner said than done.

PAMPHILUS [*horrified*]: Throw her out?

DAVOS: In no time.

PAMPHILUS: Then tell me what I can do.

DAVOS: Agree to marry.

PAMPHILUS: What!

DAVOS: What's the matter?

PAMPHILUS: How can I do that?

DAVOS: Why not?

PAMPHILUS: I absolutely refuse.

DAVOS: I shouldn't do that, sir.

PAMPHILUS: I don't want any of your advice.

DAVOS: Think of the effect –

PAMPHILUS: I know. Cut off from *her* and shut up in *there* [*indicating* GLYCERIUM'S *and* SIMO'S *houses*].

DAVOS: No, no, you're wrong. What'll happen I'm sure is that your father will say he wants the wedding today. You'll say you're ready. He can't quarrel with that, and then you'll be able to upset all his well-laid plans without any risk to yourself, for it's quite certain that Chremes will refuse to give you his daughter. Only don't alter your present behaviour, or there's the danger he'll change his mind. Tell your father you're willing, so that he can't be angry with you whenever he wants. You may hope it'll be easy to fend off a wife – 'with a character like mine no one will give me one' is what you'll say, but he's more likely to produce a penniless bride for you than leave you to go to the bad. But if he finds you take it calmly he'll fuss less and take his time to look for someone else for you. Meanwhile your luck may turn.

PAMPHILUS [*dubiously*]: Do you really think so?

DAVOS: I'm positive, sir.

PAMPHILUS: Think where you may land me.

DAVOS: Now, don't argue.

PAMPHILUS: All right, I'll agree. But he mustn't know about

Glycerium's child, for I've promised to acknowledge it as mine.

DAVOS: *That* was rash!

PAMPHILUS: It was a promise she begged of me, to make sure I wouldn't abandon her.

DAVOS: We'll keep it. But here's your father. Take care he doesn't see you looking worried.

[SIMO *comes on right, not seeing the others as they draw back.*]

SIMO: I'm back to see what they're up to and what plans they're laying.

DAVOS [*to* PAMPHILUS]: You see he's quite certain you'll refuse to marry. He's been rehearsing his speech in some lonely spot and now he comes hoping it'll make mincemeat of you. Mind you keep your wits about you.

PAMPHILUS: I only hope I can!

DAVOS: Believe me, sir, just say you'll agree to take a wife and your father won't breathe another word.

[BYRRIA *comes on left, and stands unseen by the other three.*]

BYRRIA: Young Charinus told me to drop everything and spend the day watching Pamphilus, to find out his intentions about this marriage. That's why I'm trailing this one now [*indicating* SIMO]. Why, there *is* Pamphilus with Davos – watch it, Byrria [*moving nearer*].

SIMO [*turning to see* PAMPHILUS *and* DAVOS]: There they are, the pair of them.

DAVOS [*to* PAMPHILUS]: Now, remember!

SIMO: Pamphilus!

DAVOS: Turn round as if you hadn't seen him.

PAMPHILUS [*with marked surprise*]: Why, father, is that you?

DAVOS [*aside*]: Well done!

SIMO [*watching him closely*]: Today, as I told you before, is the day on which I wish you to take a wife.

BYRRIA [*aside*]: What'll he answer? I'm nervous on our behalf.

PAMPHILUS [*sweetly*]: Neither in this nor in anything else will you meet with any opposition from me, father.

BYRRIA: What!

DAVOS: He's struck dumb.

BYRRIA: What did he say?

SIMO [*somewhat nonplussed*]: It is very right and proper of you to accede to my request with a good grace.

DAVOS [*in triumph*]: There, was I right?

BYRRIA: It sounds as though my master's done out of a wife.

SIMO: Go indoors now, and don't keep us waiting when you're wanted.

PAMPHILUS: All right. [*He goes into* SIMO's *house.*]

BYRRIA [*indignantly*]: Oh, you can't trust anyone in anything! It's quite true what you're always hearing, that no one thinks of anyone but himself. I've seen that girl, and I remember she was a real beauty, so I can understand Pamphilus if he chose to have her sleeping in his own arms and not in my master's. . . . Well, I'll have to break the news – a blow for him and blows for me.

[*He goes off left, still unseen by the other two.*]

DAVOS [*aside*]: Now he thinks I've stayed behind because I've got a trick up my sleeve.

SIMO: And what has Davos to say to this?

DAVOS [*aloud*]: Nothing, same as before.

SIMO: Really?

DAVOS: Nothing at all.

SIMO [*aside*]: All the same I really thought –

DAVOS [*aside*]: He didn't expect this, I can see, and it's put him out of his stride.

SIMO: Are you capable of telling me the truth?

DAVOS: Of course, sir, that's easy.

SIMO: Doesn't my son find the prospect of marriage at all unwelcome on account of his association with this foreigner?

DAVOS: No, sir, not at all; or if he did, it would only worry him for two or three days, you know, and then he'd get over it. He's thought it all over properly in his own mind.

SIMO: Very creditable of him.

DAVOS: It was an affair of his youth, sir, which he only carried on as long as he could, and what's more, he kept it dark and took care his reputation shouldn't suffer, as a decent man should. Now it's time he took a wife, and it's a wife he's got in mind.

SIMO: I thought he was looking a little bit depressed?

DAVOS: He may be a bit cross with you, sir, but that's another matter.

SIMO: What is it then?

DAVOS: Oh it's too childish –

SIMO: What *is* it?

DAVOS: Nothing, sir.

SIMO: What is it? Tell me at once.

DAVOS [*with a show of reluctance*]: He says you're, well, mean with your money.

SIMO: *I* am?

DAVOS: Yes, you, sir. 'Scarcely ten drachmas spent on the wedding-breakfast' is what he's saying. 'That doesn't look like a wedding for a son. I'll have to pick and choose among my friends if I'm to send out any invitations.' And if I may say so, sir, you really are terribly careful with your money. I can't say I like it.

SIMO: Be quiet.

DAVOS [*aside*]: That stung him.

SIMO: I shall have this put right at once. [*Aside*] But there's something queer here. Is he up to his old tricks? If it means mischief, you can be sure he's at the bottom of it.

[*They stand back as* MYSIS *returns, right, with* LESBIA, *the midwife, and her assistant,* CANTHARA.]

MYSIS: The fact is, Lesbia, as you said, there's scarcely a man to be found who'll stay faithful to a woman.

SIMO [*to* DAVOS]: It's the Andrian girl's servant.

DAVOS: What's that? So it is.

MYSIS: But Pamphilus –

SIMO: What!

MYSIS: – has confirmed our belief in him –

SIMO [*groans*]

DAVOS: If only he were deaf or she were dumb!

MYSIS: – by declaring that the child shall be acknowledged.

SIMO: My God, what do I hear? If what she says is true – it's the end.

LESBIA: You make him sound a really nice young gentleman.

MYSIS: He couldn't be better. But come in with me now, you mustn't keep my lady waiting.

LESBIA: After you.

[*They go into* GLYCERIUM's *house.*]

DAVOS [*aside*]: Now I've got to find a way out of *this* mess.

SIMO: Good heavens, how can he be so crazy? A foreign woman's child? [*After a pause*] Now I know! How slow I've been. At last I'm beginning to understand. . . .

DAVOS [*aside*]: *What* does he say he understands?

SIMO: This is the first stage of his plan to deceive me; the baby is all a pretence to frighten off Chremes.

GLYCERIUM [*calling from the house*]: Oh Juno Lucina, help me, save me, please!

SIMO [*whistling in surprise*]: As quick as that? It's absurd. She must have decided to speed up when she heard I was outside the door. There's something wrong with your timing, Davos.

DAVOS: Me, sir?

SIMO: Your pupils don't seem to know their parts.

DAVOS: I don't know what you mean, sir.

SIMO [*aside*]: If it had been a real marriage and this fellow had caught me unprepared, how he'd have had the laugh on me! As it is, he's the one in danger and my ship's in safe harbour.

[*The midwife comes out of the house, calling her instructions inside.*]

LESBIA: So far everything seems normal, Archylis, and she should be quite all right. First of all then, see that she has a bath; after that, give her the drink I ordered for her, just as much as I prescribed. I shall soon be back. [*Coming forward*] Bless me, that's a fine boy for Pamphilus! I pray heaven he'll live, for his father's a real gentleman and wouldn't have dreamed of wronging such a nice young lady.

[*She goes off, right.*]

SIMO: Wouldn't anyone who knows you believe you're at the bottom of this?

DAVOS: Bottom of what, sir?

SIMO: She didn't give instructions at the bedside about what was to be done for the mother, but waited to come out and shout indoors from the street. Really, Davos, do you take me for a fool? Do I appear a proper dupe for such barefaced trickery? You might at least take the trouble to *pretend* I'm a man to be feared if I find out.

DAVOS [*aside*]: He's fooling himself this time, nothing to do with me.

SIMO: I told you and warned you not to be up to your tricks. Have you no sense of shame? What's the point of it? Am I really to believe your story that this woman has borne Pamphilus a child?

DAVOS [*aside*]: That's where he's wrong, and I see what I can do.

SIMO: Can't you speak?

DAVOS: What's this about believing? Anyone would think you hadn't been *told* what would happen.

SIMO: *Did* anyone tell me?

DAVOS: You don't mean to say you found out for yourself it was all made up?

SIMO: You're laughing at me.

DAVOS: You must have been told; how else could you have suspected this?

SIMO: I can tell you how: I know *you*.

DAVOS: That's as much as saying I put them up to it.

SIMO: And I'm positive you did.

DAVOS: Really, sir, you've got me all wrong.

SIMO: Have I?

DAVOS: Whenever I try to tell you something, you take me up at once for fooling you.

SIMO: And I suppose I'm wrong?

DAVOS: The result is I daren't open my mouth.

SIMO: One thing I do know: no one has had a baby here.

DAVOS: Quite right, sir! But all the same, it won't be long before someone leaves a baby out here on the doorstep. I'm only telling you this now, sir, so that you can't say you weren't warned, and don't go around afterwards saying that Davos put them up to it and it was one of his tricks. I'd be glad of a change in your opinion of me, I must say.

SIMO: How do you know about this?

DAVOS: I believe what I've heard. A lot of things have given me the idea, and they all hang together. Earlier on, the girl said she was pregnant by Pamphilus,[1] and we've found that's not true. Now she sees preparations for a wedding in your house, so she sends her maid to fetch a midwife and bring in a baby at the same time. She knows if she can't

1. There is no mention of this elsewhere in the play.

make you see the child that nothing will stop the marriage.

SIMO: Yes, but once you'd discovered this plan, why didn't you tell Pamphilus at once?

DAVOS [*virtuously*]: Who was it, pray, who got him to break with her if it wasn't me? We all know he used to be crazy about her, but now he's looking for a wife. Just you leave everything to me, sir. Carry on with these wedding arrangements as you are doing, and I only hope the gods are on our side.

SIMO: No, I'd rather you went in. Make all the necessary preparations and wait for me there. [DAVOS *goes into* SIMO's *house*.] He hasn't entirely convinced me; and yet perhaps all he said may be true. It doesn't really matter. Much the most important thing is the promise I had from my son's own lips. Now I'll find Chremes and beg him to give us his daughter. If he agrees, what better time for the wedding than today? And if Pamphilus proves unwilling to keep his promise, I'm sure I've every right to put pressure on him. Why, here *is* Chremes, just when I want him. [CHREMES *comes on left*.] Chremes, I hope –

CHREMES: Ah, Simo, I was looking for you.

SIMO: As I was for you. I'm glad you've come.

CHREMES [*stiffly*]: Several people have approached me to say they had heard from you that my daughter is to be married to your son today. I have come to see whether this is a delusion of theirs – or yours.

SIMO [*anxiously*]: Listen a moment, and you'll know what I want of you and will have the answer to your question.

CHREMES: I'm listening. Say what you want.

SIMO: In the name of heaven, Chremes, and of our friendship which started in boyhood and has increased with our years – in the name of your only daughter and my son whose only chance of salvation rests in your hands – I beg you to help me in this matter and let the marriage take place as it was planned.

CHREMES: Don't beg me – it doesn't take entreaties to win my consent. Do you suppose *I* have changed since the time when I made the offer? If this marriage is going to benefit them both, have her fetched. But if more harm than good will come out of it for either of them, I must ask you to take thought for our joint interests, as if my girl were your own daughter and I were the father of your son.

SIMO: That is precisely the spirit in which I want this marriage, and am pressing for it to take place. I wouldn't do so, Chremes, if I weren't prompted by the facts.

CHREMES: What do you mean?

SIMO: My son has quarrelled with Glycerium.

CHREMES [*sceptically*]: So I hear.

SIMO: Seriously enough for me to have hopes he will break with her.

CHREMES: Nonsense!

SIMO: It's a fact.

CHREMES: And I can tell you what sort of a fact; lovers' quarrels are a renewal of love.

SIMO: That is exactly what I want to convince you we should forestall. Now is the time, when his passion is stifled while they bandy insults. Before these women's false tears and wicked ways can lure his lovesick mind back to tender feelings, we must get him a wife. Once he has a settled relationship with a wife of good birth I am hopeful that he will find it easy to shake off his bad habits.

CHREMES: That's what you think. Personally I don't believe he can, any more than he can carry on with that woman for long or I can put up with his conduct.

SIMO: How do you know he can't change if you don't make the experiment?

CHREMES: That sort of experiment's too risky to try on a daughter.

SIMO: But in fact, all the possible disadvantages come to this: there might be a separation, which God forbid. On the other hand, look at all the advantages if he reforms. To begin with, you'll have restored a son to your friend, and then you'll have a husband for your daughter and a steady son-in-law for yourself.

CHREMES [*dubiously*]: All right, have it your own way, if you've convinced yourself that this is a good thing. I don't want to stand in your path.

SIMO: Thank you, Chremes. No wonder I've always had the highest opinion of you.

CHREMES: But I say –

SIMO: What?

CHREMES: How do you know those two really have quarrelled?

SIMO: I had it from Davos himself who's in on all their secrets. He's urging me to hurry on the wedding as fast as I can, and you can't think he would do that if he didn't know my son wanted it too. You shall hear it from him yourself. [*Calling indoors*] Send Davos out here! Look, here he comes.

[DAVOS *comes out of the house.*]

DAVOS: I was just coming for you, sir.

SIMO: What for?

DAVOS: Why aren't we fetching the bride? It's getting late.

SIMO [*to* CHREMES]: Did you hear that? Now, Davos, I once used to have my doubts about you, thinking you might follow the common run of servants and play some trick on me because my son is having an affair.

DAVOS: Should I do such a thing?

SIMO: I was afraid you would, and so I kept from you the truth you are now to hear.

DAVOS: What is it?

SIMO: I'll tell you. [*After a doubtful pause*] I *think* you're to be trusted.

DAVOS: Then you've discovered my true character at last, sir.

SIMO: There wouldn't have been any wedding.

DAVOS: What, no wedding?

SIMO: No. It was all a pretence to test the pair of you.

DAVOS: You don't say so, sir.

SIMO: It's true.

DAVOS: Well I never! I could never have discovered that. What a clever notion!

SIMO: Now listen. After I sent you indoors I had the good fortune to meet my friend Chremes here.

DAVOS [*aside*]: Now we're for it.

SIMO: I told him what you told me just now.

DAVOS [*aside*]: Oh no, no . . .

SIMO: I begged him for his daughter, and in the end I won his consent.

DAVOS [*aside*]: I'm done for.

SIMO: What's that you said?

DAVOS [*hastily*]: Delighted, sir, I said I'm delighted.

SIMO: There'll be no further difficulties on his side.

CHREMES: I'll just go home and tell them to get ready and be back to tell you. [*He goes off, left.*]

SIMO: Now, Davos, as your unaided efforts have brought about this marriage, I beg you –

DAVOS [*aside*]: My own unaided efforts!

SIMO: – to set about reforming my son from now on.

DAVOS [*miserably*]: I'll do my best, sir.

SIMO: You'll succeed now, in his present state of irritation with that girl.

DAVOS: Don't you worry any more, sir.

SIMO: Very well then, where is he now?

DAVOS: I suppose he's at home.

SIMO: I'll go and tell him what I've said to you.

[*He goes into his house.*]

DAVOS: And that's the end of *me*. Nothing now to stop me going straight from here to the mill – no chance of begging for mercy. I've messed up everything, deceived my master, pushed his son into marriage, fixed up the wedding for to-day – which the old man never expected nor Pamphilus wanted. Clever, aren't I. If I'd kept quiet there'd have been none of this trouble. Now here he is. I'm done for. I wish I'd something to fall on [*with gesture of stabbing himself as* PAMPHILUS *bursts out of* SIMO's *house*].

PAMPHILUS [*aside*]: Where's that scoundrel who's destroyed me?

DAVOS: *And* himself.

PAMPHILUS: It's my own fault, I admit, for being such a stupid fool and trusting my affairs to a slave who can't keep his mouth shut! I'm paying the price for my folly, but he shan't escape unpunished!

DAVOS: I'll keep a whole skin for the rest of my life if I can only get out of this scrape.

PAMPHILUS: What am I to say to my father now? Refuse to marry when I've just said I would? How'd I have the nerve? I just can't think what to do with myself.

DAVOS: Neither can I, and I'm trying hard. I'd better say I'll work out something, so as to put off the evil hour.

PAMPHILUS [*seeing* DAVOS]: Hi, you!

DAVOS: He's seen me.

PAMPHILUS: Look here, my good man, do you realize the wretched trap your good advice has sprung on me?

DAVOS: I'll soon get you out of it, sir.

PAMPHILUS: Will you, indeed!

DAVOS: Of course I will, sir.

PAMPHILUS: The same way as before, I suppose.

DAVOS: Oh no, sir, I hope to do better this time.

PAMPHILUS: And I'm to trust a rascal like you? Can *you* clear up this appalling muddle? Didn't I rely on you? And now you've taken me out of my peaceful state and pushed me into marriage. Didn't I tell you this would happen?

DAVOS: You did, sir.

PAMPHILUS: What do you deserve?

DAVOS: Crucifixion. But just give me a moment to recover myself and I'll see daylight.

PAMPHILUS: Damn you, I can't wait now to deal with you as I'd like – I've only got time to look after myself. Your punishment must wait.

[CHARINUS *rushes on left, without seeing them.*]

CHARINUS: Is this credible or conceivable? For men to be so heartless that they delight in evil and seek to profit by the misfortunes of their friends? Can this be honest? Surely not – it's the lowest class of men who have some scruples about saying no at the time, but later, when the moment comes for them to carry out their promise, are forced unavoidably to reveal their true selves. They hesitate to refuse, but circumstances drive them to it. And did you ever hear such insolence? 'Who are you?' and 'What do I care?' they say. 'Why should you have my girl? Number one comes first with me.' Suppose you remind them of their promise – you'll soon find they've no scruples when scruples are needed, but all too many when they're not.

Now what am I to do? Find him and protest about the wrong he's done me? Heap abuse on him? Someone will tell me that gets me nowhere. But it will, quite a bit; at least I shall have annoyed him and relieved my feelings.

PAMPHILUS [*coming forward nervously*]: Charinus, unless heaven helps us I've destroyed us both – but I never meant to.

CHARINUS: 'Never meant to'? Well, there's an excuse at last; you've broken your word.

PAMPHILUS: What do you mean, 'at last'?

CHARINUS: Do you expect you can still lead me on with talk like that?

PAMPHILUS: I don't know what you're talking about.

CHARINUS: It was only *after* I told you I loved her that you took a fancy to her – the more fool me, to judge your nature by my own!

PAMPHILUS: You're wrong.

CHARINUS: I suppose you thought there was no solid satisfaction to be won except by deceiving a man in love and leading him on with false hopes. Very well, keep her.

PAMPHILUS: Keep her? Oh, you've no idea of all the trouble I'm in, and the misery and worry that worthless man of mine has brought about with his schemes!

CHARINUS: What's so surprising about that – if he takes his cue from you?

PAMPHILUS: You wouldn't talk like that if you knew me and my feelings.

CHARINUS: I see; you've just quarrelled with your father, so now he's angry with you, and he hasn't been able to fix up your wedding today.

PAMPHILUS: No, no, it's worse than that – and to show you how little you know of my troubles: this marriage was *not* being arranged, and no one was trying to provide me with a wife just now.

CHARINUS [*scornfully*]: I see; you were forced into it – of your own free will.

PAMPHILUS: Wait – you still don't see –

CHARINUS: I can see quite well that you're going to marry my girl.

PAMPHILUS: Oh, do stop, you'll drive me mad. Just *listen*. He never stopped badgering me to tell my father I'd agree to marry. He begged and prayed till he drove me to it.

CHARINUS: Who are you talking about?

PAMPHILUS: Davos.

CHARINUS: *Davos?*

PAMPHILUS: He's the trouble-maker.

CHARINUS: Why?

PAMPHILUS: I've no idea. All I know is that it was an evil hour for me when I listened to him.

CHARINUS: Is this correct, Davos?

DAVOS [*unwillingly*]: Yes.

CHARINUS: You scoundrel, do you realize what you're saying? God damn you as you deserve! If all his enemies wanted to push him into matrimony, isn't this just what they'd tell him to do? Answer me that.

DAVOS [*with dignity*]: I've been disappointed, but I'm not discouraged.

PAMPHILUS: So I see!

DAVOS: This way hasn't succeeded, so we'll try something else – unless you think that because the first attempt didn't do very well it's impossible to put things right.

PAMPHILUS [*bitterly*]: Certainly not. And moreover, I'm pretty sure that if you carry on with your efforts, instead of one marriage you'll present me with two.

DAVOS: As your slave, sir, it's my duty to work hand and foot, night and day, and risk my life if only I can be of service to you. If things don't always go according to plan, you only have to forgive me. My efforts may not be successful, sir, but I do my best. Of course if you like, you can think up something better yourself and get rid of me.

PAMPHILUS: That's what I want; but first you'll have to put me back where you found me.

DAVOS: Very good, sir.

PAMPHILUS: And do it *now*.

DAVOS [*playing for time*]: Well ... Just a minute, that's Glycerium's door.

PAMPHILUS: That's none of your business.

DAVOS: I'm thinking. ...

PAMPHILUS: Really? At last?

DAVOS: And soon I'll have a plan ready for you.

[GLYCERIUM'*s door opens and* MYSIS *comes out, talking to her mistress inside.*]

MYSIS: I'll be sure to find your Pamphilus wherever he is and bring him back with me. Now don't you worry yourself, my dear.

PAMPHILUS: Mysis!

MYSIS [*turning round*]: Who's that? Ah, Pamphilus, that's good.

PAMPHILUS: What's the matter?

MYSIS: She told me to beg you, if you love her, my mistress that is, to come to her at once. She's longing to see you, she says.

PAMPHILUS: Oh, this is terrible – it's starting all over again. [*To* DAVOS] All this distress and worry for us both is entirely your doing. She's sending for me now because she's heard of those wedding preparations.

CHARINUS: And how easily you could have kept clear of them if he'd only kept quiet!

DAVOS [*to* CHARINUS]: That's right, send him crazy, if he isn't bad enough already without your interference.

MYSIS [*to* PAMPHILUS]: Yes indeed, sir, that's the very reason why my poor lady's so distressed.

PAMPHILUS [*earnestly*]: Mysis, by all the gods in heaven, I swear to you that I will never desert her, not if I knew that I should make the whole world my enemy. I sought her out and won her; we were made for each other. To hell with

712] THE GIRL FROM ANDROS 73

those who want to part us! Nothing shall take her from me
but death.

MYSIS: I can breathe again.

PAMPHILUS: I assure you, it's as true as the oracle of Apollo!
Now, if it's possible to make my father believe that it's
nothing to do with me that the wedding's broken off, all the
better; but if that proves impossible, I'll see that he thinks it
was my doing, and that's easy. [*Turning to* CHARINUS *for
approval*] What do you think of me?

CHARINUS [*gloomily*]: That you're in trouble, same as me.

DAVOS: I'm thinking up a plan –

PAMPHILUS [*sarcastically*]: Clever boy! I know your efforts –

DAVOS: This one, I tell you, will be all worked out.

PAMPHILUS: Yes, but it's needed *now*.

DAVOS: It's ready.

CHARINUS: What is it?

DAVOS: Let's get this clear: it's for him, not you.

CHARINUS: Oh, all right.

PAMPHILUS [*still sceptical*]: Well then, what will you do?

DAVOS [*with growing importance*]: I doubt if this day's long
enough for all I have to see to, so don't imagine I've time to
waste on talking. Clear off, you two, you're in my way.

PAMPHILUS: I shall go and see Glycerium.

[*He goes into her house.*]

DAVOS: And where will *you* go?

CHARINUS: Shall I speak frankly?

DAVOS: Yes, of course. [*Aside*] Here begins a long rigmarole.

CHARINUS: What'll be done for *me*?

DAVOS: You've got a nerve! Isn't it enough that I'm giving
you a short reprieve, so long as I can postpone this wedding?

CHARINUS: But all the same, Davos –

DAVOS: Well, what?

CHARINUS: Fix up *my* wedding . . .

DAVOS: Don't be silly.

CHARINUS [*moving off, left*]: Do come to me if you can manage anything.

DAVOS: Why should I? I've no plan for you.

CHARINUS: But all the same, if there *is* anything –

DAVOS: All right, I'll come.

CHARINUS: – if there is anything I'll be at home.
   [*He goes off.*]

DAVOS: Now, Mysis, you wait for me here a minute till I come out.

MYSIS: What for?

DAVOS: Because you must.

MYSIS: Be quick.

DAVOS: I'll be back in a minute, I say.
   [*He goes into* GLYCERIUM's *house.*]

MYSIS: God help us, nothing lasts in this world! I used to think Pamphilus was the greatest blessing my mistress could have, friend, lover and husband, always ready to help with anything, and now look at the sorrow he's brought her, poor dear, more trouble as things are than any good he was to her before. Here's Davos back again. [*The door opens and* DAVOS *comes out, carrying the baby.*] Good heavens, man, what are you doing? Where are you taking the child?

DAVOS: Mysis, I need all your wits and presence of mind now, to help me with this.

MYSIS: What are you going to do?

DAVOS: Take this baby from me quickly and put it on our doorstep.

MYSIS: Mercy me, on the ground?

DAVOS: Take some branches from the altar[1] there and spread them under it.

1. There was an altar to 'Apollo of the Streets' outside the street-door of a Greek house.

MYSIS: Why don't you do it yourself?

DAVOS: If I have to swear to my master I didn't put it there, then I can do so with a clear conscience.

MYSIS: I see. It's something new for you to be so particular. Give it to me. [*Takes the baby and dandles it.*]

DAVOS: Hurry up; I want to explain what I'm doing. Heavens above! [*looking left along the street*].

MYSIS [*as she puts the baby on* SIMO's *doorstep*]: What is it?

DAVOS: Here's the bride's father. I'll have to give up my first plan.

MYSIS: I don't know what you're talking about.

DAVOS: I'll have to pretend I've just arrived too from the other direction. [*He hurries off, right.*] Mind you follow my lead when I need you.

MYSIS: I've no idea what you're up to, but if I can help you at all, as you can see further than I do, I'll stay here. I don't want to spoil your chances.

[CHREMES *comes on, left.*]

CHREMES: I've made all the necessary preparations for my daughter's wedding and now I've come to tell them to fetch her. Why, what's this? Good God, a baby! You there, woman, did you put it here?

MYSIS [*aside*]: Oh, where's Davos?

CHREMES: Answer me!

MYSIS: He's nowhere to be seen. Oh dear, dear me, he's gone and left me.

[DAVOS *re-enters.*]

DAVOS: Gracious me, what a hubbub in the market! Crowds of people arguing! Food prices up! [*Aside*] What else can I say?

MYSIS [*going to meet him*]: Why on earth did you leave me here alone?

DAVOS [*pretending he has just seen the baby*]: What's this

nonsense? Look here, Mysis, where did this child come from? Who brought it here?

MYSIS: Are you crazy, asking me a question like that?

DAVOS: Who else can I ask? There's no one else.

CHREMES [*aside*]: I wonder where it came from.

DAVOS: Will you answer my question?

MYSIS [*indignantly*]: Oh!

DAVOS [*speaking low*]: Come over here [*taking her aside*].

MYSIS: You're mad. Didn't you –

DAVOS [*low*]: Just you answer my questions – not another word, or else – [*Aloud*] Abusive, are you? Where did it come from? [*Low*] Speak up.

MYSIS: Our house.

DAVOS [*laughing*]: Oho! Of course! You can't expect decent behaviour from a kept woman like that!

CHREMES [*aside*]: I believe she's a servant of the Andrian girl's.

DAVOS: Do you think we're the sort of people you can fool with your tricks?

CHREMES: A good thing I'm here.

DAVOS: Hurry up now and take that baby off our doorstep. [*Low*] Stop – don't move an inch from where you are.

MYSIS [*bewildered*]: Heaven strike you dead for terrifying a poor woman out of her wits!

DAVOS: Do you realize I'm speaking to you?

MYSIS: What do you want?

DAVOS: Must you go on asking? Come on, whose is that baby you put here? Tell me.

MYSIS: Don't you know?

DAVOS [*low*]: Never mind if I know: answer my question.

MYSIS: It's your master's.

DAVOS: Which master's?

MYSIS: Pamphilus.

DAVOS: *What*! Pamphilus!

MYSIS: Well, isn't it?

CHREMES: I never liked this marriage, and how right I was.

DAVOS: What a monstrous crime!

MYSIS: What's the fuss about?

DAVOS: Isn't that the baby I saw carried into your house yesterday evening?

MYSIS: You impudent rascal!

DAVOS: It's a fact; I saw Canthara with something stuffed under her cloak.

MYSIS: Thank Heaven there were some honest women present to witness the birth!

DAVOS: She doesn't know her man, if she thinks she can get at him with this. 'If Chremes sees a baby on the doorstep he won't allow Pamphilus to marry his daughter' is what she thinks, but believe me, he will, all the more.

CHREMES: Believe me, he won't!

DAVOS: And now I'll have you know that if you don't pick that baby up at once I'll kick it into the middle of the street and roll you in the mud with it.

MYSIS: Mercy me, the man's drunk!

DAVOS: One trick leads straight on to another; now I hear it rumoured that the woman's a citizen of Attica.

CHREMES: What!

DAVOS: And he'll be compelled by law to marry her.

MYSIS: Who ever said she wasn't?

CHREMES: A ludicrous situation, and I nearly found myself in it unawares.

DAVOS: Who's that speaking? Why, you've come at the right moment, sir. Just listen.

CHREMES: I've heard everything already.

DAVOS: Everything, did you say?

CHREMES: Yes, I was listening from the start.

DAVOS: Oh, were you listening, sir? It's a shocking story! She ought to be done away with. [*To* MYSIS] This is the gentleman I mentioned – don't think it's Davos you're trying to fool.

MYSIS: Oh dear me, sir, I swear I spoke nothing but the truth.

CHREMES: I know the whole story. Is Simo at home?

DAVOS: Yes, sir.

[CHREMES *goes into* SIMO'*s house*.]

MYSIS: Don't touch me, you brute. I'm going straight to my lady to –

DAVOS [*stopping her*]: You stupid woman, don't you know what we've done?

MYSIS: How can I know?

DAVOS: That's the father-in-law. It was the only way of telling him what we want him to know.

MYSIS: What? You might have told me before.

DAVOS: Can't you see the difference between behaving freely and naturally and planning the part you'll play?

[CRITO *comes on left, a middle-aged countryman dressed for travelling.*]

CRITO [*looking round*]: This is the street they say Chrysis lived in, when she preferred riches acquired here by dishonest means to honourable poverty in her own country. Now she's dead, and all her wealth is mine by law. Ah, here's someone I can ask. Good evening.

MYSIS: Mercy me, who's that I see? Isn't it Chrysis' cousin Crito? Yes, it is.

CRITO: Mysis! How are you?

MYSIS: And how are you, sir?

CRITO: Is it true that Chrysis –

MYSIS: Alas, to our sorrow she's left us.

CRITO: And the rest of you? How are you managing here? Fairly well?

MYSIS: Oh, so so; as well as we can, as they say, since it can't be as well as we'd like.

CRITO: What about Glycerium? Has she found her parents yet?

MYSIS [*sighing*]: If only she had!

CRITO: Not yet? I seem to have chosen a bad moment. If I'd known, of course I would never have come. She was always thought and spoken of as Chrysis' sister, and now she's in possession of her property. I'm a stranger here, and I know quite well from other people's experience just how *easy* and *useful* it will be for me to go to law. At the same time I expect she's found a friend and protector already, for she was quite a big girl when she left. I'll only get myself talked about for sharp practice and cadging and legacy-hunting. In any case I shouldn't want to leave her penniless.

MYSIS: There's an honest man for you! The same old Crito.

CRITO: Take me to see her, now I'm here.

MYSIS: With pleasure, sir.

[*They go into* GLYCERIUM's *house.*]

DAVOS: I'll go too. I don't want my old man to see me just now.

[*He follows them in. There is a short pause, and then* CHREMES *and* SIMO *come out of* SIMO's *house.*]

CHREMES: You've had ample proof of my friendly feeling for you, Simo, and I've been running quite enough risks. Please stop trying to persuade me. In my willingness to fall in with your wishes I nearly gambled away my daughter's life.

SIMO: No, no, Chremes. I must beg and pray you now more than ever to carry out the promise you made me just now.

CHREMES: See how unreasonable your enthusiasm makes you. As long as you can get what you want you don't think what you're asking of me, or whether there should be limits to good-nature. If you paused to think, you would stop trying to wear me down with your unjust demands.

SIMO: What demands?

CHREMES: Need you ask? You forced me to promise my daughter to a young man who is completely wrapped up in a love-affair and has no interest in taking a wife. She faces the prospect of quarrels in the home and the break-up of her marriage, simply so that your son can be cured by *her* pain and distress. You got your way, and I agreed to the arrangement while the situation made it possible. Now that has changed, and you must put up with it. People are saying that his mistress is a free citizen; and now there's a baby born. That settles it, as far as we're concerned.

SIMO: For Heaven's sake don't allow yourself to believe them! Their only interest is to present the boy in the worst possible light. All these schemes and false rumours are only intended to put an end to his marriage. Remove their motive and they'll soon stop.

CHREMES: You're wrong. I was present myself when the woman's servant was quarrelling with Davos.

SIMO [*impatiently*]: Yes, yes, I know.

CHREMES: Quite openly too, as neither of them was aware of my presence.

SIMO: I know, I know, Davos told me earlier on what the women would do. I meant to tell you, but somehow I forgot.

[DAVOS *comes out of* GLYCERIUM's *house, talking back to her.*]

DAVOS: I tell you there's no need to worry now –

CHREMES: There you are, there's Davos.

SIMO [*indignantly*]: Coming out of that house!

DAVOS: – thanks to me, with the help of the foreign gentleman.

SIMO: Now what's he up to?

DAVOS: I've never seen anything so opportune! Man, arrival, time —

SIMO: The rascal! Who can he mean?

DAVOS: Everything safe with a happy landing.

SIMO [*moving towards him*]: I'll speak to him.

DAVOS [*aside*]: It's the master! What shall I do?

SIMO: Well, Davos, my good man —

DAVOS [*hastily*]: Oh sir, and you too, sir, everything's ready indoors.

SIMO: You've done well.

DAVOS: You can fetch the lady whenever you like.

SIMO: Very good. That's all we need. [*Grimly*] And now: will you kindly tell me what took you into that house?

DAVOS [*taken aback*]: M-me, sir?

SIMO: Yes, you.

DAVOS: M-me?

SIMO: So I said.

DAVOS: I went in just now —

SIMO: I'm not asking you *when* you went in.

DAVOS: — with your son.

SIMO: What! Is Pamphilus in there now? Oh, this is too much to bear! Didn't you tell me they were quarrelling, you wretch?

DAVOS: So they are.

SIMO: Then what's he doing there?

CHREMES [*sarcastically*]: What do you suppose? Arguing with her, no doubt.

DAVOS [*trying to recover himself*]: No, sir, please, I'll have to tell you some shocking news. An old man came here just now, and what a type he was! Impudent and artful — to look at him you'd think him worth the earth, with his face all earnest and solemn and an honest way of talking —

SIMO: What's he got to do with us?

DAVOS: Nothing, sir, except for what I heard him say.

SIMO: And what was that?

DAVOS: He said he knew Glycerium was a citizen of Attica.

SIMO: Did he! [*Crossing to his house and opening the door*] Dromo! Dromo!

DAVOS: What's the matter, sir?

SIMO: Dromo!

DAVOS: Listen, sir –

SIMO: If you say another word – Dromo!

DAVOS: Sir, do please listen –

[*The servant* DROMO *comes out, a heavily-built man carrying a leather strap.*]

DROMO: What is it, sir?

SIMO: Take him in and string him up, quick as you can.

DROMO: Who?

SIMO: Davos.

DROMO: Why?

SIMO: Because I want it. Go on, take him.

DAVOS: What have I done?

SIMO: Take him away.

DAVOS: If you find anything I've said isn't true, you can kill me, sir.

SIMO: I'm not listening.

DROMO [*menacingly*]: I'll tickle you up a bit, see?

DAVOS [*struggling in* DROMO's *grasp*]: Even if it's the truth?

SIMO: Yes. [*To* DROMO] See that he's kept tied up, and listen! Tie him hands-to-feet. Go on! And as sure as I live I'll show you and Pamphilus here and now what a dangerous game you've been playing, thinking you could deceive me – your master and his father.

[DROMO *hustles* DAVOS *in.*]

CHREMES: Please don't be so violent.

SIMO: Oh, Chremes, what gratitude! You should be sorry for me. So much trouble I've taken for such a son! [*Opening* GLYCERIUM's *door and shouting*] Here, Pamphilus! Come out, Pamphilus! Have you no shame?

[PAMPHILUS *hurries out.*]

PAMPHILUS: Who wants me? How awful, it's my father.

SIMO: What's that, you —

CHREMES: Never mind about abusing him, stick to facts.

SIMO: Could any words be too harsh for him? Do you dare to tell me that girl is a free-born citizen?

PAMPHILUS: So they say.

SIMO: 'So they say'? What impudence! Does he think what he's saying? Is he ashamed of his conduct? Look at him — does any sign of a blush mark his shame? Is he so lacking in self-control that he ignores his country's laws and customs and defies his father's wishes simply because he has set his heart on possessing this woman — to his everlasting disgrace?

PAMPHILUS [*overwhelmed*]: I'm a miserable wretch!

SIMO [*warming up to his scene*]: What? Have you only just realized that, Pamphilus? At the time when you made up your mind to satisfy your desires, no matter how — *that* was the moment for these words to fit you. What about *me*? Why should I suffer? Why torment myself? Why harass my old age with the folly of a boy like this? Must I pay the penalty for his misdeeds? No, no, let him keep her and live with her; I've done with him.

PAMPHILUS: Father!

SIMO: Why call me father? Have you any need of me as a father? Home, wife and children you've found for yourself, against your father's wishes. You've brought your witnesses to swear she is free-born; you win.

PAMPHILUS: Father, may I just say something —

SIMO: What can you say – to me?

CHREMES: Hear him, Simo, all the same.

SIMO: Hear him, Chremes? What am I to hear?

CHREMES: Just let him speak.

SIMO: Very well, he can speak. I'm not stopping him.

PAMPHILUS [with emotion]: I admit I love her, and if that is doing wrong, then I admit that too. I surrender, father. Give me your orders, lay on me what burdens you like. Do you want me to marry? And must I send her away? I'll bear this somehow, as well as I can. Only one thing I beg of you; don't believe that this old gentleman was fetched here by me. Let me bring him out to meet you and clear myself.

SIMO: Bring him out here?

PAMPHILUS: Please, father.

CHREMES: It's a reasonable request. You ought to grant it.

PAMPHILUS: Please do as I ask.

SIMO: All right. [PAMPHILUS goes into GLYCERIUM's house.] Anything to find out that he's not deceiving me, Chremes.

CHREMES: A father shouldn't be too hard on his children whatever their faults.

[CRITO and PAMPHILUS come out, talking.]

CRITO: Say no more. Any one of these is a good enough reason for my doing what you want – consideration for you, goodwill towards Glycerium, or the simple truth.

CHREMES: Why, isn't that Crito from Andros? Yes, it is.

CRITO: Chremes! I hope I find you well.

CHREMES: You're a rare visitor to Athens. What brings you here?

CRITO: Oh, just chance. Is this Simo?

CHREMES: It is.

CRITO [advancing with outstretched hand]: Simo –

SIMO [ignoring this]: Do you want me? Here, is it you who say that Glycerium's a free-born citizen?

CRITO: Are you saying she's not?

SIMO: You've come here properly primed, haven't you?

CRITO: What do you mean?

SIMO: You know very well. Do you expect to get away with this? Coming here and leading young men astray who've been properly brought up and are ignorant of the world, working on their minds with temptations and promises?

CRITO: Are you in your right mind?

SIMO: Tying up affairs with kept women in the bonds of matrimony?

PAMPHILUS [aside]: Oh dear, I'm afraid he'll never stand up to this.

CHREMES: If you knew my friend properly, Simo, you would not think this of him. He's an honest man.

SIMO: *He's* an honest man? When he turned up so smartly the very day of the wedding, though he's never been here before? Yes, yes, Chremes, just the sort of man to trust.

PAMPHILUS [aside]: If I weren't so afraid of my father there's a bit of good advice I could give him.

SIMO: Impostor!

CRITO: What!

CHREMES: It's just his manner, Crito. Take no notice.

CRITO: Let him mind his manners. If he persists in talking to me exactly as he likes, he will hear a few things that he *won't* like. [To SIMO] I'm not interfering with your affairs; they're no concern of mine. They're *your* troubles; grin and bear them! Anyway, we can soon find out whether the information I gave you was true or false. Some time ago a citizen of Attica was shipwrecked on the coast of Andros. With him was a small girl – the woman we're talking about. He lost everything, and the first person he approached for help happened to be Chrysis' father.

SIMO [scornfully]: Here the story starts.

CHREMES: Let him go on.

CRITO: Why is he interrupting?

CHREMES: Continue.

CRITO: Well, this man who gave him shelter was a relative of mine, and it was in his house that the stranger told me himself that he was an Attic citizen; there too he died.

CHREMES [*eagerly*]: His name?

CRITO: Dear, dear, sprung on me like that . . . was it Phania? Yes, Phania, I do believe it was. I'm quite positive anyway that he said he came from Rhamnus.

CHREMES [*aside*]: Heavens above!

CRITO: All this was known to a lot of other people in Andros at the time.

CHREMES [*aside*]: If only . . . Dare I hope? [*To* CRITO] Quick, tell me, what about the girl? Did he say she was his daughter?

CRITO: No.

CHREMES: Whose was she then?

CRITO: His brother's.

CHREMES: It's true! She's mine!

CRITO: What!

SIMO: What's that, Chremes?

PAMPHILUS [*aside*]: Mark this, Pamphilus.

SIMO: What makes you think so?

CHREMES: Phania was my brother.

SIMO: Of course he was. I knew him.

CHREMES: He left Athens to get away from the war and intended to follow me across to Asia. He was afraid to leave the girl here at such a time. Since then I've never heard what happened to him until today.

PAMPHILUS: Oh, I'm beside myself, my head's in a whirl with hope and fear and delight at this marvellous, unexpected, immense good fortune!

SIMO [*to* CHREMES]: I'm delighted too in every way that she's found to be your daughter.

PAMPHILUS: I'm sure you are, father.

CHREMES: There's still just one small thing which worries me.

PAMPHILUS [*aside*]: Oh, you and your scruples, you tiresome old fool; you'd look for knots in a bulrush.

CRITO: What is it?

CHREMES: The name's not right.

CRITO: She had a different one when she was small.

CHREMES: What was it, Crito? Can't you remember?

CRITO: I'm trying to think. . . .

PAMPHILUS [*impatiently*]: I'm not going to have my happiness held up by his memory when the remedy's in my own hands. Listen, Chremes, the name you want is Pasibula.

CHREMES: Right!

CRITO: That's it.

PAMPHILUS: She's told me it herself thousands of times.

SIMO: I am sure you know that we are all delighted about this, Chremes.

CHREMES: Indeed I do.

PAMPHILUS: And now, father –

SIMO: The truth has reconciled me to everything.

PAMPHILUS [*hugging him*]: Father, you're splendid. And as regards my right to possess her as my wife? Does Chremes raise any objection?

CHREMES [*drily*]: You've a sound case; so long as your father agrees.

PAMPHILUS: Of course there's the –

SIMO: Yes indeed.

CHREMES: Her dowry is sixty thousand drachmas, Pamphilus.

PAMPHILUS: I accept.

CHREMES: I can't wait to see my daughter. Come with me, Crito – I suppose she won't know me.

SIMO: Why not have her brought over to my house?

PAMPHILUS: A good suggestion! I'll tell Davos to see to it at once.

[CHREMES *and* CRITO *go into* GLYCERIUM's *house.*]

SIMO: That's impossible.

PAMPHILUS: Why?

SIMO: There's something more urgent – for which he's better suited – that's stopping him.

PAMPHILUS: What's that?

SIMO: He's tied up.

PAMPHILUS [*indignantly*]: I don't think that was a proper thing to do, father.

SIMO: Well, I told them to do it properly.

PAMPHILUS: Tell them to undo him, please.

SIMO: All right.

PAMPHILUS: Quickly!

SIMO: I'm just going.

[*He goes into his house.*]

PAMPHILUS: Oh what a lovely lucky day!

[CHARINUS *comes on, left.*]

CHARINUS: I just want to see how Pamphilus is getting on. Why, there he is.

PAMPHILUS [*not seeing him*]: Some people might fancy I think this too good to be true, but I want to believe it and I shall! If the gods enjoy eternal life I'm sure it's because their joys are everlasting, so my immortality is won so long as trouble doesn't interrupt my happiness. But who do I want here most to hear the news?

CHARINUS: What's he so happy about?

[DAVOS *comes out, rubbing his arms and shoulders.*]

PAMPHILUS: Here's Davos, he's the man I want. I know he's the only one who'll be genuinely glad to see me happy.

DAVOS: Where's Pamphilus?

PAMPHILUS: Davos!

DAVOS: Who's that?

PAMPHILUS: It's me.

DAVOS: Oh sir –

PAMPHILUS: You don't know what's happened to me!

DAVOS: No, I don't. But I know what's happened to *me*.

PAMPHILUS [*patting him on the shoulder*]: So do I.

DAVOS: There you are, you've heard of my troubles before I know your good news; the usual thing.

PAMPHILUS: My Glycerium has found her parents!

DAVOS [*genuinely pleased*]: That's good.

CHARINUS: What!

PAMPHILUS: Her father's a great friend of ours.

DAVOS: Who is he?

PAMPHILUS: Chremes.

DAVOS: That's splendid news.

PAMPHILUS: There's nothing to stop me marrying her now.

CHARINUS [*aside*]: His heart's desire! Can he be dreaming?

PAMPHILUS: Then there's the baby, Davos –

DAVOS: That's enough, sir. He's sure to be first favourite of the gods.

CHARINUS [*coming forward*]: If this is true – it'll save my life. I'll speak to them.

PAMPHILUS: Who's that? Charinus, just when we want you!

CHARINUS: Congratulations.

PAMPHILUS: Did you hear?

CHARINUS: Everything. And now, have a thought for me in your good fortune. You've got Chremes just where you want him – I'm sure he'll do anything for you.

PAMPHILUS: I haven't forgotten you.[1] What's more, it would take too long if we wait for him to come out. Come in with me – he's there now with Glycerium. Davos, you hurry

1. Alternative ending starts from here.

home and send people to bring her over to us. Come on, be quick, don't stand about.

[PAMPHILUS *and* CHARINUS *go into* GLYCERIUM'*s house.*]

DAVOS: I'm going. [*To the audience*] You needn't wait for them to come out again; the other betrothal and any other business will take place in there. Now give us your applause.[1]

[*He goes into* SIMO'*s house.*]

ALTERNATIVE ENDING

(*The following lines exist in some late* MSS., *written at the end of the play, but originally intended to follow line 976. They were known to the commentators Donatus and Eugraphius, who agree that they were not by Terence, but it is impossible to determine when and by whom they were written, evidently with a view to making sure of a happy outcome for Charinus and his Philumena.*)

[CHREMES *comes out of the house;* CHARINUS *and* DAVOS *stand aside.*]

PAMPHILUS: Ah, Chremes, I was waiting for you. I'd like to talk to you about a matter which concerns you. I was anxious for you not to say that I've forgotten your other daughter. I believe I've found a husband for her who will be worthy of you both.

CHARINUS: Oh I can't bear this, Davos. My love and life are both at stake.

CHREMES: There's nothing new to me in your proposal, Pamphilus – if I'd wanted it.

CHARINUS: There, I'm done for, Davos.

1. In the Latin text all the plays end with an appeal to the audience, indicated by ω (i.e. the last speaker). This is generally thought to be the *cantor* referred to by Horace in *Ars poetica* 155 (*donec cantor 'vos plaudite' dicat*).

DAVOS: Wait a bit.

CHARINUS: I'm finished.

CHREMES: But I'll tell you why I didn't want it. It wasn't because I was altogether against the young man as one of my family –

CHARINUS: What?

DAVOS: Hush.

CHREMES: – but because I wanted the friendship which Simo and I inherited from our fathers to be passed on to our children and even somewhat strengthened. But now that I have the opportunity and good fortune to make both my daughters happy, I give my consent.

PAMPHILUS: That's fine.

DAVOS: Come and thank him.

CHARINUS [coming forward]: Good evening, Chremes, kindest of all my friends! And this is something which is as great a joy to me as to have obtained what I want and expect from you and beg with all my heart – namely, to have found out what opinion you had of me before.

CHREMES: Whatever a man sets his mind upon, Charinus, the firmness of his intentions will shape other people's opinion of him. The truth of this may be inferred from my own attitude towards you, for though I was unfriendly, I still knew the sort of man you were.

CHARINUS: I see.

CHREMES: And so I promise you my daughter Philumena for your wife, with a dowry of thirty-six thousand drachmas.

THE SELF-TORMENTOR

[HEAUTON TIMORUMENOS]

INTRODUCTORY NOTE

ALL the MSS. and the Production Notice list *The Self-Tormentor* as Terence's third play (and *The Eunuch* as second), but as it was produced in 163 B.C. and *The Eunuch* in 161, most modern editors place it second. Between it and *The Girl from Andros* came the first attempt to present *The Mother-in-Law* in 165, which was withdrawn half-way through, and possibly the first of the two successful productions of *The Eunuch*.

It is a puzzling play in more than one sense. Terence warns us in the Prologue that there is little action and everything depends on the dialogue, and it is indeed the least dramatic of all the plays. It demands hard concentration on the part of an audience if they are not to be as confused as Syrus's dupes by the complexities of double plot and counter-plot, and many may feel that here the clever young playwright has overreached himself. But there is a certain astringency about the dialogue, and the sort of logic one enjoys following in reading the exchanges of Ivy Compton-Burnett's highly articulate characters.

Of the characters, Syrus is a typical nimble-witted house slave who endeavours to carry on several intrigues simultaneously and can generally think of an alternative when one plan fails, and Clinia's feeling for Antiphila is treated romantically in a way which recalls *The Girl from Andros*. The main interest concentrates in the pair of older men, who are as clearly differentiated as Demea and Micio in *The Brothers*. The effect of the intrigues on them concerns Terence more than the actual progress of the intrigue (contrast *Phormio*). Chremes in the earlier scenes is always sure he is right and in control of the situation and has to be made to recognize his self-delusion;

Menedemus's self-mortification and settled melancholy gradually slip from him, until in the end he obviously enjoys turning the tables on Chremes and repeating his own advice to his self-appointed mentor.

It was a popular play in antiquity, much quoted by Cicero, and also by Horace and Seneca. A reference to Menedemus's shabby dress in Varro (*Rerum Rusticarum*, 2. 2) suggests that it was still staged in his day. Yet this is the play which is not only the least dramatic but the one which bears traces of careless adaptation. At line 170 Chremes makes a very awkward exit, ostensibly to invite a neighbour, Phania, who plays no part in the play, and the stage is left empty. (A later hand suggested that the interval might be filled by a dance of dinner-guests.) Again, at line 497 Chremes mentions a boundary-dispute between neighbours, and goes off only to return a few lines later. This is quite irrelevant to the play, and one cannot help feeling that it was something Terence took over from a scene where it might have had more point. But it remains a puzzle why a normally careful craftsman did not remove these irrelevancies on revision, especially in this elaborately constructed 'literary' play.

The title also suggests that Terence moved away from his original without considering that 'The Self-Tormentor' was not really very apt as a title for the comedy in its final form. After the first scene the interest largely shifts from the inner conflicts of Menedemus to the progressive stages of the discomfiture of Chremes – who may well be Terence's own creation as an addition to the main character of the single-plot original.

PRODUCTION NOTICE

THE SELF-TORMENTOR by Terence: performed at the Megalensian Games[1] during the curule aedileship of Lucius Cornelius Lentulus and Lucius Valerius Flaccus.

Produced by Lucius Ambivius Turpio and Lucius Atilius (*or* Hatilius) of Praeneste.

Music composed by Flaccus, slave of Claudius, first for unequal pipes, afterwards for two right-hand pipes.

Greek original by Menander.

The author's third play, written during the consulship of Manius Juventus and Titus Sempronius.[2]

1. Celebrated annually in April in honour of the Great Mother, the goddess Cybele.
2. i.e. 163 B.C.

SYNOPSIS

Clinia, who is in love with Antiphila, was forced to serve abroad as a soldier by his stern father, who afterwards tortured himself with remorse for his action. Clinia returns, and, unknown to his father, goes to stay with Clitipho, lover of the courtesan, Bacchis. When Clinia sends for Antiphila in his longing to see her, Bacchis appears on the scene as if she were his mistress, with Antiphila dressed as her servant. This was all arranged to enable Clitipho to conceal Bacchis from his father, from whom, by means of Syrus's tricks, he obtains a thousand drachmas to give her. Antiphila is found to be Clitipho's sister and Clinia marries her, while Clitipho accepts another woman for wife.

CHARACTERS

CHREMES   *an Athenian gentleman*
MENEDEMUS   *his neighbour in the country*
CLITIPHO   *son of Chremes*
CLINIA   *son of Menedemus*
SYRUS   *a slave, attendant on Clitipho*
DROMO   *a slave, attendant on Clinia*
BACCHIS   *a courtesan, mistress of Clitipho*
ANTIPHILA   *a young girl, beloved by Clinia*
SOSTRATA   *wife of Chremes*
PHRYGIA   *maidservant of Bacchis*
CANTHARA(?)[1]   *a nurse in the household of Chremes*

★

*The scene is laid in Attica, in front of the farmhouses of Chremes
and Menedemus. To the audience's right the road leads to Athens,
to their left further into the country*

1. Named only in one MS at l. 614, but Canthara is the old
nurse in *The Brothers*.

AUTHOR'S PROLOGUE TO
THE SELF-TORMENTOR

(*Spoken by Lucius Ambivius Turpio[1]*)

SOME of you may be wondering why the poet has given an old man the part usually assigned to a young actor. I will explain this before going on to the speech I am here to deliver. Today I am presenting *The Self-Tormentor*, a fresh comedy from a fresh Greek source, a double plot made out of a single one. Having told you it is a new play and given its name, I should go on to say who wrote it and who wrote the Greek original, if I didn't think most of you know already. Now I'll say briefly why you see me in this part. The author wanted me to represent him, instead of delivering the usual prologue; he has called on you to be his judges and me to plead his case. I only hope that my eloquence can match his skill in marshalling his thoughts when he wrote this speech for me to deliver.

As to the rumours spread by the malicious that he creates a few Latin plays by taking a lot of Greek ones and 'spoiling'[2] them for others, he doesn't deny this; in fact he is quite unrepentant and declares he will do the same again. He has the precedent of good authors, and sees no reason why he shouldn't follow it in doing what they have done.

Then there's the assertion of that malevolent old playwright[3] that he took up the art of poetry too suddenly, and depends on the talents of his friends[4] rather than on his native genius. This

1. Terence's producer and leading actor.
2. See Introduction, p. 19.
3. Luscius Lanuvinus, Terence's rival.
4. i.e. members of the 'Scipionic circle'. See Introduction, p. 13, and *The Brothers* 15 ff.

is something which your judgement and opinion will have to decide, and that is why I want to appeal to you all not to listen to the voice of prejudice instead of that of honest truth. Be fair to authors, and when they give you the opportunity to see something new and free from faults, give them in return a chance to get on in the world. There is one author who needn't think this applies to him – I mean the one who showed us that scene the other day with a running slave pushing his way through a crowd: why further the interests of anyone so crazy? My author will have more to say about his faults when he puts on further new plays, unless the other puts a stop to his slanderous remarks.

Now listen with open minds, don't interrupt, and allow me to present a play which doesn't depend on action. I'm getting on in years, and can't always be shouting at the top of my voice and wearing myself out playing a running slave, angry old man, greedy sponger, shameless impostor and rapacious pimp.[1] Put yourselves in the mood to see the justice of this, if only for my sake, and give me some respite from my labours, for the writers of the new plays today have no consideration for an elderly man like me; they come running to me if they have an exacting part, while the easy ones go to some other company.

This play depends on the natural purity of its spoken words, so you will be able to see what my talents can do in either style. Set a precedent in me, and then young actors will aim to please you, their audience, rather than themselves.

1. Stock types of comic character; cf. *The Eunuch* 37 ff. A *leno* or slave-dealer in attractive female slaves often appears no better than a pimp.

[MENEDEMUS, *haggard and shabbily dressed, is wearily trudging home carrying a heavy pronged hoe when his neighbour* CHREMES *comes out of his house to speak to him.*]

CHREMES [*in some embarrassment as* MENEDEMUS *takes no notice*]: I know it's not long since we became acquainted, in fact it all started with your buying the farm next to mine, and this is the first time we've really had much to do with each other. . . . All the same, there's something about you – or maybe it's the fact that we're neighbours, which I always think is the next best thing to being friends – which makes me feel that I ought to speak out frankly and give you some friendly advice. [*He waits until* MENEDEMUS *looks up.*] Your behaviour doesn't seem to me to be right for a man of your age and circumstances. What does it all mean, for heaven's sake? What on earth do you want? You're sixty, if not more, I imagine, and no one hereabouts has better land worth more than yours; you've plenty of slaves to work it, and yet you continue to do their work as if you'd no one at all. However early I go out in the morning, however late I come home in the evening, I always see you at work in the fields, digging or ploughing or moving something about. You never slack off for a moment or think of yourself, and it isn't as if you get any pleasure out of it, I'm sure. You may tell me you're not satisfied with the amount of work done on the place, but if you'd only apply the effort you spend on doing everything yourself to making your people get on with the job, you'd do better.

MENEDEMUS: Chremes, can you spare a moment from your

own affairs to listen to someone else's – even if they don't really concern you?

CHREMES: I'm human, so any human interest *is* my concern. Call it solicitude or curiosity on my part, whichever you like. If you're right I'll copy you, and if you're wrong I'll try to make you mend your ways.

MENEDEMUS: This is something *I* have to do; you can do what suits your case.

CHREMES: Does anyone have to torment himself?

MENEDEMUS: Yes, I do.

CHREMES: If you're in trouble, I'm sorry. But what's wrong? What can you have done to deserve this?

MENEDEMUS [*sighs*]

CHREMES: Come now, don't cry; let me know your trouble whatever it is. Don't be afraid, don't keep anything back, you can trust me. I'll give you all the comfort or advice or practical help I can.

MENEDEMUS [*struggling with his tears*]: Do you really want to know?

CHREMES: Yes, of course I do, for the reason I've just given you.

MENEDEMUS: I'll tell you . . .

CHREMES: Then just put down that mattock while you do so, and stop working.

MENEDEMUS: No!

CHREMES: Don't be so silly.

MENEDEMUS: You shan't stop me if I refuse to take time off from my labours.

CHREMES [*cheerfully, as he takes the mattock*]: Well, I am stopping you.

MENEDEMUS [*hopelessly*]: Oh, it's wrong of you.

CHREMES [*leaning the mattock against the wall*]: My goodness, what a weight!

MENEDEMUS: No more than I deserve.

CHREMES: Now then, tell me.

MENEDEMUS: I have an only son, just a boy ... Have one? No, Chremes, I did have one, but whether I still have him or not I've no idea.

CHREMES: What do you mean?

MENEDEMUS: I'll tell you. There's a foreigner here from Corinth, an old woman of humble means. My son fell madly in love with her daughter, in fact he practically treated the girl as his wife. I knew nothing of this at first, but when I did find out I could have shown some humanity and decency in my handling of the boy's love-sick feelings. Instead of which I took the harsh line that parents commonly do in these cases, and was on at him every day. 'Do you hope you'll be allowed to carry on much longer like this in your father's lifetime, setting up a mistress almost as if she were a wife? If that's your idea,' I said, 'you're wrong, Clinia; you don't know me. I'm willing for you to be called my son just as long as you do what's proper in your position – if you don't, I'll find the proper way to deal with you. There's a simple explanation for all this: you haven't got enough to do. When I was your age I'd no thought of love – no, I was a poor man and went off to Asia[1] on active service, and there I won fame and fortune.' The result was that in the end the boy was worn down by having the same things perpetually dinned into him, and he thought my age and concern for him made me wiser and better able to judge his interests than he could himself. So he went off to Asia to serve in the king's army.

CHREMES: No!

1. i.e. Asia Minor. Service in the army of one of the Asiatic rulers was both a career for the penniless and an escape for young men anxious to leave home.

MENEDEMUS: He left without a word to me and has been gone three months.

CHREMES: You're both to blame, though his venture does show spirit as well as respect for you.

MENEDEMUS: When I found this out from the friends who were in his confidence, I came home utterly miserable, almost out of my mind with anxiety and grief. I sat down, and my servants came running to take off my shoes. I saw the others hurrying about, making up a couch, preparing my dinner, everyone doing his best to relieve my distress, and watching them made me think: 'Are all these people worrying solely on my account, just to give me satisfaction? Do I need all these maids to look after my clothes? Must I spend so much in the house for myself, when my only son who should have enjoyed everything as I do – or even more, as he's at a better age to do so – has been driven from home, poor boy, by my own injustice? Why, I'll deserve any fate if I continue like this. As long as he leads that wretched existence far away from home, and all because of the wrong I did him, I'll do penance for it; I'll toil and save and scrape and slave for him.' That's what I've been doing ever since. I've kept nothing in the house, not a dish nor a rag. I gathered up everything I had, all the slaves too, man and woman, except those who could easily earn their keep working in the fields, and auctioned and sold the lot. I put up my house for immediate sale and made about 90,000 drachmas, bought this bit of land, and here I'm working. I've made up my mind that I can lessen the wrong done to my boy by making myself miserable, and I've no right to enjoy any pleasure here until he's safely home to share it with me.

CHREMES: I think you've the makings of a considerate father, and he could be an obedient son if he were tactfully handled in the right way. But you've never succeeded in knowing each other well enough, and for the usual reason: lack of sincerity in your way of life. You never showed him how much he meant to you, and he didn't dare trust you as a son should his father. If you had done, this would never have happened.

MENEDEMUS: You're right, I admit. I've made a terrible mistake.

CHREMES: But I'm hopeful for the future, Menedemus. I feel certain he'll soon come back to you safe and sound.

MENEDEMUS: I pray he will!

CHREMES: Your prayer'll be answered. Come now, it's a public holiday;[1] please spend the day with me, if it's convenient.

MENEDEMUS: I can't.

CHREMES: Why not? Do please relax, only for a little while; your son would want it even though he's not here.

MENEDEMUS: I forced him to hard labour. It's not right for me to shirk it now.

CHREMES: You've made up your mind then?

MENEDEMUS: Yes.

CHREMES: Then I'll say good-bye.

MENEDEMUS: Good-bye.

[*He picks up the mattock and goes into his house.*]

CHREMES: He brings tears to my eyes, I'm so sorry for him. But it's getting late; high time I reminded my neighbour Phania about coming to dinner. I'll go and see if he's at home.

[*He goes off, right. After a short interval when perhaps music is played and dinner-guests assemble and enter* CHREMES' *house,* CHREMES *returns.*]

CHREMES: He didn't need reminding; they say he's been at

1. Probably the spring festival of Dionysus in Athens.

my house some time, so I'm the one who's keeping my guests waiting. I'll go in at once. [*As he turns to go in, the door creaks and opens.*] But who's that at my door? Someone's coming out. I'll step aside.

[*His son* CLITIPHO *comes out without seeing him, talking to someone inside.*]

CLITIPHO: There's nothing to worry about so far, Clinia. They're not late yet, and I'm sure she'll be here soon with the messenger. Do stop torturing yourself with imaginary fears.

CHREMES [*aside*]: Who's my son talking to?

CLITIPHO [*overhearing*]: Why, there's father, the very man I wanted. I'll speak to him. Father, you've come at the right time.

CHREMES: What do you mean?

CLITIPHO: Do you know this neighbour of ours, Menedemus?

CHREMES: Of course I do.

CLITIPHO: Did you realize he has a son?

CHREMES: I'd heard about one. He's in Asia, I believe.

CLITIPHO: No he isn't, father; he's in our house.

CHREMES: What!

CLITIPHO: He's just arrived. I met him as he left his ship and carried him off to dinner. He and I have always been good friends since we were boys.

CHREMES: This is good news! I'm delighted. I only wish I'd been more pressing with my invitation to Menedemus to join us, so that I could have been the first to give him this unexpected pleasure in my own house. But there's still time.

[*He moves towards* MENEDEMUS's *house.*]

CLITIPHO: No, don't, father; you mustn't.

CHREMES: Why not?

CLITIPHO: He hasn't made up his mind yet what to do with

himself. He's only just come, and he's full of fears about his father's anger and his girl's feelings for him. He's crazy about her – she's the cause of all this trouble and the reason why he left home.

CHREMES: I know.

CLITIPHO: He's just sent his boy into town with a message for her, and I've sent our Syrus along too.

CHREMES: What has he to say?

CLITIPHO: Clinia? He can only talk about his misery.

CHREMES: *Misery*? Can you imagine anyone *less* miserable? Are there any of the so-called blessings of mankind he doesn't possess? Parents, a safe homeland, friends, family, relatives, money, he's got the lot. But I suppose these things take their value from the disposition of their owners, blessings if you know how to use them and curses if you don't.

CLITIPHO: But the old father was always difficult, and what I'm afraid of now is that he'll go too far in his anger against his son.

CHREMES: Menedemus? [*Aside*] No, I mustn't speak; it'll help him if his son's afraid of him.

CLITIPHO: What's that you're saying?

CHREMES: I'll tell you. Whatever the situation, your friend ought to have stayed at home. Maybe his father was a bit too strict for his liking, but he could have put up with it. Who was there he should bear with if not his own father? Which would have been right – was the son to adapt himself to the father's ways or the father to the son's? As for his making out his father was hard on him, it's not true. Parents are strict pretty much to the same pattern, provided that they're fairly reasonable men. They don't want their boys to be forever running after women and taking to drink and they keep them on a small allowance, but all this is intended to form their character. But once the mind is the slave of a base passion, Clitipho, inevitably it takes to schemes of the same kind. The sensible thing is to see in others an example you can profit by yourself.

CLITIPHO [*anxious to cut him short*]: Yes, of course.

CHREMES: I am going in to see what there is for dinner. It's late, so don't you go far away.

[*He goes into his house.*]

CLITIPHO: How unfairly all we young men are judged by our fathers! They think we ought to be old men at birth, with no interest in the things which appeal to youth. They try to control us in the light of their present desires, not those they had at our age. If I ever have a son, you may be sure he'll find me an easy father. I shan't seek a means of finding out his faults unless I can forgive them too – not like my own father, who's always taking cover behind someone else to express his views. Damn it all, when he's taken a glass too many he's got plenty to say! But now it's nothing but 'see in others an example you can profit by yourself'; artful, isn't he! Ah, but he little knows that his words fall on deaf ears! At the moment I'm far more concerned about my mistress and her 'give me' and 'fetch me', to which I've no answer. I doubt if there's anyone worse off than I am. Why, even Clinia here, who's got his own share of trouble, has a decent, well-brought-up girl with none of the professional's tricks, while mine is masterful and insolent, prides herself on being a lady, and costs me the earth. All I can give her at present is a soft answer, for I can't bring myself to confess I'm penniless. I've only just realized it myself, and my father hasn't found out yet.

[CLINIA *comes out of* CHREMES' *house, looking anxiously down the road.*]

CLINIA: If I had any luck in love I'm sure they'd have been here long ago, but I'm terribly afraid someone seduced her while I was away. A lot of things taken together increase my worry – opportunity, situation, her youth, and the fact that she's under the thumb of her wicked old mother who cares for nothing but cash.

CLITIPHO: Clinia!

CLINIA: I'm so miserable . . .

CLITIPHO: Do please be careful, or someone coming out of your father's house might see you.

CLINIA: All right; but I'm certain there's trouble brewing for me.

CLITIPHO: Do you *have* to be sure of that before you know the facts?

CLINIA: If it weren't trouble they'd be here by now.

CLITIPHO: They'll be here soon.

CLINIA: What do you mean by 'soon'?

CLITIPHO: You forget she's got quite a way to come, and you know what women are. Plans and preparations can take them a year.

CLINIA: I'm so nervous, Clitipho.

CLITIPHO [*looking down road, right*]: You can breathe again. Here come Dromo and Syrus; there they are!
[DROMO, *a smart young house-slave, and* SYRUS, *a rather older man, appear from right, and the two couples continue to talk without seeing each other.*]

SYRUS: Really?

DROMO: Yes, truly.

SYRUS [*looking back*]: But while we are talking away like this the girls are left behind.

CLITIPHO: She's here, Clinia. Did you hear that?

CLINIA: Yes, I hear, and now I can see and live again!

DROMO: No wonder, they've got such piles of luggage, and they're bringing a whole troop of servants along.

CLINIA: Damn it, where did she get those from?

CLITIPHO: Don't ask me.

SYRUS: We shouldn't have left them like this. Think what they've got to carry.

CLINIA: Oh, no, no!

SYRUS: All those jewels and dresses; and it's getting dark, and they don't know the way. We've been fools. You go back and meet them, Dromo. Hurry up! What are you waiting for? [DROMO *goes off, right*.]

CLINIA: O misery, the end of all my hopes!

CLITIPHO: What's the matter now? What's worrying you?

CLINIA: Need you ask? Can't you see? Servants, jewels, dresses! And I left her with one little maid. Where do you suppose those came from?

CLITIPHO [*looking down the road*]: Oh, *now* I see.

SYRUS [*also looking*]: My God, what a crowd! I don't believe the house will hold them, and think what they'll eat and drink! Nothing will be more pitiable than my poor old master. [*Seeing* CLINIA *and* CLITIPHO] Ah, there are the two I wanted.

CLINIA [*coming forward*]: God in heaven, where is constancy? I was a homeless wanderer on your account, Antiphila, fool that I was, and you seized your chance meanwhile to get rich and abandon me in my troubles. It's all because of you that I'm in such disgrace and a disobedient son to my father. I'm ashamed and sorry now when I think how he was always warning me about the habits of women like this, advice all wasted, for he could never get me to give the girl up. I shall have to do it now, though at the time when I might have been glad to, I refused. No one knows misery like mine.

SYRUS [*aside*]: He seems to have got it all wrong, what we

were saying. [*To* CLINIA] Look, sir, you're mistaken about
your lady. Her life hasn't changed at all, nor her feelings for
you, as far as we could judge from what we saw.

CLINIA: What do you mean, please? There's nothing in the
world I'd like better now than to have my suspicions proved
false.

SYRUS: First let's make sure you know the whole story. That
old woman wasn't her mother, as people used to say, and
now she's dead. I happened to hear the girl telling the other
one herself as we walked along.

CLITIPHO: What other one?

SYRUS: Wait a bit, sir; let me finish telling the story I began.
I'm coming to that later.

CLITIPHO: Be quick, then.

SYRUS: Well, first of all, when we came to the house, Dromo
knocked at the door. An old woman came out, and as soon
as she'd opened the door, in he darted, with me at his heels.
The woman shot the bolt and went back to her spinning.
Now, this is where you could have seen as nowhere else, sir,
the life she's been leading in your absence, I mean when we
burst in on her without warning. It gave us a chance to
judge her ordinary everyday habits, and that's what best
reveals a person's character. We found her busy weaving at
her loom, simply dressed and in mourning, I suppose for the
old lady who'd died; no sign of jewels, or anything beyond
what you'd see on women who dress only to please themselves, with none of those nasty feminine refinements; her
hair not done up, but just combed down round her head and
carelessly tossed back. I needn't say more.

CLINIA [*clutching him*]: Syrus, dear man, please don't raise my
spirits with false hopes.

SYRUS: The old woman was spinning yarn, and there was

only one little maid besides, helping with the weaving, a grubby little slut in rags and tatters.

CLITIPHO: If this is true, Clinia, as I'm sure it is, you're the luckiest man alive! Do you get the point about the maid being shabby and dirty? When go-betweens are uncared-for, it's another sure sign that their mistress is beyond reproach, for it's general practice for men who want access to the mistress to tip the servants first.

CLINIA: Go on, please, Syrus, but don't try to curry favour on false pretences. What did she say when you mentioned my name?

SYRUS: As soon as we said you were back and asked her to come to you she left her loom at once, tears streaming down her face; it was clear to see how much she had felt your absence.

CLINIA: My God, I don't know where I am for joy! I was terribly afraid.

CLITIPHO: I knew all along there was nothing to be afraid of. Now, Syrus, it's my turn. Who's that other girl?

SYRUS: It's your Bacchis we're bringing along too, sir.

CLITIPHO: *What*? Bacchis? You wretch, where are you taking her?

SYRUS: Where should I? To our house, of course.

CLITIPHO: To meet my father?

SYRUS: Why not?

CLITIPHO [*to* CLINIA]: The brazen impudence of the man!

SYRUS: Look, sir, this is something really big and serious; you've got to take risks.

CLITIPHO: But are you intending to win glory by gambling on my life? One little slip on your part and I'm finished. [*To* CLINIA] What am I to do with him?

SYRUS: But in fact –

CLITIPHO: What fact?

SYRUS: If you'll let me, I'll tell you.

CLINIA: Let him speak.

CLITIPHO: I'm not stopping him.

SYRUS [*gaining time*]: At present things are – as if – when –

CLITIPHO: Damn the man, must he speak in riddles?

CLINIA: He's right, Syrus. Drop it, and come to the point.

SYRUS [*injured*]: Indeed, I can't keep silence. You're utterly unfair, sir. I find you quite insufferable.

CLINIA [*forestalling* CLITIPHO]: Do be quiet. We really must listen to him.

SYRUS: You want a love-affair, you want your girl and some ready cash to give her; what you don't want is the risk you must take to have her. Not bad reasoning, I suppose, if it really makes sense to cry for the moon. You've got to accept the bad with the good, or else drop both; these are the only alternatives, so choose which you like. All the same, I know my plan's safe and sure, and it'll give you a chance to have your girl with you in your father's house with nothing to fear. Then there's the money you've promised her; I can get it in the same way – you've just about burst my eardrums going on and on at me to find it. What more do you want?

CLITIPHO [*dubiously*]: If it really works out . . .

SYRUS: *If?* Try it and see.

CLITIPHO: Very well, let's hear your plan. What is it?

SYRUS: We'll pretend your girl belongs to Clinia.

CLITIPHO [*with heavy sarcasm*]: Splendid! And what will he do with his own? Shall she be called his too, in case one isn't disgrace enough?

SYRUS: We'll hand her over to your mother.

CLITIPHO: Why there?

SYRUS: It'd take too long to explain, sir. I've got good reason.

CLITIPHO: Rubbish! I can't see how I gain anything by accepting such a risky situation.

SYRUS: Just a minute, sir. If you're afraid of that risk, I've another, which you'll both admit has no danger at all.

CLITIPHO: That's more like it. Let's hear it, please.

CLINIA: Yes, tell us.

SYRUS: I'll meet them and tell them to return home.

CLITIPHO: *What* did you say?

SYRUS [*injured*]: I'm only trying to remove all your fears so that you can sleep sound on either ear.

CLITIPHO: Whatever am I to do now?

CLINIA: Well, it's a good chance –

CLITIPHO: Syrus! Please tell me the truth!

SYRUS: Come on, sir; soon you'll be willing when it's too late, and that won't help.

CLINIA: – and I'd take it while you can, for you never know ...

CLITIPHO: Syrus, please –

SYRUS: Do as you like, but I shall stick to what I mean to do. [*Turning to go.*]

CLINIA: – if you'll ever have the opportunity again.

CLITIPHO: My God, you're right. Syrus, Syrus! Here, Syrus, come back!

SYRUS [*aside*]: He's warmed up. [*Coming back*] Anything I can do, sir?

CLITIPHO: Come back, come back!

SYRUS: Here I am. Tell me what you want. I suppose you'll soon be saying you don't like that either.

CLITIPHO: No, no, Syrus, I'm putting myself and my love and reputation in your hands. You're the judge; only take care you don't find yourself in the dock.

SYRUS: That's a silly bit of advice, sir, as if my interests were less at stake than yours. If anything happens to go wrong for us you won't get more than a talking-to, but it'll be a thrashing for me. I'm not likely to be careless. Now persuade your friend to pretend the lady's his.

CLINIA: I'm quite ready. As things are, I've no choice.

CLITIPHO: And I'm really grateful, Clinia.

CLINIA: But be careful *she* doesn't slip up.

SYRUS: She's been well drilled in the part.

CLITIPHO: I simply can't understand how you found it so easy to persuade her. She's said no to all sorts of people.

SYRUS: I caught her at the right moment, always the first essential. In fact I found her with an officer who was pitifully begging her for a single night, and she was handling him in her artful way so as to inflame his desire by his frustration, and at the same time keep in your own good graces. But do watch your step, sir, and don't wreck everything by being careless. You know what a sharp eye your father has for such things, and I know you and how you can let yourself go. Double meanings, side-glances, clearing your throat, sighing and coughing and laughing – none of that.

CLITIPHO: You'll congratulate me.

SYRUS [*looking along the road*]: Careful, please.

CLITIPHO: Even you will be surprised.

SYRUS: How quickly the women have caught up!

CLITIPHO: Where are they? [*Struggling to free himself from* SYRUS's *grasp*] Why are you stopping me?

SYRUS: She's not yours now.

CLITIPHO: I know, when my father's there, but until then –

SYRUS: It makes no difference.

CLITIPHO: Let me go!

SYRUS: No, I won't.

CLITIPHO: Please, just for a minute –

SYRUS: No, you shan't.

CLITIPHO: Just one kiss –

SYRUS: If you've any sense you'll go.

CLITIPHO: All right, I'm going. What about *him*?

SYRUS: He's staying.

CLITIPHO: Lucky man!

SYRUS: Get moving!

[*He pushes* CLITIPHO *into* CHREMES' *house as an elegant young woman,* BACCHIS, *appears, right, with the girl,* ANTI- PHILA, *followed by maids and servants with baggage.*]

BACCHIS [*rather condescending and consciously refined*]: My dear Antiphila, I congratulate you. You really have been fortu- nate, I think, in seeing that your morals match your beauty. Heaven knows I'm not surprised that everyone wants to make you his own, for your conversation has given me a clear idea of your character. When I think of your way of life and that of those like you who keep the vulgar crowd at a distance, I don't wonder that you are as you are and the rest of us are so different. Your virtue is a positive asset; but the men we deal with simply don't let us be good. It's only our looks which attract lovers to wait on us, and when these fade they take their attentions elsewhere; and if meanwhile we've made no provision for the future, we're left to a soli- tary life. You and your kind have only to make up your mind to spend your life with a husband whose character most resembles your own, and he's devoted to you at once; with the happy result that you are truly bound together, so that your love is untouched by any misfortune.

ANTIPHILA: I can't answer for the others, but I know I've always done my best to make his interests my own.

CLINIA [*unseen by* ANTIPHILA]: Yes indeed Antiphila, my darling, nothing but you brought me back home today – for all my hardships while I was away were easy to bear except having to live without you.

SYRUS: I believe you.

CLINIA: Syrus, I can hardly bear it. Oh the misery of not being able to enjoy such a girl to my heart's desire!

SYRUS: You're nowhere near that, from what I've seen of your father's attitude; he'll make life difficult for you for a long time yet.

BACCHIS: Who is that young man staring at us?

ANTIPHILA [*overcome*]: Oh, hold me, please.

BACCHIS: My dear girl, what's the matter?

ANTIPHILA: I can't bear it, it's too much . . .

BACCHIS: Antiphila, can't you speak? What is it?

ANTIPHILA: Is that really my Clinia I see?

BACCHIS: Who is it?

CLINIA [*running to catch her in his arms*]: Dear heart . . .

ANTIPHILA: Clinia, my darling . . .

CLINIA: How are you?

ANTIPHILA: Happy, now that you're safely home.

CLINIA: Is it really you, Antiphila? Oh, I've longed for you with all my heart.

SYRUS [*edging them towards* CHREMES' *house*]: Go in, please. The master's been expecting you for ages.[1]

[*They all go in. The stage is left empty to indicate passage of time. When* CHREMES *comes out of his house again, it is next morning.*]

CHREMES: Dawn's breaking, so I think I might knock at my neighbour's door and be the first with the news that his son has returned. I believe the boy would rather I didn't, but when I see how his unhappy father is torturing himself over his son's departure, why should I deny him this unexpected joy, especially when the boy is in no danger from the disclosure? No, I shall help the old man in what way I can. I

1. Presumably for the party mentioned on p. 107.

see my own son devoting himself to his friend, who's a lad
of his own age, acting as his ally in all his affairs, so it's only
right that we old people should support each other.

[MENEDEMUS *comes out of his house, talking to himself.*]

MENEDEMUS: Either I was born with an exceptional disposition for misery, or else there's no truth in the popular saying
that time is the healer of man's suffering. In my case what I
suffer for my son increases day by day, and the longer he's
away the more I miss him and long for his return.

CHREMES: Why, here he is, coming out. I'll go and speak to
him. Good morning, Menedemus; I've news for you, news
which I know you are longing to hear.

MENEDEMUS: Chremes! Can you have heard anything about
my son?

CHREMES: He is alive and well.

MENEDEMUS: Where is he, please?

CHREMES: In my house.

MENEDEMUS [*overwhelmed*]: My son, did you say?

CHREMES: Yes, your son.

MENEDEMUS: He's come?

CHREMES: He has indeed.

MENEDEMUS: My Clinia has come?

CHREMES: So I said.

MENEDEMUS [*taking* CHREMES *by the arm*]: Come along,
please take me to him.

CHREMES: He doesn't want you to know he's back, and he's
trying to keep out of your sight. He knows he did wrong,
and that makes him fear that your old severity may even
have increased.

MENEDEMUS: Didn't you tell him about me?

CHREMES: No, I didn't.

MENEDEMUS: Why not?

CHREMES: Because the worst thing you can do, in your own interests and in his, is to be seen in such a subdued and compliant state of mind.

MENEDEMUS: I can't help it. I've played the heavy father long enough.

CHREMES: You always run to extremes, Menedemus, one way or the other. Either you're too lavish with your money or else you're too strict, and you'll make yourself misunderstood as much by what you propose to do now as you did before. Formerly, sooner than allow your son to frequent a young woman who was content at the time with little and grateful for everything, you frightened him out of the house. She was then forced against her inclinations to make a living in the usual way. Today when she can only be kept at vast expense,[1] you're all eagerness to give him anything. Just let me tell you how well she's equipped now for ruining a man. In the first place, she's brought about a dozen maids with her, each one of them laden with her dresses and jewels; she might have a foreign viceroy for a lover, but he'd never be able to meet her expenses, and you certainly can't.

MENEDEMUS [not really listening]: Is she in your house?

CHREMES: Isn't she! I ought to know, for last night I provided dinner for her and her companions. Another meal like that would ruin me. Apart from everything else, there's all the wine she's wasted with tasting and spitting: 'This wine's too rough, father,' she'd say; 'have you nothing milder to offer?' I opened every jar and cask I had, kept everyone on the jump – and that's only one night. What's going to become of you, do you think, when they're continually eating you out of house and home? I'm sorry for your savings, Menedemus, God knows.

1. Chremes has been told that *Bacchis* is Clinia's mistress.

MENEDEMUS: Let him do what he likes – take, spend, squander. I'm determined to accept anything, as long as I can keep him with me.

CHREMES: Well, if you've really made up your mind, I think the important thing is that he shouldn't guess that you know the truth but are willing to keep him supplied.

MENEDEMUS: What am I to do?

CHREMES: Anything rather than what you're proposing. Pay out through someone else, let yourself be duped by his man's tricks – that's something I've already spotted: they're at it already, plotting on the sly. Syrus and that lad of yours are whispering with their heads together and passing on their schemes to the young men, and you'd do better to lose a thousand on my plan than a hundred on theirs. It's no longer a question of money, but the problem of how to give it to the boy with the minimum of risk. If he once has an inkling of your state of mind and sees that you'd throw away your life and all you have rather than lose him, you'll have opened the floodgates for dissipation, and farewell to any future pleasure in life! The fact is that all of us deteriorate when restrictions are removed. He'll fancy whatever comes into his head without a thought of right or wrong, and go straight for it. You won't be able to endure the ruin of your fortune *and* your son. But on the other hand, if you cut off supplies altogether he'll turn at once to what he thinks gives him most hold over you; he'll threaten to leave you on the spot.

MENEDEMUS [*doubtfully*]: I suppose that's true . . . yes, you must be right.

CHREMES: Believe me, I didn't sleep a wink all last night for thinking how I could restore your son to you.

MENEDEMUS: Give me your hand, Chremes. Carry on, please, as you are doing.

CHREMES: I'm ready.

MENEDEMUS: Do you know what I'd like you to do now?

CHREMES: Tell me.

MENEDEMUS: As you've noticed that they are planning to trick me, try to hurry them up. I can't wait to give my boy what he wants and set eyes on him in person.

CHREMES: I'll do my best. There's just a small matter delaying me; our neighbours Simus and Crito are involved in a boundary dispute, and have asked me to arbitrate. I'd promised to see to this, but I'll go and tell them it can't be today. I'll be back in a minute.

MENEDEMUS: Please do. [CHREMES *goes off, right.*] Heavens above, to think that human nature is so designed that we can all judge another man's affairs better than our own! Is it because in our own case we are blinded by extremes of joy or sorrow? How much wiser this man is on my behalf than I am for myself.

[CHREMES *returns.*]

CHREMES: I've excused myself, and now I'm free to give you my assistance. I must catch Syrus and tell him what we want of him. [*His door is heard opening.*] Here's someone coming out; you go home, Menedemus, or they'll see that we are working together.

[MENEDEMUS *goes into his house.* SYRUS *comes out, talking to himself.*]

SYRUS: Go on, run round in circles, but you've got to find that money somehow. You must set a trap for the old man.

CHREMES [*aside*]: You see I was right about their plans. I suppose Clinia's man is too slow for the job, so they've handed it over to this fellow of mine.

SYRUS: Who's that? Oh, how frightful! Could he have heard?

CHREMES: Syrus!

SYRUS [*makes some inarticulate response*]

CHREMES: What's the matter with you?

SYRUS [*trying to gain time*]: Oh I'm all right, sir, only I'm surprised to see you out so early, after all you drank last night.

CHREMES [*stiffly*]: Nothing out of the ordinary.

SYRUS: Don't you think so, sir? Well, it looked to me like what they call life in the old dog yet.

CHREMES [*snorts*]

SYRUS: Attractive young person, isn't she, sir? Witty too.

CHREMES: No doubt she is.

SYRUS: You thought so too, sir? Marvellous figure as well.

CHREMES: Not bad.

SYRUS: Not like the girls were in your time, of course, sir, but quite good for today. No wonder Clinia's crazy about her. But he's got a mean old miser for a father in our neighbour here – do you know him? Rolling in money, and yet his son ran away from home because he hadn't a penny. It's quite true; had you heard?

CHREMES: Of course I have. Hard labour at the mill is what he deserves!

SYRUS [*puzzled*]: Who, sir?

CHREMES: Young Clinia's servant, of course . . .

SYRUS [*aside*]: That gave you a nasty fright, Syrus.

CHREMES: . . . who allowed that to happen.

SYRUS: What could he do?

CHREMES: Don't ask silly questions. He could have found some way out, devised some scheme to produce the means for the boy to give what he wanted to his mistress and to save that tiresome old father in spite of himself.

SYRUS: You're joking, sir.

CHREMES: That is what he should have done.

SYRUS: Tell me, sir, do you approve of servants' deceiving their masters?

CHREMES: Yes, on occasion, I do.

SYRUS: Quite right too!

CHREMES: It's often the solution for serious trouble. In this case, an only son would have stayed at home.

SYRUS [aside]: I can't tell whether he's joking or in earnest. Anyway, it puts me in a mood to enjoy myself.

CHREMES: What's the fellow waiting for now, Syrus? Is he waiting till the son goes off again because he can't meet that young woman's expenses? Why can't he think up some trick to play on the old father?

SYRUS: He's not very bright, sir.

CHREMES: Then you ought to help him, for the young man's sake.

SYRUS [eagerly]: I can easily do so, if you give the word, sir. I know a bit about how these things are generally done –

CHREMES: So much the better.

SYRUS: Of course it's against my principles to tell lies . . .

CHREMES: You see to it, then.

SYRUS: Only do remember all this, sir, should it ever happen that your own son does something of this kind, human nature being what it is.

CHREMES: The situation won't arise, I hope.

SYRUS: I'm sure I hope so too, sir, and I don't mean to suggest I've noticed anything about him at present. But if ever . . . don't you . . . As you see, he's young. . . . [Eagerly] Anyway, if it comes to that, sir, I'd be able to handle you in grand style.

CHREMES [drily]: We'll see what's needed when the occasion arises. Meanwhile, attend to the business in hand.

[He goes into his house.]

SYRUS: Never in my life have I heard my master speak more to the point! Nor could I have believed I'd be allowed to make trouble without paying for it! Now who's coming out?

[CHREMES *bursts out again, dragging* CLITIPHO.]

CHREMES: What on earth do you think you are doing? Can you explain your conduct? Is this the way to behave?

CLITIPHO [*sulkily*]: What have *I* done?

CHREMES: Didn't I just see you putting your hand down the front of that woman's dress?

SYRUS [*aside*]: That's finished me; I'm done for.

CLITIPHO: What, me?

CHREMES: I saw you with my own eyes, don't deny it. Clinia has done nothing to deserve such disgraceful treatment; you should keep your hands to yourself. It's grossly insulting to your friend to receive him in your own house and then make advances to his mistress. And yesterday, when you were drinking, you were positively indecent –

SYRUS: That's a fact.

CHREMES: – and offensive. God help me, I dreaded to think how it would end. I know very well what lovers are, and how they take offence in a way you might not expect.

CLITIPHO: But he trusts me not to do anything like that, father.

CHREMES: Maybe, but at least you could take yourself out of their sight for a while. Passion leads to a lot of things where your presence would only be a hindrance. I know how I should feel, for not one of my friends is the sort of man I'd dare to tell all my secrets. With one my pride stops me, with another I'm ashamed of what I've done, not wanting to look a fool or a hot-head, and you may be sure Clinia feels the same. Our duty is to try to find out where and when we can best fall in with his wishes.

SYRUS [*joining them*]: What's this I hear?

CLITIPHO: Oh, damn it all!

SYRUS [*to* CLITIPHO, *in scandalized tones*]: Is this how you carry out my instructions, sir? Do you call that proper behaviour for a self-restrained and honourable man?

CLITIPHO: Be quiet, can't you.

SYRUS: A nice way to behave.

CLITIPHO: I'm sorry, Syrus.

SYRUS: I dare say you are, and so you should be. I'm very much upset.

CLITIPHO: You'll be the death of me, I swear.

SYRUS: I'm only speaking the truth, as I see it.

CLITIPHO [to CHREMES]: Can't I go anywhere near that couple?

CHREMES: Have you more than one way of going near them?

SYRUS [aside]: It's hopeless. He'll give himself away before I've had a chance to get the money. [To CHREMES] I don't profess to be clever, sir, but would you be willing to listen to me?

CHREMES: What shall I do?

SYRUS: Tell him to go off somewhere.

CLITIPHO: Where to?

SYRUS: Anywhere you like, only leave them to themselves. You go for a walk.

CLITIPHO: Where shall I go for a walk?

SYRUS: Good heavens, aren't there plenty of places? [Pushing him off, left] Go that way, over there, anywhere.

CHREMES: He's quite right. I say the same.

CLITIPHO [calling back as he goes]: To hell with you, Syrus, pushing me off like this!

SYRUS [laughing]: Then keep your hands to yourself next time! [CLITIPHO goes.] Do you really say the same, sir? He needs you to watch him, and all the correction and guidance heaven has given you, or I don't know what he'll do one day, do you, sir?

CHREMES [*shortly*] : I'll see to that.

SYRUS: Yes, sir, you're the one who'll have to look after him now.

CHREMES: I intend to.

SYRUS: You will if you're wise, for he takes less and less notice of me.

CHREMES: And what have *you* been doing? Have you done anything about what I spoke to you about just now, or thought of anything yet which would do?

SYRUS: You mean that trick,[1] sir? Yes, I've just thought of one.

CHREMES: Good boy. What is it?

SYRUS: I'll tell you, sir, but first things first –

CHREMES: What do you mean?

SYRUS: That's a thoroughly bad woman, sir.

CHREMES: So she seems.

SYRUS: But if you only knew! Oh, the wickedness she's plotting. There was an old woman from Corinth living here, to whom she'd lent a thousand drachmas.

CHREMES: What then?

SYRUS: The old woman died, leaving a young daughter who was pledged to the other as security for the loan.

CHREMES: I see.

SYRUS: The girl was brought along here, in fact she's the one indoors with your wife now.

CHREMES: What then?

SYRUS: Bacchis is asking Clinia to give her the money at once, and says he can have the girl when he does. She's demanding the thousand in cash.

CHREMES: *Demanding*, did you say?

SYRUS: Well, do you doubt it? That's what it sounded like to me.

1. cf. ll. 545 ff.

CHREMES: What do you propose to do now?

SYRUS: I'll go to Menedemus and say the girl was kidnapped from Caria, that she's well-born and rich, and if he buys her he'll do very well out of it.

CHREMES: That's a mistake.

SYRUS: Why, sir?

CHREMES: I can give you Menedemus's answer myself, straight off: 'I'm not buying.' What will you do then?

SYRUS: That's the very answer I want.

CHREMES: Why?

SYRUS: It doesn't matter.

CHREMES [*mystified*]: Doesn't matter?

SYRUS: Good lord, no.

CHREMES: I wonder what you mean.

SYRUS: You'll soon find out, sir. [*Turns to go in.*]

CHREMES: Here, wait a minute! What's that noise at our door?

[*They stand aside as* CHREMES' *wife,* SOSTRATA, *and a* NURSE *come out.*]

SOSTRATA: Unless I'm much mistaken, this is the very ring I take it to be, and the one which was with my baby daughter when she was exposed.

CHREMES [*aside, to* SYRUS]: What does she mean by that?

SOSTRATA: What do you think, nurse? Isn't it the same?

NURSE: I said so the moment you showed me it.

SOSTRATA: But are you sure you looked at it properly?

NURSE: Yes, I did.

SOSTRATA: Go in at once and tell me if she's had her bath. I shall wait out here for my husband.

[*The* NURSE *goes in.*]

SYRUS: It's you she wants, sir. Find out what it's about. Something's upset her, and there must be a reason. I feel quite nervous.

CHREMES: Do you? She makes a lot of fuss about what she has to say, but it's generally a lot of nonsense.

SOSTRATA: Why, my dear husband –

CHREMES [*sarcastically*]: Why, my dear wife.

SOSTRATA: I was looking for you.

CHREMES: Tell me what you want.

SOSTRATA: First of all, let me beg you to believe that I've never ventured to act against your instructions.

CHREMES: If you want me to believe the incredible – all right, I will.

SYRUS [*aside*]: She must have done something wrong, or she wouldn't start with these excuses.

SOSTRATA: Do you remember that time when I was pregnant and you gave me strict orders not to rear the child if it was a girl?

CHREMES: Then I know what you did; you brought it up.

SYRUS [*aside*]: Exactly, which means another mistress for me and a dead loss for my master.

SOSTRATA: I did not. But there was a woman from Corinth living here, quite a decent old thing, and I gave her the baby to expose.

CHREMES: Good God, the stupidity of the woman!

SOSTRATA: Oh dear, what have I done?

CHREMES: Can't you see?

SOSTRATA: If I did wrong, Chremes, I didn't mean to.

CHREMES: One thing I'm sure about, even if you deny it: there's never any sense or reflection in anything you say and do. There are any number of things wrong about this. In the first place, if you had really intended to carry out my order you should have destroyed the child at once, instead of pretending it was dead while in fact you were giving it a chance to survive. But let that pass; it was pity, you'll say, a mother's love; very well. Just think how you made proper provision for carrying out your intention! Why, you entirely abandoned your daughter to that old woman, and for all you could do she might have made a living out of the child or it could have been sold into slavery. I suppose you thought anything would do as long as it stayed alive. How can one deal with people who have no conception of what is just or right or good? Better or worse, gain or loss, they can see only what they want to see.

SOSTRATA: I was wrong, Chremes, I admit. I'm not trying to defend myself. All I'm asking of you now, as the years have brought you greater wisdom and forgiveness, is that my folly shall find protection in your sense of justice.

CHREMES: I must forgive you, I suppose, for what you did, Sostrata, but my indulgence is a poor example for you in many ways. Well, whatever your reason was for introducing this subject, let's have it.

SOSTRATA: Like any other silly superstitious woman, when I gave the baby to the woman to expose I took a ring from my finger and told her to put it out with the child. I didn't want it to die with nothing at all from us.

CHREMES [sarcastically]: Well done. It was a safeguard for your own conscience as well as for the child.

SOSTRATA [showing him a ring]: This is the ring.

CHREMES: Where did you get it from?

SOSTRATA: The girl who came here with Bacchis —

SYRUS [lets out a cry of astonishment]

CHREMES: What has she to say?

SOSTRATA: — gave it to me to look after while she went to have a bath. I didn't pay much attention at first, but then when I looked at it I recognized it at once and hurried out to you.

CHREMES: Have you noticed or suspected anything about the girl?

SOSTRATA: I don't know ... You might ask her straight out where she got it from, if that's something we could find out.

SYRUS [*aside*]: Damn it, things look much too hopeful for my liking.[1] If it's true, this must be our girl.

CHREMES: Is the old woman still alive?

SOSTRATA: I don't know.

CHREMES: What did she say at the time?

SOSTRATA: That she'd carried out her instructions.

CHREMES: Tell me her name, so that I can make inquiries.

SOSTRATA: Philtera.

SYRUS [*aside*]: That's her! The girl's found for certain, and I'm lost!

CHREMES: Come indoors with me, Sostrata.

SOSTRATA: This is more than I could have hoped. I was so afraid, Chremes, that you'd be as stony-hearted now as you were then about bringing her up.

CHREMES: A man can't always be what he chooses; circumstances don't always permit. As things are now I'm anxious for a daughter; before, there was nothing I wanted less.

[*They go into their house.*]

SYRUS: Unless I'm much mistaken, disaster's waiting for me round the corner. This has put me and my plans in a very tight place, unless I can see a way of stopping old Menedemus from discovering the girl's his son's mistress. As for my hopes about money, or my idea of being able to trick him, all that's off. It'll be a triumph if I can cover my flanks and beat a retreat. It's sheer torture to have such a morsel snatched from my lips, but what can I do? I must think up something; there's got to be a new plan of action. [*He paces about the stage.*] Nothing's too difficult for hard thinking not

1. If Antiphila is free-born, she cannot be security for a loan; which puts an end to Syrus's plan of getting money out of Menedemus in ll. 603 ff.

to find a way out. I might start this way . . . no, it won't do.
What about that . . . no go either. Well, then, this . . .
impossible. No, it isn't, it's perfect! Hurrah, I've a perfect
plan! I do believe I'll lay hands on that runaway cash after
all.

[CLINIA *hurries out of* CHREMES' *house, in a state of high
excitement.*]

CLINIA: Nothing can ever happen to me now to cast a
shadow on the happiness which has dawned so bright for
me! Henceforth I'll put myself entirely in my father's hands,
and he'll find me as deserving as he could wish.

SYRUS: I was right; she's been recognized, if I've understood
what he said. [*Coming forward*] I'm delighted to hear that
things have turned out as you wanted, sir.

CLINIA: My dear Syrus, have you heard?

SYRUS: Of course. I was in on it all the time.

CLINIA: Did you ever know anyone have such luck?

SYRUS: No one.

CLINIA: And I swear to heaven I'm not so happy just on my
own account – it's for her too. I know she deserves every
mark of respect.

SYRUS: I'm sure she does. But now it's your turn to listen to
what I've got to say. We must make sure that your friend's
affairs are safely settled too, so that his old father doesn't
hear about his mistress Bacchis.

CLINIA [*taking no notice*]: O Gods above!

SYRUS: Do be quiet.

CLINIA: My Antiphila will marry me!

SYRUS: *Must* you interrupt like this?

CLINIA [*hugging him*]: What am I to do? Syrus, dear man, I'm
so happy; bear with me.

SYRUS: That's exactly what I am doing.

CLINIA: We've won a place among the gods!

SYRUS [*crossly*]: It seems to me I'm just wasting my time.

CLINIA: Carry on; I'm listening now.

SYRUS: But you won't next minute.

CLINIA: Yes I will.

SYRUS: What I said, sir, was that we must make sure that your friend's affairs are also safely settled. If you move out of our house and leave Bacchis behind, my master'll find out straight away that she's Clitipho's mistress. If you take her away with you, the secret won't come out any more than it has done up to now.

CLINIA [*dismayed*]: Yes, but Syrus, nothing is more likely to stand in the way of my wedding. What sort of face am I to put on when I approach my father? Can you suggest what I'm to say?

SYRUS: Yes, of course.

CLINIA: Then what *am* I to say? What reason can I give?

SYRUS: I don't intend you to go telling a lot of lies. Be quite frank with him, and tell him the truth.

CLINIA: What!

SYRUS: I mean it. Say you love Antiphila and want to marry her, and the other girl is Clitipho's.

CLINIA [*with heavy sarcasm*]: A very right and proper suggestion; so easy to carry out too. And I suppose you'd also like me to beg my father to keep it from your old master?

SYRUS: On the contrary, get him to tell the whole story, straight out.

CLINIA: You must be mad or drunk. You're the one who'll ruin Clitipho, that's obvious. What's 'safely settled' for him in that, pray?

SYRUS: That's my prize plan, the one I'm really proud of! [*Drawing himself up*] It reveals in me such a power and force of ingenuity that I can deceive the pair of them simply by telling the truth! Don't you see – when my old man hears from your father that Bacchis is his son's mistress, he simply won't believe it.

CLINIA: Yes, but this plan of yours will once again destroy all my hopes of marriage. So long as your master thinks Bacchis is *my* mistress, he won't trust me with his daughter. Maybe you think it doesn't matter what becomes of me, so long as you can look after Clitipho.

SYRUS: Damn it all, sir, are you suggesting that I want this pretence kept up for ever? It's only for one day, while I can get the money out of him, that's all; not a minute more.

CLINIA: But do you think that gives you enough time? And what are we to do if his father finds out the truth?

SYRUS: Well, all I can say is that there are people who say 'what if the sky falls?'

CLINIA: I'm afraid of what I've got to do.

SYRUS: No need to be afraid; you can extricate yourself whenever you like, simply by publishing the facts.

CLINIA [*reluctantly*]: All right then. Bring Bacchis over to us.

SYRUS [*as* CHREMES' *door opens*]: Luckily she's coming out herself.

[BACCHIS *comes out, in a very bad temper, with her maid; the others stand back.*]

BACCHIS: Damn Syrus for his impudence, bringing me here with his promises of a thousand drachmas! If he's deceived me this time he'll ask and ask in future, but his errand will be in vain. Or else I'll say I'll come and fix a time, and then when he's taken back the message and raised Clitipho's hopes I can play the deceiver and not turn up, and Syrus's back shall smart for it.

CLINIA [*to* SYRUS]: That's a nice promise to make you.

SYRUS: And do you think she's joking? She'll do it if I don't look out.

BACCHIS [*aside*]: They're asleep. I'll make them sit up. [*Aloud*] Phrygia, my dear, did you hear which house it was that man told us was Charinus's?

PHRYGIA: Yes, I did.

BACCHIS: Was it the next one on the right, after this farm?

PHRYGIA: That's what I remember.

BACCHIS: Just run on ahead. My captain's celebrating the holiday with him –

SYRUS: Now what's she up to?

BACCHIS: – and you can tell him I'm here, detained against my will, but somehow I'll manage to outwit these people and come.

SYRUS: That'll finish me. Stop, Bacchis, stop! Where are you sending that girl, please? Tell her to stop.

BACCHIS [*to* PHRYGIA]: Go on.
    [PHRYGIA *starts to move off, left.*]

SYRUS: But the money's there, waiting for you.

BACCHIS: Well then, I'll stay.
    [PHRYGIA *returns.*]

SYRUS: You'll have it at once.

BACCHIS [*graciously*]: At your convenience. I'm not pressing you.

SYRUS: But have you heard this, if you please –

BACCHIS: What?

SYRUS: You're to move over to Menedemus's at once and take all the maids with you.

BACCHIS: What on earth do you mean by that, you rascal?

SYRUS: Well, I'm . . . I'm coining money, you might say, to give you.

BACCHIS: Do you think I'm a proper object for your jokes?

SYRUS: I'm quite serious.

BACCHIS: In that case, have we any more to say to each other?

SYRUS: No, I was only paying you your due.

BACCHIS: Let us go, then.

SYRUS: Come this way. [*He knocks at* MENEDEMUS'*s door*.] Hi, Dromo!

[DROMO *comes out*.]

DROMO: Who's calling me?

SYRUS: It's me, Syrus.

DROMO: What's the matter?

SYRUS: Take all Bacchis's maids across to your place, and look sharp.

DROMO: What for?

SYRUS: Don't ask. See that they take away what they brought with them. [DROMO *goes into* CHREMES' *house and soon reappears with the maids and all the luggage*.] My old master'll hope to cut down his expenses by this exodus, but he little knows how much this small gain is going to cost him! You'll forget about all this, Dromo, if you're wise.

DROMO: You can count me dumb.

[*He shepherds all the women into* MENEDEMUS'*s house and* CLINIA *follows*.[1] *Almost at once* CHREMES *comes out*.]

CHREMES: God knows I'm sorry for Menedemus and the wretched lot that's befallen him! Fancy having to support that female and all her set-up! I know he's been so anxious to see his son again that he won't notice it for the next few days, but once he realizes the huge expenses he'll have in his home every day, and no end to them, he'll be only too glad to see the back of him again. Ah, here's Syrus; that's luck.

SYRUS [*aside*]: Now for it!

CHREMES: Syrus!

SYRUS [*with exaggerated pleasure*]: Well I never!

CHREMES: What do you mean?

SYRUS: I've been hoping to run into you for ages, sir.

1. He is in the house at l. 842, but one would expect more to be made of his first entry into his father's home.

CHREMES: You look as though you'd already fixed up something with our neighbour.

SYRUS: In the matter we were just ... Yes, sir, no sooner said than done.

CHREMES: Upon your honour?

SYRUS: Upon my honour, sir.

CHREMES [*genially*]: You'll have to have a pat on the head for that, Syrus. Come over here. I'll do you a good turn for this, and gladly.

SYRUS: Ah, if you only knew the bright idea I had!

CHREMES [*laughing*]: Now, now, are you boasting that everything went according to plan?

SYRUS: Certainly not, sir, I was only telling the truth.

CHREMES: Well then, tell it.

SYRUS: Clinia has told his father that this woman Bacchis is your Clitipho's mistress, and that he's only brought her with him to prevent your finding out.

CHREMES [*laughing*]: Good.

SYRUS: What have you to say to that!

CHREMES: Excellent, I say.

SYRUS [*aside*]: Ah, if you only knew ... But let me tell you the rest of the trick. Clinia is also pretending that he's seen your daughter and fallen in love with her beauty at first sight, and wants to make her his wife.

CHREMES: My newly discovered daughter?

SYRUS: Yes; and he'll get his father to ask for her.

CHREMES: What's all this about, Syrus? I don't quite get that.

SYRUS: You're a bit slow, sir.

CHREMES: Perhaps I am.

SYRUS: Clinia'll be given money for the *wedding*, for jewels and dresses and so on – got it now?

CHREMES: You mean, to buy them?

SYRUS: Yes, of course.

CHREMES [*still obtuse*]: But I'm not giving him nor promising him my daughter.

SYRUS: Won't you, sir? Why not?

CHREMES: Why not? What a question! A man who ...

SYRUS [*hastily*]: Yes, yes, of course. I wasn't suggesting anything *permanent*, sir, only that you should *pretend* to let him have her.

CHREMES: I'm not given to pretence. Carry on with your concoctions, but don't mix me up in them. Am I likely to promise her to a man I've no intention of giving her to?

SYRUS: I just thought you might.

CHREMES: Certainly not.

SYRUS [*crestfallen*]: It was such a bright idea. And I only started on it because you'd been badgering me so long to do something.

CHREMES: I dare say.

SYRUS: Anyway, your attitude is quite correct and proper, sir. I accept that.

CHREMES: But I'm still very anxious for you to make a success of this, only by some other way.

SYRUS: All right, we must think of something else. But there's still that money which I told you was owed to Bacchis on account of your daughter.[1] It's got to be paid at once, and I'm sure you're not one to make excuses that it's nothing to do with you, because you never saw the money or gave any instructions, and the old woman had no power to pledge your daughter without your consent. It's a true saying that 'strictest law means greatest hardship'.

CHREMES: I shan't do anything like that.

SYRUS: No, sir, others may, but not you; you're well known to be well set up in a nice little fortune.

CHREMES: In fact I shall take the money to her now myself.

1. The supposed loan for which Antiphila was security. See ll. 600 ff.

SYRUS [*hastily*]: I shouldn't do that, sir; tell your son to take it.

CHREMES: Why?

SYRUS: Because the suspicion of being her lover has been transferred to *him*.

CHREMES: What's that got to do with it?

SYRUS: It'll seem more plausible if he's the one to hand over the money; and it'll also make it easier for me to carry out what I've in mind. [*Looking along the road, left*] Why, here he comes. You go in, sir, and fetch the money.

CHREMES: I will.

[*He goes into his house as* CLITIPHO *walks wearily on, left.*]

CLITIPHO: Anything easy seems difficult when you don't want to do it. This wasn't really a tiring walk but I'm exhausted. The one thing I dread at the moment is to be pushed off again, just to make me miserable and keep me away from Bacchis. [*He sees* SYRUS.] May all the gods in heaven confound you, Syrus, with your schemes and inventions! You're always thinking up things like this to make my life a misery.

SYRUS: Go to hell, can't you, where you belong. You nearly did for me altogether, the liberties you take.[1]

CLITIPHO: My God, I wish I had done; it's what you deserved!

SYRUS: I deserve it? How? I'm glad you told me that *before* you got your hands on the money I was going to give you.

CLITIPHO: What do you want me to say then? You went off and fetched my mistress, and then I wasn't allowed to touch her.

SYRUS: I'm not angry with you now. But do you know where your Bacchis is at the present moment?

CLITIPHO: In our house.

SYRUS: No.

1. Clitipho's behaviour with Bacchis, noticed by Chremes in ll. 562 ff.

CLITIPHO: Where is she then?

SYRUS: At Clinia's.

CLITIPHO [*horrified*]: What!

SYRUS: Cheer up. You're going to take her the money you promised her.

CLITIPHO: Nonsense. Where can I get it from?

SYRUS: Your father.

CLITIPHO: I suppose that's your idea of a joke.

SYRUS: Events will show.

CLITIPHO: Then I'm a lucky man! [*Seizing him*] Syrus, I adore you!

SYRUS: Here's your father coming out. Be careful not to show surprise at any reason for this. Humour him at the right moment, do what he says, say as little as possible.

[CHREMES *comes out, with money.*]

CHREMES: Where's Clitipho?

SYRUS [*whispers*]: Say 'here I am!'

CLITIPHO: Here I am, father.

CHREMES: How much have you told him?

SYRUS: Pretty well everything.

CHREMES: Take this money then, and hand it over.

[CLITIPHO *is thunderstruck.*]

SYRUS: Go on, don't stand there like a log; take it.

CLITIPHO: All right, give it to me.

SYRUS: Come along with me, and hurry up. You wait here, sir, until we come out. There's nothing to keep us there long.

[*He takes* CLITIPHO *into* MENEDEMUS'*s house.*]

CHREMES: That means that my daughter has already cost me a thousand drachmas, which I reckon as covering her maintenance; now there'll be another thousand for a trousseau, and then a further twelve thousand for her dowry. How many unjust and unnatural demands convention makes on us! And now I have to lay everything aside and look for someone to whom I can hand over my hard-earned wealth.

[MENEDEMUS *comes out, speaking to* CLINIA *within.*]

MENEDEMUS: I count myself the happiest man in the whole world, Clinia, now that I see you restored to your senses.[1]

CHREMES [*aside*]: That's where he's wrong!

MENEDEMUS: Why, Chremes, I was looking for you. Please do all you can to bring happiness to my son, myself and all of us!

CHREMES: What do you want me to do?

MENEDEMUS: Today you have found a daughter –

CHREMES: Yes, what of it?

MENEDEMUS: Clinia wants her for his wife.

CHREMES: What sort of a man are you, I wonder?

MENEDEMUS: What do you mean?

CHREMES: Have you already forgotten our conversation about that trick – which was to be a way of getting money out of you?[2]

MENEDEMUS: I remember.

CHREMES: This *is* the trick.

MENEDEMUS: What do you say, Chremes? Am I mistaken? Is this what they've done? Oh, it's the end of all my high hopes! But that woman in my house is Clitipho's mistress, not Clinia's; they told me so.

CHREMES: And you believe it all. They also tell you Clinia wants to marry simply so that once you've arranged the wedding you'll give him money to buy jewels and dresses and everything else that's needed.

MENEDEMUS [*after a shocked pause*]: Yes, that must be right. And it'll all go to his mistress.

CHREMES: Of course it will.

1. Clinia has told his father that Bacchis is really Clitipho's mistress.
2. ll. 470–5.

MENEDEMUS [*sighing*]: So all my rejoicing was in vain – just my luck. But even now I'd rather lose anything than my boy. What answer can I take back from you, Chremes, so that he won't know I know and be angry with me?

CHREMES: *Angry*? Really, Menedemus, you're much too good to him.

MENEDEMUS: Don't try to change me, Chremes. I've chosen my course, help me to carry it through to the end.

CHREMES: Tell him you met me and discussed the marriage.

MENEDEMUS: I will. And then?

CHREMES: Tell him I was quite agreeable, and approved of him as a son-in-law. If you like, you can also say that I've agreed he can have her.

MENEDEMUS: That's exactly what I wanted!

CHREMES [*scornfully*]: So that he'll be all the quicker with his demands on you, and you can give him the money as soon as possible: which is your main object.

MENEDEMUS: Yes it is.

CHREMES: As far as I can see, you'll soon be sick of the whole business. But in any event, if you're wise you'll be cautious and pay out small sums.

MENEDEMUS: All right.

CHREMES: Go in then, and find out how much he asks for. I shall be at home if you need me.

MENEDEMUS: I *do* need you, for I want to keep you informed of what I do.

[*They both go into their houses, and there is a short interval, after which* MENEDEMUS *comes out again, looking happier, as he now has evidence of the truth.*]

MENEDEMUS: I know I'm not as bright as some and not so quick in the uptake, but that guide and mentor of mine, that self-appointed manager of my affairs Chremes outdoes me in this. Any of the usual epithets for the stupid suit me –

blockhead, numskull, nit-wit, ass – but what can you say about him? His stupidity's beyond description.

[CHREMES *comes out, talking back to* SOSTRATA *within.*]

CHREMES: For heaven's sake, woman, stop bothering the gods with thanks for the discovery of your daughter; unless you think they take after you and imagine they can't grasp anything unless it's repeated a hundred times. Meanwhile, what's that son of ours doing all this time, waiting about with Syrus?

MENEDEMUS: Who do you say is waiting about, Chremes?

CHREMES: Oh, Menedemus, there you are. Have you told Clinia what I said?

MENEDEMUS: Every word.

CHREMES: What did he say?

MENEDEMUS: He showed his delight at once, like anyone who wants to marry.

CHREMES [*laughs*]

MENEDEMUS: What are you laughing at?

CHREMES: I just thought of Syrus and his tricks.

MENEDEMUS: In what way?

CHREMES: He can even make up people's faces, the rascal!

MENEDEMUS: You mean my son's delight was simply put on?

CHREMES: Of course.

MENEDEMUS [*humouring him*]: The same thing occurred to me.

CHREMES: Just one of his old devices!

MENEDEMUS [*with irony*]: You'll be even more sure of this if you hear more.

CHREMES: Really?

MENEDEMUS: Just you listen –

CHREMES: Wait a bit, I'd like to know first what it's cost you so far. When you told your son he could have my daughter, I expect Dromo put in a word about all the dresses and jewels and maids they'd need for the bride, in order to get some money out of you.

MENEDEMUS: No.

CHREMES: What! He didn't?

MENEDEMUS: No, I say.

CHREMES: Then didn't your son?

MENEDEMUS: Not a word of that, Chremes. The one thing he insisted on was that the wedding should take place today.

CHREMES: That's amazing. What about Syrus? Had *he* nothing to say?

MENEDEMUS: Nothing.

CHREMES: I can't think why.

MENEDEMUS [*with satisfaction*]: Personally, I find *that* amazing, when you're so well informed about other things. But that Syrus of yours certainly did an amazingly good job of make-up on *your* son; there's not the slightest reason to suspect now that Bacchis is *Clinia's* mistress.

CHREMES: Clitipho? What's he doing?

MENEDEMUS: To say nothing of kisses in each other's arms, I don't count those –

CHREMES: How can pretence go further?

MENEDEMUS [*cryptically*]: Aha!

CHREMES: What do you mean?

MENEDEMUS: Just listen. I've a room right at the back of the house. A bed was taken in and made up.

CHREMES: What happened then?

MENEDEMUS: In darted Clitipho, like a flash.

CHREMES: Alone?

MENEDEMUS: Alone.

CHREMES: I don't like the sound of this . . .

MENEDEMUS: Bacchis followed at once –

CHREMES: Alone?

MENEDEMUS: Alone.

CHREMES: Damn!

MENEDEMUS: Once inside, they shut the door . . .

CHREMES: What! And did Clinia see this?

MENEDEMUS: Of course. He was there, with me.

CHREMES: So Bacchis is my son's mistress! Oh Menedemus, I'm ruined.

MENEDEMUS: Why?

CHREMES: My household can scarcely stand it ten days.

MENEDEMUS [*enjoying himself*]: Why, are you so alarmed because he's trying to help his friend?

CHREMES: It's his *girl*-friend that's worrying me.

MENEDEMUS: If that's how things are.

CHREMES: Can you doubt it? Do you suppose anyone could be so free-and-easy as to allow his mistress . . . under his nose . . .

MENEDEMUS [*laughing*]: Well, why not? It might be all part of the trick against *me*.

CHREMES: You're laughing at me, and no wonder. I'm furious with myself now. There were so many indications which could have pointed the way to the truth if I hadn't been so obtuse. The things I saw! What a fool I am! But they shan't get away with this while I'm alive. I'll –

MENEDEMUS: Have you no self-control? No regard for yourself? Am I not warning enough for you?

CHREMES: I'm beside myself with rage.

MENEDEMUS: How can you talk like that! It's scandalous: you give advice to others and are sensible abroad but you can't help yourself at home.

CHREMES: What am I to do?

MENEDEMUS: What you kept telling me I failed to do. Make the boy feel that you are a true father, one he dare trust with everything, to whom he can come with his requests and demands; otherwise he'll look for help elsewhere and abandon you.

CHREMES: No. I would rather he went off to the ends of the earth than stayed here to reduce his father to beggary by his misdeeds. For if I continue to meet his expenses, Menedemus, I'll be the one who has to make a living by the mattock.

MENEDEMUS: What trouble you'll create for yourself if you're not careful! You'll let him see you're unsympathetic, then you'll forgive him later all the same and get no thanks for it.

CHREMES: You've no idea what I suffer . . .

MENEDEMUS: Very well, have it your own way. And now, what about my request that your daughter should marry my son? Unless, of course, there's anything you'd like better.

CHREMES: No, no, I've no objection to the match or the boy's connections.

MENEDEMUS: What dowry shall I tell him you mentioned? [*There is an uncomfortable pause.*] Can't you speak?

CHREMES [*lost in thought*]: Dowry?

MENEDEMUS: That's what I said.

CHREMES: Well. . . .

MENEDEMUS: Don't worry, Chremes, if it's not much; the dowry doesn't matter to us.

CHREMES [*slowly*]: I was thinking that twelve thousand drachmas was about right for my means; but if you want to save me and my fortune *and* my son, you can say that the dowry I'm giving her is everything I have.

MENEDEMUS: Why are you doing this?

CHREMES: Pretend to be astonished, and at the same time ask Clitipho why he thinks I'm doing it.

MENEDEMUS: I've really no idea why.

CHREMES: Haven't you? Well, at the moment he's abandoning himself to loose living and extravagance. I want to curb his high spirits – he won't know where to turn when I've finished with him.

MENEDEMUS: What *are* you up to?

CHREMES: Never mind, just let me manage this in my own way.

MENEDEMUS: All right, if that's what you want.

CHREMES: Yes, it is.

MENEDEMUS: Very well.

CHREMES: Tell Clinia to get ready to fetch his wife. I'll silence *my* son with a good talking-to, the proper way to deal with children. As for Syrus –

MENEDEMUS: What about him?

CHREMES: Sure as I live, I'll give him such a dressing-down, such a beating that he'll remember me to the end of his days – thinking he could have his fun making a laughing-stock out of *me*! Good heavens, he wouldn't dare to try out on a helpless widow what he's done to me!

[*During this short speech* MENEDEMUS *has gone into his house;* CHREMES *paces up and down, fuming, until he returns with* CLITIPHO *and* SYRUS.]

CLITIPHO: Is that really so, Menedemus? Has my father shed all paternal feeling for me in so short a time? What have I done? Oh dear me, what crime have I committed? I've only done what everyone does.

MENEDEMUS: I'm just as much upset as you are, though I know it's much harder and more painful for you as the real sufferer. I can't understand it at all. I don't know what I can do except assure you of my warm sympathy.

CLITIPHO: You said my father was out here?

MENEDEMUS: There he is.

[MENEDEMUS *goes in again.*]

CHREMES: What have you to complain about, Clitipho? Whatever I've done was done to save you from yourself and your folly. When I saw you so heedless, giving first place to the pleasures of the moment and incapable of taking a longer view, I thought of a plan to keep you from beggary and make it impossible for you to lose all we have. You have only yourself to blame if I could not give you the inheritance on which you have first claim. I therefore turned to your next-of-kin, and have put everything securely in his hands.[1] You will always find a refuge from your folly with him, Clitipho, and food and clothing and a roof over your head.

CLITIPHO [*tearfully*]: Oh dear!

CHREMES: It was better than leaving everything to you for Bacchis to lay her hands on.

SYRUS [*aside*]: Damn me for a mischief-maker! Look at the trouble I've stirred up unawares!

CLITIPHO: I wish I were dead!

CHREMES [*drily*]: You'd better learn first what it is to live. When you know that, if you've no use for life you can try dying.

SYRUS: Please, sir, may I . . . ?

CHREMES: Speak.

SYRUS: But – is it safe?

CHREMES: Speak.

SYRUS: Don't you think it's all wrong of you, sir, quite crazy in fact, to visit my faults on the young master here?

CHREMES [*calmly*]: Run away, and don't interfere. No one's accusing *you*, Syrus. You needn't look for sanctuary nor anyone to beg you off.

SYRUS: I don't understand what –

1. i.e. Clinia, as his brother-in-law.

CHREMES: I'm not angry with you; nor with you, Clitipho; so neither of you has any right to complain about what I'm doing.

    [*He walks firmly into his house and shuts the door.*]

SYRUS: Has he gone? Oh, I wanted to ask him –

CLITIPHO [*gloomily*]: What?

SYRUS: Where I was to seek my daily bread. Look how he's cast us off! Though *you* can go to your sister I hear.

CLITIPHO: Things have come to a pretty pass, Syrus, if I'm in danger of starving.

SYRUS: So long as there's life, there's hope –

CLITIPHO: Hope of what?

SYRUS: – that we'll be hungry for meals.

CLITIPHO: How can you joke at a time like this! Haven't you any helpful suggestion?

SYRUS: Well, as a matter of fact, I have, and I was thinking about it all the time your father was talking. As far as I can see –

CLITIPHO: What?

SYRUS [*playing for time*]: It'll come to me soon . . .

CLITIPHO: What is it then?

SYRUS: Got it! I don't believe you can be their son.

CLITIPHO: What on earth do you mean, Syrus? You must be crazy.

SYRUS: Let me tell you what I've thought of, then you can judge. So long as you were their only child, their chief and sole delight, they spoilt you and gave you anything you wanted. Now that they've found a true daughter of their own, they've also found an excuse to get rid of you.

CLITIPHO [*only half-convinced*]: It seems likely . . .

SYRUS: Do you suppose it was really your bad behaviour which annoyed your father?

CLITIPHO: No, I don't.

SYRUS: Here's another point; all mothers stand up for their sons in disgrace and always help them when their fathers are unjust, but there's nothing like that now.

CLITIPHO: You're right, Syrus. So what am I to do now?

SYRUS: Question them about your suspicions, bring the whole thing into the open. If it isn't true you'll soon make them sorry for you or else you'll find out whose son you really are.

CLITIPHO: That's good advice. I'll take it.

[*He goes into* CHREMES' *house.*]

SYRUS: A very happy thought of mine! The more genuinely the boy appears to have suspicions and the more deeply he despairs, the easier it'll be for him to dictate peace to his father on his own terms. I wouldn't be surprised if he married in the end, though there'll be small thanks for Syrus if he does! Now what's that? Master's coming out; I'm off. After what's happened I wonder he didn't order me to be packed off at once. I'll go across to Menedemus and get him to intercede for me; I don't trust our old man.

[*He goes into* MENEDEMUS's *house;* CHREMES *and* SOS-TRATA *come out after a short interval.*]

SOSTRATA: You must be careful, Chremes, or you'll do our son an injury. I simply can't imagine how such a foolish thought could enter your head.

CHREMES: Just like a woman! I never wanted anything in my life, but you set yourself against me. But if I ask you where I'm wrong or why you behave like this, you don't know, and now you remain as obstinate as ever, you stupid creature.

SOSTRATA [*indignantly*]: Do you say I don't know?

CHREMES: All right, you do know; anything rather than going all over the same ground again.

SOSTRATA: Oh, you're quite unjust! This is something so important, and you forbid me to speak.

CHREMES: I'm not stopping you; speak now; but I shall carry on just the same.

SOSTRATA: Will you?

CHREMES: Indeed I shall.

SOSTRATA: But can't you see the wrong you'll do him? He's already suspecting that he's not our son.

CHREMES: Not our son, did you say?

SOSTRATA: That's what it'll come to, husband.

CHREMES [*sarcastically*]: And do you admit it?

SOSTRATA: For Heaven's sake, leave that for our enemies! Why ever should I admit that he's not my son when he is?

CHREMES: Why, are you afraid you can't prove he's yours whenever you like?

SOSTRATA [*puzzled*]: Because I've done this for my long-lost daughter, do you mean?

CHREMES: No, there's a much more plausible reason; he's so like you in his ways, you can easily prove he's your son. He's exactly like you, not a single fault in him which isn't the same as yours; nobody but you could possibly be the mother of such a son. [CLITIPHO *comes out.*] Here he comes now, sunk in gloom! You've only got to look at him to guess the truth.

CLITIPHO: Mother, if there was ever a time when I brought you pleasure, and you were both glad to call me your son, remember it now, I beseech you, and take pity on my present plight. My sole desire, my only request is to hear from you who my parents were.

SOSTRATA: My son, I implore you not to get it into your head that you are someone else's child.

CLITIPHO: But it's true, isn't it?

SOSTRATA: Oh dear me, how could you ask such a question? You are as truly my son and his as I pray you may survive us both. If you love me, please don't let me ever hear you say such a thing again.

CHREMES: But if you respect *my* wishes, make sure I see you change your ways.

CLITIPHO: What ways?

CHREMES: I can tell you, if you want to know. You're an idle, good-for-nothing fraud, and a damned loose-living spend-thrift. Believe that, and then believe you're our son.

CLITIPHO: That doesn't sound like a father.

CHREMES: If you'd been born out of my head, as they say Minerva sprang from Jove's, it wouldn't make it any easier for me to bear the disgrace you've brought on me by your misdeeds.

SOSTRATA: Heaven preserve us from anything like that!

CHREMES [*grimly*]: I can't answer for heaven; I can only do my best for myself. You're looking for parents, and these you've got. You don't think of looking for what you haven't got – the will to obey your father and preserve what he won by honest toil. Didn't you resort to trickery to bring into my house, under my own eyes a – Oh, I'm ashamed to use such a shocking word before your mother. But you weren't ashamed to do what you did.

CLITIPHO [*aside*]: Oh God, how I hate myself now. I'm so ashamed, and I've no idea how to set about placating him.

[MENEDEMUS *comes out of his house.*]

MENEDEMUS: Chremes is certainly too hard on the boy. It's quite inhuman, the way he torments him. So I'm coming out to make peace between them. Ah, good, there they are.

CHREMES: I say, Menedemus, why don't you send for my daughter and make sure of the dowry I offered?

SOSTRATA: My dear husband, I implore you not to do this.

CLITIPHO: Father, I implore you to forgive me.

MENEDEMUS: Take my advice, Chremes, and pardon him.

CHREMES: And make a present of my fortune to Bacchis with my eyes open? Certainly not.

MENEDEMUS: But we are here to stop that.

CLITIPHO: If you want me to stay alive, father, you must forgive me.

SOSTRATA: Come, Chremes, my dear.

MENEDEMUS: Come, Chremes, please don't be so obstinate.

CHREMES [reluctantly]: Very well. I see I'm not allowed to carry out my intention.

MENEDEMUS: There, now you're doing the right thing.

CHREMES: I'll forgive him on one condition: that he does what I think is proper for him.

CLITIPHO [eagerly]: Just tell me, father, and I'll do anything.

CHREMES: You can take a wife.

CLITIPHO [astounded]: Father!

CHREMES: That's no answer.

SOSTRATA: I'll answer for him; he'll do it.

CHREMES: No answer from him yet.

CLITIPHO [to himself]: Oh no, no . . .

SOSTRATA: Are you hesitating, Clitipho?

CHREMES: It's for him to decide.

SOSTRATA: He'll do everything.

MENEDEMUS [patting him on the back]: The first plunge seems hard, when it's all new to you, but you'll find it's quite easy once you've tried it.

CLITIPHO [with an effort]: All right, father, I will.

SOSTRATA: And I'll find you such a charming bride, Clitipho, it'll be easy to love her – our friend Phanocrates' daughter.

CLITIPHO [outraged]: That red-headed, hook-nosed girl with green eyes and a spotty face? I'm not having her.

CHREMES: Good gracious, how choosy he is! You'd think his mind runs on marriage.

SOSTRATA: I'll find you someone else.

CLITIPHO: No, if I must marry, I've someone in mind whom I like quite well.

CHREMES [*drily*]: Congratulations, my son.

CLITIPHO: It's the daughter of our neighbour Archonides.

SOSTRATA [*eagerly*]: Oh, I like her *very* much.

CLITIPHO: There's still one thing, father –

CHREMES: What?

CLITIPHO: I'd like you to forgive Syrus. What he did was for my sake.

CHREMES [*cheerfully*]: All right, I will.

[*To the audience, as they all go in*] Farewell, and give us your applause.

THE EUNUCH

[EUNUCHUS]

INTRODUCTORY NOTE

The Eunuch was Terence's most successful play in his lifetime, and according to Suetonius's *Life* 'it was staged twice in a day and won 8,000 sesterces, the highest fee ever paid for a comedy'. All the MSS. say it was his second play; so does the Production Notice, but gives the date as 161 B.C., after the known dates of *The Girl from Andros* and *The Self-Tormentor*, while Donatus says it was his third production. Perhaps the date refers to the second performance, if Suetonius's information is correct, and there was an earlier one before *The Self-Tormentor*, but most modern editors list it as third.

It is the most high-spirited and Plautine play Terence wrote, and Gnatho's monologue at lines 232 ff. is the only instance in his plays of a humorous scene which is not integrated into the plot. Though none of the characters is very subtly conceived, the light touch is consistent and dramatically right. Thais is a courtesan, but that is a matter of social status rather than morals, and she has charm and personality in marked contrast with the conventional views expressed about her profession. Pythias' gift for repartee makes her much more than a stock maidservant, and she is given an excellent scene where she pricks Parmeno's bubble of self-satisfaction. The awkward young countryman Chremes is artfully drawn as a foil to the more sophisticated brothers, Phaedria and the ebullient young Chaerea, who is the prototype perhaps for Beaumarchais' Cherubin. The inherent improbabilities in the play (too little time is allowed for Chaerea's escapade, and Chremes sobers up remarkably quickly) escape notice in the rapid development of surprises. Inevitably *The Eunuch* has been criticized for its amoral handling of Chaerea's conduct and the heartless solution of the rivalry between Phaedria and Thraso, but this is a comedy essentially aimed at amusing its audience. Robert Graves has even suggested that *The Eunuch* could be 'recast as a modern musical with great success'.

PRODUCTION NOTICE

THE EUNUCH by Terence: performed at the Megalensian Games[1] during the curule aedileship of Lucius Postumius Albinus and Lucius Cornelius Merula.

Produced by Lucius Ambivius Turpio and Lucius Atilius (*or* Hatilius) of Praeneste.

Music composed by Flaccus, slave of Claudius, for two right-hand pipes.[2]

Greek original by Menander.

The author's second play, written during the consulship of Marcus Valerius and Gaius Fannius.[3]

1. Celebrated annually in April in honour of the Great Mother, the goddess Cybele.
2. Two pipes could be played, one by each hand; see Introduction, p. 26.
3. i.e. 161 B.C.

SYNOPSIS

A girl was wrongly said to be the sister of Thais; unaware of this, the soldier Thraso brought her with him as a present for Thais. In fact, she was a freeborn Athenian. Thais's lover, Phaedria, gives orders for a eunuch he has bought to be given to her, is persuaded to yield his place to Thraso for two days, and departs for the country. Phaedria's young brother is desperately in love with the girl given to Thais; on Parmeno's suggestion he dresses up as the eunuch, gains admission to the house, and seduces the girl. But an Athenian citizen is found to be her brother and gives her in marriage to her seducer. Thraso persuades Phaedria to come to terms.

CHARACTERS

DEMEA[1]	*an Athenian gentleman*
PHAEDRIA	*his elder son, in love with Thais*
CHAEREA	*his younger son, in love with Pamphila*
ANTIPHO	*a friend of Chaerea*
CHREMES	*a young countryman of Attica*
THRASO	*an army officer*
GNATHO	*his hanger-on*
DORUS	*a eunuch*
PARMENO	*Demea's chief slave, attendant on Phaedria*
DONAX	
SANGA	
SIMALIO	*slaves of Thraso*
SYRISCUS	
Two others	
THAIS	*a courtesan*
PYTHIAS	*her maidservant and chief slave*
DORIAS	
Two other maids	*slaves of Thais*
PAMPHILA	*Chremes' young sister, at present a slave of Thraso*
SOPHRONA	*her old nurse*
An Ethiopian girl slave	

*

The scene is laid in Athens in front of the houses of Demea and Thais. To the audience's right the street leads to the centre of the town and the harbour and docks of the Peiraeus, and to their left to the countryside of Attica

1. He is never addressed by name in the play, and in the scene-headings the MSS. are divided between Demea and Laches.

AUTHOR'S PROLOGUE TO
THE EUNUCH

IF there are people who try to please as many and hurt as few honest men as possible, the poet begs to announce himself one of their number.

Furthermore, if someone[1] has thought something too harsh has been said against him, he must realize that this was not an attack but an answer, for he launched the first assault. For all his competence as a translator, his poor style of writing has turned good Greek plays into bad Latin ones. He is also the man who has just given us *The Spectre* of Menander, and in his *Treasure* made the defendant state his claim to the money before the plaintiff puts his own case saying how he came by the treasure, and how it found its way into his father's tomb. He must not deceive himself and fancy that he has made an end of this and I shall have no more to say; I warn him, he is wrong and must not provoke me further. There are plenty of other things which I am overlooking for the moment, but can produce later on, if he continues to attack me in the way he set out to do.

The play we shall present today is *The Eunuch* of Menander. After the aediles had bought it, he managed to get an opportunity to see it. When the official was present, the performance began.[2] At once he cried out that this was not the work of a poet but of a thief, though he had not taken anyone in – there was already a *Flatterer*, an old play of Naevius and Plautus,

1. Luscius Lanuvinus, Terence's rival and critic.
2. There is no other reference to a preliminary performance before the public showing of a play, evidently for censorship. The aediles seem to have bought the play at the producer's recommendation.

from which the characters of the sponger and the soldier had been stolen.

If that is the author's fault, it is due to inadvertence, not to any intention on his part to steal from a play. You, the audience, will soon be able to judge if this is so. Certainly Menander's *Flatterer* exists, and in it there are a sponger who flatters and a soldier who boasts. The author admits that he has transferred these characters from the Greek play into his *Eunuch*: but the suggestion that he knew that these plays had already been translated into Latin he absolutely denies. If he is not allowed to make use of the same characters as other writers, how can he still bring on a running slave, virtuous wives and dishonest courtesans, greedy spongers and braggart soldiers? How can he show substitution of a child, deception of an old man by his slave, love, hatred, and suspicion? Nothing in fact is ever said which has not been said before.

It is only right that you should recognize this, and forgive new authors if they do what earlier writers have repeatedly done. Give us your support, pay attention in silence, and understand what *The Eunuch* has to say.

[*The young man* PHAEDRIA *comes out of his father's house talking to his slave* PARMENO, *a middle-aged attendant.*]

PHAEDRIA: Well then, what am I to do? I can't refuse to go now she's asking me herself, can I? Or had I better think of making a stand against these insults from such women? She slammed her door on me once, and now she opens it again. Shall I go back? No, not if she goes down on bended knees.

PARMENO: Of course, sir, if you can do that, it's the best and boldest course. But if you make a start and can't stick it out, and then go running back to her when you can't stand it any longer, unasked and no terms fixed, letting her see you're in love and can't bear it – then it'll all be over and done with. It will be the end of *you*, sir; she'll stop play once she finds you're beaten. So while there's time, do think, and think again, sir. Reason can't solve what hasn't got rhyme nor reason, and all these upsets – insults, jealousies, quarrels, reconciliations, war, then peace again – they're all part of love, and if you insist on a method to settle all your uncertainties, why, you might as well think up a method for madness. You're angry now, muttering away to yourself: 'I'll show her! She ... with him ... and me ... and then not ... just let her try! I'd rather die! She'll learn what sort of a man I am!' But believe me, it won't take more than a single tiny false tear – which she can hardly squeeze out by force after all that rubbing of her eyes – to damp down all those hot words. Then she'll turn the attack on you, and you'll be the one to suffer.

PHAEDRIA: Monstrous! At last I can see her wickedness and my own sorry state. I'm eaten up with love and I'm sick of it, I'm dying on my feet, eyes open, awake and aware, but what on earth can I do?

PARMENO: Do? Buy your freedom as cheap as possible, and if you can't get it cheap, pay up what you can and stop worrying yourself to death.

PHAEDRIA: That's your advice?

PARMENO: Yes, if you've any sense. Love provides enough troubles anyway – just you face up to those properly and don't go adding to them. Look, she's coming out, that blight on our fortunes! Every penny we ought to have goes to *her*.

[THAIS *comes out of her house without seeing them: she is an attractive young woman.*]

THAIS: Oh dear, I'm afraid Phaedria was annoyed and misunderstood me when I wouldn't let him in yesterday.

PHAEDRIA [*clutching* PARMENO]: The mere sight of her sets me all trembling and shivering.

PARMENO: Courage, sir! Go nearer the fire and you'll warm up all right.

THAIS [*coming forward*]: Who's that? Phaedria my dear, is that you? Why are you waiting here? You should have come straight in.

PARMENO: Not a word about shutting her door to him!

THAIS: Why don't you say something?

PHAEDRIA [*bitterly*]: I always find the door open, don't I – I always come first with you.

THAIS: Please, no more.

PHAEDRIA: Why 'no more'? Oh Thais, Thais, if only love meant the same thing to you as it does to me and we were on equal terms! Then you would suffer for this as much as I do, or I would think nothing of what you have done!

THAIS: Phaedria, my own, my darling, don't torture yourself, please. I swear I didn't do this because I care for anyone or love anyone more than you. In the circumstances it had to be done.

PARMENO: Quite so. Poor soul, I suppose you shut the door for love of him!

THAIS: You think that of me, Parmeno? All right: but let me tell you why I sent for you.

PHAEDRIA [*eagerly*]: Tell me.

THAIS: First of all, can *he* keep his mouth shut?

PARMENO: Me? Of course I can. Listen, I stick to a promise – but there are conditions. When I hear the truth spoken I can hold my tongue and keep quiet as well as anyone, but if it's a lie or an invention or a trumped-up tale, it's out at once; I'm full of cracks and leak all over. So if you want a secret kept, madam, tell the truth.

THAIS [*ignoring him*]: My mother came from Samos and lived in Rhodes.

PARMENO: I can keep *that* secret.

THAIS: While she was there, a merchant made her a present of a little girl stolen from here, from Attica.

PHAEDRIA: A citizen born?

THAIS: I think so, but we can't be sure. All she could tell us herself was her father's and mother's name, and she didn't know her country or anything else to identify her – she was too young. The merchant added that he had heard from the pirates who sold her that she had been carried off from Sunium. As soon as my mother had taken her in she took care to teach her all she could and bring her up as her own child. She was generally believed to be my sister. Then I found a protector, my first and only one, and came here to Athens with him. It was he who set me up with all I have.

PARMENO: Two lies: they'll both leak out.

THAIS: What do you mean?

PARMENO: One wasn't enough for you and he wasn't the

only one to give you something. My master here has also made a handsome contribution.

THAIS: Very well, but let me come to my point. It wasn't long before my soldier friend went off to Caria, and that was when I came to know you. You know yourself how dear you have been to me ever since and how I have always told you everything.

PHAEDRIA [*bitterly*]: There's another thing for Parmeno to let out.

PARMENO: No doubt about that, sir.

THAIS: Please listen, both of you. My mother died recently at Rhodes, leaving a brother who is always greedy for money. Seeing the girl was a beauty and knew how to play the lyre, he hoped she would fetch a good price, so he put her up for sale and sold her on the spot. Luckily my friend happened to be there and bought her as a present for me, knowing nothing of course of all I've just told you. Now he's back in Athens, but since he found out about my relations with you too he's busy finding excuses not to give me her. He says he'd be willing to do so if he could be sure he came first with me and wasn't afraid I should leave him once I had her, only that is what he *is* afraid of. Personally I have my suspicions that he's taken a fancy to the girl.

PHAEDRIA: Is it more than a fancy?

THAIS: No; I have made inquiries. Now there are many reasons, Phaedria dear, why I want to get her away from him. In the first place she's spoken of as my sister, and then there's the chance I may be able to restore her to her family. I'm alone here, Phaedria, without a single friend or relative, and I should like to make some friends by doing a kindness. Please help me with this and make things easier: let the man have first place with me for the next few days.... Can't you answer me?

PHAEDRIA: You wretched woman, what answer can I give to conduct like yours?

PARMENO: Well done, sir, congratulations! It's come home to you at last; you're a man!

PHAEDRIA: Do you think I couldn't see what you were leading up to? 'A little girl was carried off from here, my mother brought her up as her own, she was taken for my sister and I want to get her away to restore her to her family.' In fact all you've just said amounts to this – I'm kept out and he's let in. And why? Obviously because you love him more than you love me; and now you're afraid that girl he brought here may snatch him from you – for what he's worth.

THAIS: *I'm* afraid of *that*?

PHAEDRIA: What else is worrying you? Tell me that. Is he the only one who gives you presents? Have you ever known me set a limit to my generosity? When you told me you wanted an Ethiopian slave-girl, didn't I leave everything to look for one? And then you said you'd like a eunuch because only queens employ them; well, I've found one, and only yesterday I paid two thousand drachmas for the pair. Badly treated as I was by you, I didn't forget; and in return for what I've done you kick me out!

THAIS: There, there, Phaedria. I want to get the girl away and I still think my plan is the best way to do this, but rather than lose your affection I'll do anything you bid me.

PHAEDRIA: If only you spoke from your heart and really meant 'rather than lose your affection'! If only I could believe you are sincere in what you say, I could endure anything!

PARMENO [*aside*]: He's weakening. Beaten by a word and all too soon!

THAIS: Alas, don't I speak from the heart? Have you ever

wanted anything from me, even in fun, without getting it? I can't get what *I* want – I can't persuade you to give me a mere couple of days.

PHAEDRIA: If it's only a couple ... but it might turn into twenty.

THAIS: I promise you, only a couple or –

PHAEDRIA: I'm not having 'or'.

THAIS: It shan't be more. Just let me have this.

PHAEDRIA: Oh all right, have it your own way.

THAIS [*embracing him*]: No wonder I love you, you're so kind.

PHAEDRIA: I'll leave town and endure my misery in the country – two days of it. That's settled then; Thais must have her way. Parmeno, see that those two are brought across.

PARMENO: Very good, sir.

PHAEDRIA: For two days then, Thais – good-bye.

THAIS: Good-bye, dear Phaedria. That's all, then?

PHAEDRIA: All – except this. When you are with your soldier in person, be absent in spirit. Night and day, love me, long for me, dream of me, wait for me, think of me, hope for me, find joy in me, and be all mine. You have my heart: try to give me yours.

[*He walks firmly into* DEMEA's *house without a backward glance, followed by* PARMENO.]

THAIS: Oh dear. . . . Perhaps he doesn't trust me and judges my character by other women. But knowing myself, I can swear I've told nothing but the truth, and no man is dearer to me than my Phaedria. All I have done in this I did for the girl's sake, for I have hopes that I've already found her brother, a young man of good family. He's arranged to visit me this very day, so I'll go in and wait for him.

[*She goes into her house. After a short pause* PHAEDRIA *comes out, ready for departure, followed by* PARMENO.]

PHAEDRIA: Do as I told you and have those two brought here.

PARMENO: Yes, sir.

PHAEDRIA: Get on with it!

PARMENO: Yes, sir.

PHAEDRIA: Look sharp!

PARMENO: Yes, sir.

PHAEDRIA: You know your instructions?

PARMENO: What a question! There's no difficulty about it. I only wish, sir, you were likely to get as much out of this as you're going to lose by it.

PHAEDRIA: I'm lost anyway, that matters more to me.... But don't *you* go making heavy weather of it.

PARMENO: I won't. I'll see it's done. Anything else?

PHAEDRIA: Say the best you can about my present, and do what you can to keep that rival of mine away from her.

PARMENO: No need to remind me about *that*.

PHAEDRIA: Now I'm off to the country and there I'll stay.

PARMENO: That's right, sir.

PHAEDRIA: Just a minute –

PARMENO: What is it?

PHAEDRIA: Do you think I shall be able to stick it out and not come home too soon?

PARMENO: Good lord, no, sir. You'll be back here at once, or at any rate after the first sleepless night.

PHAEDRIA: I shall work and make sure I'm so tired I'll sleep in spite of myself.

PARMENO: Then all you'll gain is that you'll be sleepless *and* tired.

PHAEDRIA: Shut up, Parmeno, that's nonsense. I'm absolutely determined from now on to be *firm*. I've been letting myself go.... Why, if it came to it, I could do without her for – *three* whole days.

PARMENO: Three days on end? Be careful what you say, sir.

PHAEDRIA: I've made up my mind.

[*He goes off left with a great air of determination.*]

PARMENO: Heaven above, what a disease this is, when a man
is so much changed by love that you'd hardly know him for
the same! There was a time when no one was as sensible,
serious, and sober as this young man. . . . But who's that
coming? Why, it's Gnatho, that hanger-on of the soldier's,
and he's got the girl with him to give to Thais. God, what a
beauty! I'll cut a poor figure today with my decrepit old
eunuch. This girl's even better looking than Thais herself.

[*He stands back as* GNATHO *comes on from the right, followed
by* PAMPHILA *and a maid, and voices his self-satisfaction to
the audience.*]

GNATHO: Ye gods, how one man can surpass another! What
a world of difference there is between a fool and a man with
brains! The thought struck me on my way here, when I ran
into a man of my own rank and position, a decent fellow
who'd guzzled up all his patrimony like I did. There he was,
unshaven, dirty, and wretched, a ragged old man. 'What's
the meaning of this get-up?' I said. 'I've been unfortunate,
lost all I had, and look what I've come to. All my friends
and acquaintances cut me now.' He filled me with contempt
when I compared him with myself. 'You great booby,' I
said, 'have you managed to lose all your self-confidence?
Did your wits disappear along with your fortune? Look at
me; my origins are the same as yours; I'm healthy, well-
groomed, and properly dressed, a fine figure of a man. I'm
penniless, but I've got everything: I've nothing of my own
and lack nothing.' 'But unhappily I haven't the talent for
playing the fool or taking a beating.' 'Are you supposing
that's how it's done? You're quite wrong. There was a time,
a generation ago, when there was money to be made by that

kind of thing, but we've new ways of setting our traps today. I can even claim to be the inventor of the new method.
There's a type of man, you know, who wants to come first
in everything and doesn't quite make it. They're the ones I
aim at, but I don't try to make them laugh at me – no, no,
I'm ready with *my* laughs and admiration for them and their
wit. I praise whatever they say, and then if they change to
the opposite I praise that too. If they say No, I say No, and
if it's Yes, it's Yes from me too. In fact, I've trained myself
to agree with anything. There's a fat lot to be made out of
it today, I can tell you, nothing better.'

PARMENO [*aside*]: My word, that's a clever one! He can turn a
fool into a gibbering idiot in no time.

GNATHO [*still not seeing him*]: During this conversation we
came to the market, and up came running the confectioners,
fishmongers, butchers, cooks, poulterers, and spratsellers,
all delighted to see me, people who'd profited from me
when I still had money and still often do now I've none.
They always greet me, ask me to dinner, and bid me welcome. When that poor starveling saw the honours paid me
and my easy way of making a living, he began to beg me to
let him learn from me. I told him he could be my disciple; the
philosophers have schools named after them, so I have hopes
that spongers may henceforth be known as Gnathonists.

PARMENO [*aside*]: Look what can be got out of idleness and
eating with someone else to foot the bill!

GNATHO: But I must hurry on to give this girl to Thaïs and
ask her to dine with my master. Why, there's Parmeno
standing outside her house, looking glum. He's our rival's
servant, so all must be going well. They must be having a
cool reception. I can't resist teasing the fellow.

PARMENO [*aside*]: And men like this imagine that it only
takes a present to make Thaïs theirs!

GNATHO [*going up to him ceremoniously*]: Gnatho bids a warm welcome to his dear friend Parmeno. How do I find you?

PARMENO: Standing on my feet.

GNATHO: So I see. Is there anything here [*eyeing the girl*] you would prefer not to see?

PARMENO: You.

GNATHO: Quite so, but is there anything else?

PARMENO: Why should there be?

GNATHO: You look glum.

PARMENO: It's nothing.

GNATHO: Well then, cheer up. What do you think of this for a slave girl?

PARMENO: Not bad.

GNATHO [*aside*]: He's warming up.

PARMENO [*overhearing*]: That's just where he's wrong.

GNATHO: How do you think Thais will like this present?

PARMENO: Do you mean by this that we're turned out? Well, it's a world of ups and downs.

GNATHO: Mark my words, Parmeno, I'm giving you six whole months of peace from running to and fro and staying up till daybreak. Doesn't that make you happy?

PARMENO: Me happy? Really!

GNATHO: I always try to please my friends.

PARMENO: Congratulations.

GNATHO: Don't let me keep you if you were on your way somewhere.

PARMENO: I wasn't.

GNATHO [*eagerly*]: In that case, please do me a small favour; help me to gain admission to Thais.

PARMENO: Well then, go in; now you've that girl with you the doors will open of their own accord.

[GNATHO *tries the door and it opens.*]

GNATHO: Perhaps there's someone I can send out to you?

[*He goes in with* PAMPHILA *and the maid.*]

PARMENO [*shouting after him*]: Just you wait till those two days are up! You can open doors with your little finger now your luck's in, but I'll see you're kept kicking at them without an answer!

GNATHO [*coming out*]: Still there, Parmeno? I wonder if you were left to intercept any private message passing between my master and the lady?

PARMENO: Witty, aren't you; just the sort of course to please your soldier friend. [GNATHO *goes off right.*] Now I do believe I see my master's younger son coming. He's supposed to be on guard duty at the docks[1] today, so I wonder what brings him here. Something's up – he's in such a hurry and searching everywhere.

[CHAEREA *rushes on from the right, not seeing* PARMENO: *he is a very young man in officer's uniform.*]

CHAEREA: Hell! The girl's lost and I'm lost too in losing sight of her. Where to look, where to find her, whom to ask, or which way to turn I've no idea. My only hope is that wherever she is, she can't stay hidden for long. Oh she's a beauty! I've written off all other women – I'm through with ordinary types.

PARMENO [*aside*]: Now here's the other one talking about love! Oh my poor old master! If once this boy begins, you'll say the first one was just fooling about compared with what this one's frenzy will do.

CHAEREA: Devil take the old fool who kept me, and me too for stopping and paying attention to him. But look who's there – hullo, Parmeno.

PARMENO: What's the matter with you? What's all the excitement? Where've you come from?

1. i.e. the Piraeus, the harbour town of Athens.

CHAEREA: Damned if I know – either where I've come from or where I'm going. I've completely lost my head.

PARMENO: How, may I ask?

CHAEREA [*impressively*]: I'm in love.

PARMENO: What!

CHAEREA: Now's your chance, Parmeno, to show what sort of a man you are. You know the promise you often made me: 'Just you find something to love, Chaerea, and I'll show you how useful I can be.' That was when I used to bring all the contents of my father's larder secretly to your room.

PARMENO: Don't be so silly.

CHAEREA: Well, I did, you know. Now you can please keep your promise – if you think it's worth your while to make the effort. This isn't an ordinary girl, like the ones whose mothers want them to have round shoulders and flat chests to make them look slim – and if there's one who's a bit plumper they tell her she looks like a prize-fighter and cut down her diet, so that she ends up after treatment thin as a bulrush in spite of her natural charms. What a way to find a lover!

PARMENO: What about your girl?

CHAEREA: *She*'s something quite different.

PARMENO: She would be!

CHAEREA: Natural complexion, firm figure, plump and juicy . . .

PARMENO: Age?

CHAEREA: Sixteen.

PARMENO: A perfect peach!

CHAEREA: You must get her for me, Parmeno, by force or stealth or entreaty; I don't care how, so long as I have her.

PARMENO: Well, who does she belong to?

CHAEREA: I've no idea.

PARMENO: Where does she come from?

CHAEREA: No idea.

PARMENO: Where does she live?

CHAEREA: Don't know that either.

PARMENO: Where did you see her?

CHAEREA: In the street.

PARMENO: How did you come to lose her?

CHAEREA: That was what I was cursing myself for as I came along. I don't think there's another man alive whose good luck turns against him like mine. Oh, what a dirty trick! It's done for me.

PARMENO: But what *happened*?

CHAEREA: I'll tell you. You know Archidemides, that old friend and relative of my father's –

PARMENO: Yes, of course.

CHAEREA: I ran into him while I was following the girl.

PARMENO: How inconvenient.

CHAEREA: Inconvenient's not the right word – I'd call it damned unlucky. I can swear I haven't set eyes on the man for the last six or seven months and I had to meet him now when I least wanted or needed him. A bird of ill omen, that's what I'd call him – wouldn't you?

PARMENO: I would indeed.

CHAEREA: He came running up from a mile off, hunched-up and shaking, with his slobbering old mouth wheezing away: 'Hi, Chaerea, I'm talking to you!' he said. I stopped. 'Do you know what I want you for?' 'No, tell me.' 'I've got a case on tomorrow.' 'So what?' 'Be sure to tell your father not to forget to come early to support me.' It took him an hour to get this out, and then I asked if I could go. 'Certainly,' he said, and I made off, but when I looked round for the girl she'd just turned off this way, down our street.

PARMENO [*aside*]: I do believe he means the girl who's just been given to Thais.

CHAEREA: By the time I was here she'd disappeared.

PARMENO: I suppose she'd someone with her?

CHAEREA: Yes, one of those spongers and a maid.

PARMENO [*aside*]: It's her all right. [*To* CHAEREA] Come off it, sir; the affair's finished, dead and buried.

CHAEREA: You must mean something else.

PARMENO: I mean *your* affair.

CHAEREA: But do you know who she is? Have you seen her?

PARMENO: I've seen her, I know her, and I can tell you where she was taken.

CHAEREA [*shaking him excitedly*]: Parmeno, old man, do you really know her? And where she is now?

PARMENO: She was brought here as a present for Thais and given to her.

CHAEREA: Who's in a position to make a present like that?

PARMENO: The soldier Thraso, Phaedria's rival.

CHAEREA: That doesn't leave my brother much of a part.

PARMENO: No, and you'd say so even more if you knew the present he's intending to give her himself.

CHAEREA: Well, what is it?

PARMENO: A eunuch.

CHAEREA: No, please, not that horrible individual, that old woman of a man you bought yesterday!

PARMENO: That's the one.

CHAEREA: He'll be kicked out and his present after him. But I didn't know Thais lived near us.

PARMENO: She hasn't for long.

CHAEREA: Damn it all, I've never even seen her! Come on, Parmeno, is she as lovely as they say?

PARMENO: She is.

CHAEREA: But doesn't bear comparison with my girl?

PARMENO: Ah no, that's different.

CHAEREA: Parmeno, for God's sake help me to possess her!

PARMENO: I'll do my best, I'll try everything I can. Now, sir, may I go?

CHAEREA: Where to?

PARMENO: Home. I've got to fetch those slaves your brother told me to give to Thais.

CHAEREA: Oh, lucky eunuch, to be a present for that house!

PARMENO: What do you mean?

CHAEREA: Can't you see? He'll always see his fellow slave in all her beauty around the house, he'll speak to her and be under the same roof, he may sometimes take his meals with her . . . and perhaps sleep by her side.

PARMENO [teasing him]: Suppose you were the lucky one –

CHAEREA: How could I be?

PARMENO: You could wear his clothes –

CHAEREA: His clothes? And then?

PARMENO: I could take you in instead of him –

CHAEREA: Yes –

PARMENO: And say you were him –

CHAEREA: I see!

PARMENO: You could enjoy all those advantages you just said would be his; be near her, eat with her, touch her, play with her – and sleep by her side. None of the women there can recognize you or knows who you are. [Bursts out laughing] Besides, you're just the right age and figure to be taken for a eunuch!

CHAEREA [ignoring this]: Splendid! I've never had such marvellous advice. Quick, come home at once, dress me up, bring me out, take me there this minute!

PARMENO: What? Oh no, I was only pulling your leg.

CHAEREA: Nonsense!

PARMENO: I'm a damn fool – what have I done? Where are you shoving me? You'll have me down. Stop it, I say!

CHAEREA: Come *on*.

PARMENO: You're really set on it?

CHAEREA: Of course I am.

PARMENO: You'll find things too hot for you if you don't look out.

CHAEREA: No I shan't. Let me do it.

PARMENO: Yes, but it'll be me who smarts for it.

CHAEREA [*impatiently*]: Oh –

PARMENO: We'll be doing wrong.

CHAEREA: *Wrong*? For me to be taken into a house of that reputation and pay back those tormentors who always scorn us and our youth and think up every kind of torture for us? Wrong for me to deceive them as they do us? Would you rather I duped my father? I'd be blamed all right for that if I was found out, but everyone would think this a deed well done.

PARMENO: All right, if you must do it, go ahead. Only don't go putting the blame on me later on.

CHAEREA: Of course not.

PARMENO: I'm to take it as an order then?

CHAEREA [*drawing himself up*]: Order? It's my will and command. I'm not one to shirk responsibility. Follow me.

PARMENO: And heaven be on our side!

[*They go into* DEMEA's *house. Soon* GNATHO *and his master* THRASO, *a middle-aged army officer, come on from the right.*]

THRASO: Thais really sent me many thanks?

GNATHO: Her heartfelt thanks.

THRASO: And she's really pleased?

GNATHO: Not so much pleased with the gift as with the fact that you were the giver. That's a real triumph for her.

PARMENO [*opening* DEMEA's *door*]: I must watch for the right moment to take him across. Oh, there's the soldier.

THRASO [*complacently*]: I have a real knack of giving pleasure with everything I do.

GNATHO: That is something which has always struck me.

THRASO: The king always thanked me most warmly in his own person for anything I did, in a way he never thanked anyone else.

GNATHO: It often happens that others have worked hard to win the renown which a witty man can appropriate with a word. That's so in your case.

THRASO: True.

GNATHO: Thus the king held you –

THRASO: He did indeed –

GNATHO: – in high favour.

THRASO: Yes; he entrusted his entire army to me, and all his plans.

GNATHO: How wonderful!

THRASO: Then when he was bored with his courtiers or tired of business and felt he needed a rest, as if – do you know?

GNATHO: I do: as if he would rid his mind of all his troubles –

THRASO: You've got it. At such times he would take me aside as his sole companion.

GNATHO: Ah, there's a king with good taste!

THRASO: That's the man he is; very select in his company.

GNATHO [*aside*]: *Very* select, if he chose you.

THRASO: All the court was jealous, backbiters all, but what did I care? They were miserably envious, most of all the man in charge of the Indian elephants. When he was particularly troublesome, 'Why, Strato,' I used to say, 'have you learnt ferocity from controlling those wild beasts of yours?'

GNATHO: A pretty bit of wit! Marvellous! You had him by the throat. How did he take it?

THRASO: Struck dumb.

GNATHO: I'm not surprised.

PARMENO [aside]: Good lord, what a hopeless fool the man is! And the other's a wicked liar.

THRASO: Did I ever tell you, Gnatho, about the dinner-party where I dealt with that man from Rhodes?

GNATHO: Never; do tell me now. [Aside] I've heard it thousands of times.

THRASO: This young fellow from Rhodes I was talking about was dining with me. I had a girl there, and he was cracking jokes at my expense. 'Less of your impudence,' I said: 'Why should you be a hare who runs with the hounds?'

[GNATHO breaks into exaggerated laughter at this pointless platitude.]

THRASO: What did you say?

GNATHO: Brilliant! Witty! Neat! The best thing I've heard. Is it yours? I thought it was an old one.

THRASO: Had you heard it before?

GNATHO: Often, and it always goes down well.

THRASO: It's my own.

GNATHO: I feel for him, the forward young idiot, having that said to him.

PARMENO [aside]: To hell with you!

GNATHO: What did he say?

THRASO: It finished him. Everyone present nearly died of laughter. Since then they've all stood in awe of me.

GNATHO: And so they should.

THRASO: By the way, what about this girl: should I rid Thais of her suspicions that I'm attracted to her?

GNATHO: Certainly not. You'd do better to increase them.

THRASO: Why?

GNATHO: Why? You know how it galls you if ever she praises Phaedria or even mentions his name?

THRASO: Yes, yes, I know.

GNATHO: There's only one way of stopping it. When she names Phaedria, you retaliate with Pamphila; if ever she suggests asking Phaedria in to supper, we'll invite Pamphila to sing, and if she praises his good looks, you praise hers. We can give her tit for tat and cut her to the quick.

THRASO [*sighing*]: If only she really loved me, Gnatho, that would be the thing to do.

GNATHO: She waits in for your presents and loves *them*, so I believe she's loved you for a long time; and it's long been easy for you to upset her, since she's always afraid of losing what she gets out of you now if someday you go off in a huff elsewhere.

THRASO: True: I hadn't thought of that.

GNATHO: You're joking – it's just that you hadn't given your mind to it. Otherwise you'd have thought of it yourself, and how much better!

[THAIS *comes out of her house.*]

THAIS: I'm sure I heard my soldier's voice – and there he is. Welcome, Thraso.

THRASO: Thais, my own, my sweetheart, how are you? Can you love your Thraso a little bit for the girl he's given you?

PARMENO [*aside*]: There's gallantry! What a way to start!

THAIS: Very much, as you deserve.

GNATHO: Then come along to dinner; why delay?

PARMENO [*aside*]: Listen to that one now! The man's sub-human.

THAIS: When you like; I won't keep you waiting.

PARMENO [*aside*]: Here's my cue – I can pretend I've just come out. [*Comes forward*] Are you going out, madam?

THAIS: Ah, Parmeno, I'm obliged to you. I'm just going –

PARMENO: Where?

THAIS: Can't you see? [*indicating* THRASO].

PARMENO: Oh I'm sick of seeing *him*. When it suits you, madam, I've presents for you from Phaedria.

THRASO: Must we stand around? Why can't we go?

PARMENO: By your leave, sir, I'm only asking for a moment to give the lady what we have for her and just say a few words.

THRASO: Fine presents, comparable I expect with my own!

PARMENO: We shall see. [*Calls inside the house*] Here, hurry along with those two I told to come out. [*The black slave-girl comes out.*] Come forward, you. [*To* THAIS] Now *she*'s come all the way from Ethiopia.

THRASO: Three hundred drachmas at the most!

GNATHO: Scarcely that.

PARMENO: Where are you, Dorus? Come here. [CHAEREA *comes out, dressed suitably for a eunuch.*] Now there's a eunuch for you, in the prime of life and looks like a gentleman!

THAIS [*clearly interested*]: Heavens, he is good looking.

PARMENO: Well, Gnatho? Any criticisms? What about you, sir? Silence speaks volumes. Test him on literature, music, athletics: I'll guarantee his accomplishments come up to any young gentleman's.

THRASO: I know what I'd do to that eunuch if it came to it – drunk or sober.

PARMENO [*to* THAIS]: And the donor of these gifts is not making demands on you to live with him alone, to the exclusion of everyone else. *He* doesn't recount his battles and display his scars or lie in wait for you like someone else I know. All he asks is to be received when it's convenient and you have time and feel like it.

THRASO: The man's master must be a penniless and poor-spirited creature!

GNATHO: Obviously no one with means to buy another would put up with a slave like this!

PARMENO: You shut up, you scum of the earth. I know you and your nasty ways, making up to *his* type. You'd steal from a corpse.

THRASO: Are – we – going?

THAIS: I must just take these two indoors and give some instructions. I'll be back in a minute. [*She goes in with the black slave and* CHAEREA.]

THRASO [*to* GNATHO]: I shall go. You wait here for her.

PARMENO: The High Command shouldn't be seen in the street with its lady friend!

THRASO: All I wish to say to *you* is – you take after your master.

[PARMENO *goes off laughing, down the street, right, while* GNATHO *tries to conceal his laughter.*]

THRASO [*suspiciously*]: What are you laughing at?

GNATHO: Only something you said just now – and that tale about the man from Rhodes, whenever I think of it. But here comes Thais.

[THAIS *comes out with her maids,* PYTHIAS, *a middle-aged woman, and two others.*]

THRASO: You hurry on ahead then, and have everything ready at home.

GNATHO: I will. [*He goes off right.*]

THAIS: Look after them well, Pythias, and if Chremes should call, try first to persuade him to wait; if it doesn't suit him ask him to call again, and if he can't manage that, bring him to me.

PYTHIAS: Very good, madam.

THAIS: Now, was there anything else? Yes, take great care of the girl, and mind all of you stay indoors.

THRASO: Can't we *go*?

THAIS [*to the two maids*]: You follow me.

[PYTHIAS *goes back into the house;* THRASO *and* THAIS *go off right. After a short pause,* CHREMES *comes on from the left. A shy and awkward young man, he pauses doubtfully outside* THAIS*'s door and then turns away.*]

CHREMES: The more I think of it, the more I'm convinced Thais has something unpleasant in store for me, she's been working on me so artfully from the moment she first asked me to visit her. [*To audience*] (In case any of you are wondering about my relations with her, I may say I didn't even know the woman.) When I called she found an excuse for keeping me waiting – said she'd been at her prayers and had something important to discuss with me. From then on I had suspicions this was all a plot. She sat down beside me, made advances and tried to start a conversation. When it petered out, she changed the subject. How long had my parents been dead? A long time, I said. Then she asked if I had any property at Sunium and how far it was from the sea. I suppose she's taken a fancy to it and hopes to get it from me. Lastly, had I had a little sister who disappeared from there, was anyone with her, had she anything on her at the time and could anyone identify her? Why on earth does she want to know all this? Surely she can't have the nerve to pretend *she* is the little sister who was lost years ago – if the girl's still alive she'd be no more than sixteen, and Thais is a bit older than I am. Now she's sent for me again, begging me to come. Either she must say what she wants or stop making a nuisance of herself. I'm damned if I'll come a third time. [*Knocks on the door*] Hi there, is anyone at home? It's Chremes.

PYTHIAS [*comes out and greets him eagerly*]: Oh, my dear young man!

CHREMES [*aside*]: I said there was a plot.

PYTHIAS: My mistress left an urgent message for you, asking you to call again tomorrow.

CHREMES: I shan't be in town.

PYTHIAS: Please, sir –

CHREMES: Impossible, I tell you.

PYTHIAS: Then will you please wait here till she returns?

CHREMES: Certainly not.

PYTHIAS: My dear sir, why not?

CHREMES: Go to the devil!

PYTHIAS: If you are sure you can't stay, will you please step across to where she is?

CHREMES [*sulkily*]: Very well.

PYTHIAS [*calling indoors*]: Dorias! Take this gentleman over to Thraso's at once.

[*A maid comes out of the house and goes off right with* CHREMES. *Soon after,* ANTIPHO *hurries on from the right, a cheerful young man also in uniform.*]

ANTIPHO: Some of the lads at the docks met yesterday and planned to club together for dinner today. We chose Chaerea to make the arrangements, fixed the time and place, and pledged ourselves to be there. The time's passed, nothing's ready in the place we named, and Chaerea's nowhere to be found. I don't know what to say or what to make of it. Now the others have given me the job of looking for him and I've come to see if he's at home. [THAIS's *door opens and* CHAEREA *appears.*] There's someone coming out – is it him or isn't it? It is – but what on earth's happened to the man? Dressed up like that – what's he up to? It beats me. . . . I can't imagine. . . . Whatever it is, I think I'll just step back for the moment and see if I can find out.

CHAEREA [*in a state of wild elation*]: Anyone here? Nobody. Anyone follow me from the house? Not a soul. Dare I be happy and let myself go? My God, this is the moment to face death while I can bear it, before life's troubles spoil my happiness! And there's no busybody here now wanting to follow wherever I lead, deafening me with questions and pestering me to death to know why I'm so excited and happy, where I'm going, where I've come from, where I got these clothes from and what I want, whether I'm off my head or not!

ANTIPHO: I'll go and do him the service I see he wants. Chaerea, why are you so excited? What's the meaning of these clothes? Why are you so happy? What's the idea? Are you off your head? Why are you staring at me – can't you answer?

CHAEREA [*hugging him wildly*]: Oh glorious day! Oh my dear friend, welcome! The very man I wanted to see!

ANTIPHO: I beg you, please tell me what's up.

CHAEREA: No, no, it's I who implore you to listen. You know that girl of my brother's?

ANTIPHO: Yes of course; I suppose you mean Thais.

CHAEREA: That's the one.

ANTIPHO: I thought so.

CHAEREA: Today she's been given a girl . . . no need for me to say much in praise of *her* looks. You know I've a connoisseur's eye for a lovely woman. I fell for this one.

ANTIPHO: Really?

CHAEREA: You'd give her top marks if you saw her. To cut it short, I'm in love. By a stroke of luck there was a eunuch at home that my brother had bought for Thais and not yet sent to her. Our man Parmeno made a suggestion which I jumped at –

ANTIPHO: What was it?

CHAEREA: Shut up and you'll hear. To change clothes with him and have myself taken there in his place.

ANTIPHO: Instead of the eunuch?

CHAEREA: Yes.

ANTIPHO: What on earth were you to gain by that?

CHAEREA: Why, it's obvious. I could see and hear her and be with the object of my desires. Wasn't that a sufficient reason? Not a bad scheme, Antipho. I was handed over to the lady, she accepted me and was delighted to take me into her house. She put the girl in my care.

ANTIPHO: *Your* care?

CHAEREA: Mine.

ANTIPHO: Care and protection, I suppose. . . .

CHAEREA: She gave instructions that no man was to come near the girl and told me not to go out but to stay alone with her inside the house. I bowed modestly, eyes on the ground. [*He does so.*]

ANTIPHO: Silly fool!

CHAEREA: 'I'm going out to dinner,' said Thais, and off she went with her maids, leaving a few new young ones to wait on the girl. They began at once to get her ready for a bath, while I kept telling them to hurry. Meanwhile the girl sat in her room, looking up at a picture on the wall which showed the story of Jupiter pouring the shower of gold into Danaë's lap.[1] I began to look at it too, and my spirits soared to think how he had played the same game long ago; a god turning himself into a man and crawling secretly across another man's roof, coming down to seduce a woman – down through the skylight! And what a god! 'who shakes the topmost towers of heaven with his thunder'.[2] Couldn't a mere man like me do the same? He could – and gladly. During these meditations of mine, the girl was summoned to her bath. She went, had it, and came back. Then the

1. St Augustine (*Confessions* 1. 16 and *City of God* 2.7) discusses this passage as being likely to corrupt schoolboys.

2. According to Donatus, a parody of the poet Ennius.

maids settled her on a couch. I stood around to see if they had any orders for me. Then one came up and said: 'Here, Dorus, take this fan, fan her gently with it while we have a bath, and when we've finished you can have one too if you like.' I took it with a bad grace.

ANTIPHO: What wouldn't I give to have seen your shameless face and the figure you cut, you great ass, standing there with a fan in your hand!

CHAEREA: The words were hardly out of her mouth when there was a rush for the door. They all went off to the bath, chattering as servants do when their masters are out of the house. The girl meanwhile fell asleep. I took a secret peep at her, sideways behind the fan, like this, and at the same time looked round to make sure the coast was clear. I saw it was. Then I bolted the door.

ANTIPHO: What then?

CHAEREA: What do you mean, 'what then', you fool?

ANTIPHO: Oh, all right.

CHAEREA: Was I to lose the chance offered me, an opportunity so brief, so unexpected and so much desired? My God, if I had, I should really have been what I pretended.

ANTIPHO: True, as you say. Meanwhile, what's been done about our dinner?

CHAEREA: It's ready.

ANTIPHO: Good man! Where? At your house?

CHAEREA: No, no, at Discus's.

ANTIPHO: What a way! All the more reason for us to hurry. Change your clothes.

CHAEREA: Where can I change? Damn it, I'm banished from home in case my brother's there; or my father might have got back from the country by now.

ANTIPHO: Let's go to my place, it's the nearest, and you can change there.

CHAEREA: Good, come on. On the way I want your advice on how I can make this girl my own in future.

ANTIPHO: Right you are.

[*They go off left together, and after a pause the maid* DORIAS *returns from* THRASO's *carrying* THAIS's *jewellery.*]

DORIAS: Heaven help me, from what I've seen of that man I'll swear he's mad! I'm terrified he'll make a scene or do Thais an injury. When young Chremes turned up, the girl's brother, she asked Thraso to have him brought in. That put him in a temper at once, but he didn't dare refuse, and Thais went on pressing him. Her object was to keep Chremes there, for it wasn't the right moment to tell him all she wanted about his sister. Thraso asked him in with a bad grace; Chremes stayed, and Thais immediately began to talk to him. Thraso imagined she'd brought in a rival under his very nose, so to pay her back he told a boy to fetch Pamphila 'to amuse us'. 'That girl at a dinner-party?' said Thais: 'Certainly not.' Thraso insisted, and they had words. Then Thais removed her jewels unperceived and gave them to me to take away. I know what this means – as soon as she can she'll slip away from the party.

[*She is about to go into* THAIS's *house when* PHAEDRIA *comes on from the left.*]

PHAEDRIA: On my way out to the country I began to think of this and that, always looking on the gloomy side, as you do when there's something weighing on your mind, and to cut a long story short, I passed our farm without seeing it – I'd gone a long way before I noticed. I went back, annoyed with myself, but when I reached the turning I stopped and began thinking again. 'Must I really spend two days alone here without her? And then what? I suppose it doesn't matter ... but it does.... There's no chance of touching her but at least I could *see* her – that'll surely be allowed. A long-distance view of love is better than nothing.' So this time I passed the house deliberately. [PYTHIAS *bursts out of* THAIS's *house.*] Now why the devil is Pythias rushing out in such a state?

PYTHIAS: Where is he? Brute, monster, where can he be? Oh to think he could dare to do such a wicked thing!

PHAEDRIA: Good lord, I don't like the sound of this.

PYTHIAS: And to add insult to injury, after he'd wronged the girl he tore her clothing and pulled the poor thing's hair!

PHAEDRIA: What!

PYTHIAS: Just let me get my hands on him – I'd scratch his eyes out, the poisonous snake!

PHAEDRIA: Something awful must have happened while I was away. I'll go and ask her. Pythias, what's all this? What's the hurry? Who is it you want?

PYTHIAS [*coldly*]: Phaedria! Need you ask? You go to hell – the proper place for you *and* your fine presents.

PHAEDRIA: What do you mean?

PYTHIAS: You know very well. That eunuch you gave us – Oh, what a mess we're in! And the girl, the one Thraso gave my mistress – he's had her.

PHAEDRIA: What!

PYTHIAS: Oh it's terrible!

PHAEDRIA: Nonsense, you're drunk.

PYTHIAS: I only wish my enemies felt like I do.

DORIAS: My dear Pythias, you must explain how – it's fantastic.

PHAEDRIA: You're crazy. *How* could a eunuch –

PYTHIAS: Don't ask me how: but it's quite clear from the facts that he did. The girl does nothing but cry and can't bring herself to answer any questions. The man has vanished, so much for his honesty. And oh dear me, I'm sure he's gone off with something from the house.

PHAEDRIA: I'd be very surprised if he's gone far, a poor creature like him. He's probably gone back to our house.

PYTHIAS: Then do please go and see.

PHAEDRIA: You'll soon know. [*He goes into* DEMEA's *house.*]

DORIAS: My conscience, it's monstrous! My dear, I never heard of such a thing!

PYTHIAS: Well, I've always been told their sort falls heavily for women, but they're incapable. . . . It certainly never crossed my mind – or I'd have shut him up somewhere and never trusted him with the girl.

[PHAEDRIA *returns, dragging* DORUS *dressed in* CHAEREA's *clothes.*]

PHAEDRIA: Come out, you scoundrel! Still trying to clear off, are you? Come *on*, you rotten bargain!

DORUS: Please, sir.

PHAEDRIA: Look at the face he's pulled, the brute! What do you mean, going back like that and changing your clothes? Come on, answer. If I'd waited another minute, Pythias, I'd have missed him there – he'd already planned his escape.

PYTHIAS [*mystified*]: Have you caught him, sir?

PHAEDRIA: Of course I have.

PYTHIAS: Well done!

DORIAS: Oh, how splendid!

PYTHIAS: Where is he?

PHAEDRIA: What do you mean? Can't you see him?

PYTHIAS: See who, please?

PHAEDRIA: This man, of course.

PYTHIAS: Who's *he*?

PHAEDRIA: He was brought over to you only today.

PYTHIAS: But none of us have ever set eyes on him, sir.

PHAEDRIA: What!

PYTHIAS: Did you suppose *this* was the man who was brought to us?

PHAEDRIA: I had no one else to send.

PYTHIAS: But there's no comparison! The other one was
gentlemanly and good looking.

PHAEDRIA: He only seemed so then because he was smartened
up in coloured clothes. He cuts a poor figure now because
he hasn't got them.

PYTHIAS: Nonsense, there's more to it than that. The man
brought to us today was young; you'd have found him a
pleasure to the eye yourself, sir. This is a worn-out, wrinkled
senile old man, the colour of a weasel.

PHAEDRIA: Damn it all, what are you saying? Are you trying
to make out that I'm not responsible for my actions? [*To*
DORUS] Here you, did I buy you?

DORUS: Yes, sir, you did.

PYTHIAS: Now tell him to answer *me* a question.

PHAEDRIA: Go on then.

PYTHIAS: Did you come to our house today? [DORUS *shakes
his head.*] He says No. But someone else did, a lad of sixteen,
brought by Parmeno.

PHAEDRIA: Let's get this clear first; where did you get those
clothes you are wearing? Come on, answer. You dumb
brute, can't you speak?

DORUS: Chaerea came –

PHAEDRIA: My brother?

DORUS: Yes.

PHAEDRIA: When?

DORUS: Today.

PHAEDRIA: How long ago?

DORUS: Just now.

PHAEDRIA: With anyone?

DORUS: Parmeno.

PHAEDRIA: Had you seen him before?

DORUS: No, I'd never even heard of him.

PHAEDRIA: Then how did you know he was my brother?

DORUS: Parmeno said so. Your brother gave me these clothes –

PHAEDRIA: Damn it!

DORUS: And he put on mine. Then they left the house together.

PYTHIAS: *Now* will you believe I'm not drunk? I told you the sober truth. Isn't it quite clear now what happened to the girl?

PHAEDRIA [*reluctantly*]: Come, come, you silly creature; do you believe what *he* says?

PYTHIAS: No need to believe him. The facts speak for themselves.

PHAEDRIA [*to* DORUS]: Just come over here a little; do you hear? A little further – that'll do. Now tell me again: Chaerea took your clothes –

DORUS: That's right.

PHAEDRIA: – and put them on –

DORUS: Right.

PHAEDRIA: – and was taken to that house in your place?

DORUS: Yes.

PHAEDRIA: Good God, the wanton impudence of the man!

PYTHIAS [*crying*]: Oh, it was a wicked trick to play on us! Can't you believe me now?

PHAEDRIA: Oh, you'd believe anything he says. [*Aside*] What am I to do? [*To* DORUS] Now this time answer No. [*Aloud*] I'll drag the truth out of you here and now! *Did* you see my brother Chaerea?

DORUS: No.

PHAEDRIA: He can't tell the truth without torture, I can see. Come along with me. First he says Yes, then No. [*Aside to* DORUS] Beg for mercy.

DORUS: Please, please, sir. . . .

PHAEDRIA [*kicking him into the house*]: Go in at once.
[DORUS *goes in with a howl of pain.*]
PHAEDRIA [*aside*]: How else can I get out of this without losing face? [*Shouts into the house*] If you still try fooling me, you scoundrel – you're for it. [*He follows* DORUS *into the house.*]
PYTHIAS: Sure as I live, this is one of Parmeno's tricks.
DORIAS: It must be.
PYTHIAS: I'll find some way to pay him back. What do you think we ought to do, Dorias?
DORIAS: About the girl, do you mean?
PYTHIAS: Yes. Shall I mention it or keep my mouth shut?
DORIAS: Why, if you're wise you'll know nothing of what you know either about the eunuch or what happened to the girl. That'll keep you out of all this trouble and win her gratitude. All you need say is that Dorus has run off.
PYTHIAS: All right, I will.
DORIAS [*looking down street, right*]: Look, there's Chremes. Thais'll be here soon.
PYTHIAS: What makes you think so?
DORIAS: A quarrel had broken out at Thraso's when I left.
PYTHIAS: You go and put away those jewels. I'll find out from him what's happening.
[DORIAS *goes in.* CHREMES *comes on from the right, rather drunk.*]
CHREMES: It's a cheat . . . and a swindle. . . . Damn it all, I'm drunk. So long as I sat still I seemed nice and sober. . . . Then I got up . . . head's all wrong . . . [*staggers*] legs too. . . .
PYTHIAS: Chremes!
CHREMES: Who's there? Pythias! You're a beauty . . . [*lurching towards her*] lovelier than ever!
PYTHIAS [*primly*]: You're the merrier, no doubt about that.

CHREMES: Well, it's true. . . . 'Love needs a bite and a sup to warm things up.'[1] . . . Thais been back long?

PYTHIAS: Has she left the party already?

CHREMES: Long ago . . . ages ago. . . . There was . . . a simply terrific . . . row.

PYTHIAS: But didn't she tell you to follow her?

CHREMES: All she did . . . was give me . . . a bit of a nod . . . as she left.

PYTHIAS: And wasn't that enough for you?

CHREMES: I didn't know that was what she meant . . . till Thraso put me right . . . and kicked me out. Here she is. . . . I wonder where I got ahead of her.

[THAIS *comes on right with her two maids.*]

THAIS: He'll be here in a minute, I suppose, to take Pamphila from me. Just let him come! If he lays a finger on her I'll scratch his eyes out! I can put up with his stupid ways and bragging words as long as they *are* only words, but if it comes to actions, I'll have him horse-whipped!

CHREMES: Thais, I've been here a long time.

THAIS: Chremes my dear, I was looking for you. Do you realize that you're the cause of this scene? None of it would have started but for you.

CHREMES: Me? How? What are you talking about?

THAIS: It was my eagerness to restore your sister to your keeping that brought all this on my head, and a lot more besides.

CHREMES: Where is she?

THAIS: In my house.

CHREMES: What!

THAIS: Don't worry, I've looked after her — I've done the right thing by you both.

1. Literally, 'without Ceres and Bacchus Venus is cold'.

CHREMES: Really?

THAIS: Truly. I'm making you a present of her, and I don't expect a penny in return.

CHREMES [*formally*]: Then I can only repay you by my proper gratitude, Thais.

THAIS: But watch out, or you'll lose her before you receive her from me; she's the girl Thraso is coming this very moment to carry off by force. Pythias, you go and fetch the little box with the proofs.

CHREMES: Look, he's coming –

PYTHIAS [*to* THAIS]: Where is it?

THAIS: In the chest. Oh you're so slow and tiresome!

CHREMES: Good God, look at the army he's bringing!

THAIS: My dear man, you're not afraid, are you?

CHREMES [*visibly alarmed*]: Nonsense. Who's afraid? Not me.

THAIS: That's the spirit.

CHREMES: What do you take me for, I should like to know!

THAIS: All right, I only want you to remember that you're dealing with a foreigner who is less influential and well known than you are, with fewer friends in Athens.

CHREMES: Yes, I know all that, but it's silly to sit down under things you can avoid. I'd rather we took preventive action than have to retaliate after damage is done. You go in and bolt the door while I run to the market place – I'd like some help here against what's coming to us.

THAIS: Stay here –

CHREMES: No, better not.

THAIS [*holding on to him*]: No, stay.

CHREMES: Let go; I'll soon be back.

THAIS: But it's quite unnecessary, Chremes. All you need do is to tell him she is the sister you lost when she was small and now you've recognized her. [*To* PYTHIAS *as she comes out with the box*] Show him the tokens.

PYTHIAS: Here they are.

THAIS: Take them. If he shows violence you can always give him in charge. Do you understand?

CHREMES [*dubiously*]: I suppose so.

THAIS: You must talk to him firmly.

CHREMES: I will. . . .

THAIS: Prepare yourself for action. [*Aside*] Good heavens, I'm lost. What a man to defend me! He needs a champion of his own.

> [*They all go into the house as* THRASO *marches on right with* GNATHO *and a motley band of followers – six in all.*]

THRASO: Am I to put up with a gross insult like this, Gnatho? Better death than dishonour! Simalio, Donax, Syriscus, follow me. First I'll storm the house.

GNATHO: Right, sir.

THRASO: I'll carry off the girl.

GNATHO: Very good, sir.

THRASO: And then I'll punish that female.

GNATHO: Splendid, sir.

THRASO: Centre here, Donax, with the crowbar. Simalio, on the left wing. Syriscus, you on the right. Bring up the reserves. Where's Sergeant Sanga and his kitchen squad of thieves?

SANGA [*stepping forward*]: Present, sir.

THRASO: What's that, you coward? Do you propose to fight a battle with that sponge you're carrying?

SANGA: Sir? I know my general's valour and the army's spirit. There's bound to be bloodshed, said I; I'll need something to staunch their wounds.

THRASO: Where are the others?

GNATHO: What others, damn it? There's only Sannio left on duty at home.

THRASO [*to* GNATHO]: Draw them up. I'll take up my position behind the front line; from there I'll give the order to them all.

GNATHO: Sound tactics! [*Aside*] A formation designed to give him a safe place.

THRASO [*complacently*]: I am only following Pyrrhus's practice.[1]

[CHREMES *and* THAIS *appear at a window.*[2]]

CHREMES: Look what he's doing, Thais. You see I was right about bolting the door.

THAIS: I can see the man's a great booby, though you may think him a hero. You needn't be afraid of *him*.

THRASO: Well, what now?

GNATHO: I was just wishing you had one of those big siege-engines, so that you could pick them off from a distance unseen; that would rout the lot.

THRASO: Look there – isn't that Thais?

GNATHO: How soon do we attack?

THRASO: Wait. A wise man should try everything before he has recourse to arms. For all you know I may get my own way with her without using force.

GNATHO: Heavens above, what wisdom! Every minute spent with you is something learned.

THRASO: Thais, first answer me this: when I gave you the girl, did you promise to keep the next few days for me alone?

THAIS: What if I did?

THRASO: Can you ask – when you have brought your lover into my presence, under my very nose?

THAIS: What's that to you?

THRASO: And slipped off with him when I wasn't looking?

THAIS: Well, I wanted to.

1. King of Epirus and traditional master of tactics and strategy.

2. In a production following strict Roman conventions, Thais and Chremes are better left on the stage, in the doorway.

THRASO: All right. Then give back Pamphila, unless you'd rather I took her by force.

CHREMES: Give her back! If you so much as lay a finger on her, you –

GNATHO: Now then, you shut up!

THRASO: What's that? Can't I lay hands on my own property?

CHREMES: *Your* property, you dirty brute?

GNATHO: Please be careful. You don't know the man you're insulting.

CHREMES [*to* GNATHO]: You clear off! [*To* THRASO] Do you realize what you're letting yourself in for? If you make any move to cause trouble here today, I'll give you something to make you remember the place and time – and me – for ever.

GNATHO: You're trying to make an enemy out of this grand gentleman; well, I'm sorry for you.

CHREMES: Clear off, or I'll break your head!

GNATHO: Really? So that's the way you carry on, you cur?

THRASO: Who do you think you are? What do you want? What interest have you in the girl?

CHREMES: Listen. In the first place I can tell you she is free-born –

THRASO: What!

CHREMES: – a citizen of Attica –

THRASO: No!

CHREMES: – and my sister.

THRASO: What barefaced impudence!

CHREMES: I'm just giving you warning, my man, not to use any force on her. Thais, I'm going to fetch the nurse Sophrona and show her the proofs.

THRASO: Are you trying to stop me from laying hands on my own property?

CHREMES: I'll stop you all right.

[*He leaves the window, comes out of the house, and walks off right in triumph.*]

GNATHO: Did you hear that? He proves himself guilty of theft. That's all the evidence you need.

THRASO: Do you agree with that, Thais?

THAIS: Find someone else to answer you. [*She slams the window shut.*]

THRASO: Now what do we do?

GNATHO: Go home. She'll soon come round of her own accord and eat humble pie.

THRASO: Do you really think so?

GNATHO: Of course I do. I know women and their ways. Whenever you want a thing, they won't have it, and then set their hearts on it after you've given up.

THRASO: I suppose you're right.

GNATHO: May I tell the men to fall out?

THRASO: When you like.

GNATHO: Sanga, the moment has come to take thought of hearth and home, as a true soldier should.

SANGA: My mind's been on my saucepans this long while.

GNATHO: Good fellow.

THRASO: Follow me, my men.

[*They march off right. When they have gone,* THAIS *and* PYTHIAS *come out of the house.*]

THAIS: You wretched woman, can't you stop talking in riddles? 'I know – I don't know – he ran off – so I heard – I wasn't there –' If you've anything to tell me, can't you speak plainly? The girl's dress is torn, she does nothing but cry and won't say a word. The eunuch has vanished. Why? What has happened? Can't you speak?

PYTHIAS: Oh dear, where can I begin? They say he wasn't the eunuch –

THAIS: Who was he then?

PYTHIAS: That Chaerea —

THAIS: What Chaerea?

PYTHIAS: That young brother of Phaedria's.

THAIS: Nonsense, you scandal-monger.

PYTHIAS: It's true. I'm positive.

THAIS: What on earth did he want with us? Why was he taken to my house?

PYTHIAS: I don't know, but I suppose he's in love with Pamphila.

THAIS: Oh I shall die of shame, you miserable creature, if there's any truth in what you say. Can *that* be why the girl is crying?

PYTHIAS: I think so.

THAIS: Impossible, you liar. Wasn't that the very thing I warned you against when I went out?

PYTHIAS: What was I to do? I did as you told me yourself and gave him sole charge of her.

THAIS: You wretch, it was trusting the wolf with the lamb. Oh, I'm so ashamed of being taken in like this! What sort of a man can he be?

PYTHIAS [*eagerly*]: Madam, please, say no more; we're saved. There's our man.

THAIS: Where?

PYTHIAS: Look left; can't you see him coming?

THAIS: Yes.

PYTHIAS: Have him arrested at once.

THAIS: What are we to do with him, you fool?

PYTHIAS: Need you ask? Now look carefully, madam, when he comes in sight and see if he hasn't a bold face. [CHAEREA *comes on from the right still wearing the eunuch's clothes.*] Am I right? The impudence of the man!

CHAEREA: Well, I went to Antipho's, but both his parents were there as if they'd stayed at home on purpose, so I couldn't go in without them seeing me. Then when I was standing outside the door someone I knew came along and I had to take to my heels as fast as I could down an empty alley,[1] and make my escape from one to another in agonies all the time for fear someone would recognize me. But that must be Thais I can see – yes, it is. What can I do? Will it make any difference anyway? What'll she do to me?

THAIS: Let's meet him. Dorus, my man, here you are. Now tell me: have you been trying to escape?

CHAEREA: That's right, madam.

THAIS: And you congratulate yourself on doing so?

CHAEREA: No, madam.

THAIS: Do you expect to go unpunished?

CHAEREA: Please overlook this one lapse, madam. If I ever do wrong again you can kill me.

THAIS: It wasn't because you were afraid I'd be a cruel mistress?

CHAEREA: No, madam.

THAIS: Then, what was it?

CHAEREA [*indicating* PYTHIAS]: Her. I was afraid she'd go to you complaining about me.

THAIS: What had you done?

CHAEREA: Nothing much.

PYTHIAS: Nothing much! Have you no shame? Do you call it nothing much to assault a virgin and a free-born citizen?

CHAEREA: I took her for a fellow slave.

PYTHIAS: Fellow slave! I can scarcely keep my hands off your hair, you brute! And now he's come to laugh at us.

THAIS: You're beside yourself; leave us.

PYTHIAS: What? I suppose I'd be the one to pay damages if I

1. *Angiportum*, a narrow street or alley, off stage, and sometimes a back lane behind the houses which Chaerea must have taken, as he went off left at l. 614. Cf. *Phormio* 348.

got at him, the beast – especially since he was only pretending to be your slave.

THAIS: Pythias, this must stop. Chaerea, your conduct was
unworthy of you. Even if it were right for me to be insulted
like this, it was quite wrong for you to behave in this way.
I've no idea now what I can best do for this girl – you have
thoroughly upset all my plans. It's impossible for me to
hand her back to her family now; this would have been the
right thing, and I was also anxious to do so in order to gain
some solid advantage for myself.

CHAEREA: But I'm hoping that from now on there will be a
lasting bond of good feeling between us, Thais. It often happens in a situation like this that a bad start leads to a close
friendship. It may, in fact, be heaven's will.

THAIS [*after a pause*]: Well. . . . I am willing to look at it that
way myself.

CHAEREA: Please do. And there's just one thing I should like
you to know – I hadn't any intention of insulting you. I did
it for love of her.

THAIS: I realize that, Chaerea, and it makes me all the more
ready to forgive you. I'm not altogether lacking in human
feeling or experience; I know something of the power of
love.

CHAEREA: I swear to God I love you too, Thais.

PYTHIAS: In that case, madam, I fancy you'd better watch out
on your own account.

CHAEREA: I wouldn't dare –

PYTHIAS: I don't trust you an inch.

THAIS [*laughing*]: That'll do!

CHAEREA: Now let me beg you to help me in this, Thais. I
put myself in your hands with complete confidence in your
discretion. Be my protector, hear my prayers – I shall die if
I can't marry her.

THAIS: What about your father?

CHAEREA: Him? Oh he'll be willing enough I'm sure – if only she's a free citizen.

THAIS: If you'll just wait a little her brother will be here himself. He went to fetch the nurse who looked after her as a child. Then you can be present at the recognition scene.

CHAEREA: Of course I'll stay.

THAIS: Meanwhile, would you like to wait for him indoors instead of standing here in the street?

CHAEREA: I'd like nothing better.

PYTHIAS: *Now* what are you up to, madam?

THAIS: What *is* the matter?

PYTHIAS: Need you ask? Do you really intend to receive this man in your house after what has happened?

THAIS: Why not?

PYTHIAS: Mark my words, he'll make fresh trouble.

THAIS: Hold your tongue, I say.

PYTHIAS: You can't have seen through his bold front.

CHAEREA: I shan't do anything, Pythias.

PYTHIAS: I should have to be sure what you haven't done, before I believe you, Chaerca.

CHAEREA: Well then, you can look after me.

PYTHIAS: Get along with you; I'd no more dare to look after you than give you something to look after.

THAIS [*looking down the street*]: Ah, splendid; here comes her brother.

CHAEREA: Oh no, please, Thais, do let's go indoors – I don't want him to see me in the street in these clothes.

THAIS [*amused*]: Why not? Are you bashful?

CHAEREA: Yes, I really am.

PYTHIAS: Really? Spare his maiden blushes!

THAIS: Go in, I'll follow. Wait here, Pythias, to bring Chremes in.

[*She follows* CHAEREA *into the house.*]

PYTHIAS: Oh if I could only think of something – some way of paying back that scoundrel who planted this man on us!

[CHREMES *comes on right, with the old nurse,* SOPHRONA.]

CHREMES: Do get a move on, nurse.

SOPHRONA: I am moving.

CHREMES: I can see you are, but you don't move *on*.

PYTHIAS: Have you shown her the tokens yet?

CHREMES: Yes, every one.

PYTHIAS: Please, what does she say? Does she recognize them?

CHREMES: Perfectly.

PYTHIAS: That's good news! I'm fond of the girl. Go in – the mistress has been waiting for you for ages. [*They go in.*] And now here comes our worthy friend Parmeno, sauntering along without a care in the world! Please heaven, I believe I've thought up a way of tormenting him. I'll just pop indoors to make sure of the recognition scene and then be back to terrify the life out of him for his wicked lies. [*She goes in.*]

[PARMENO *comes on right, looking pleased with himself.*]

PARMENO: Here I am again, to see how Chaerea's getting on. If he's played his cards well, my God, what glory for me – and rightly. [*Strutting about complacently*] To say nothing of the satisfactory consummation I have procured without trouble or expense of any kind in a love affair which might have proved difficult and costly, as the girl was in the power of a greedy professional – there is this further achievement, which I consider my real masterpiece: I have found a way of giving a young man a glimpse of the character and habits of loose women early in life, so that the lesson learned in time will make him hate them for ever. Met outside their own homes, dining with a lover and pecking daintily at their food, these women give an impression of perfect elegance, composure, and good taste; but just see the sordid filth and squalor and their nasty habits and greed when they're at home by themselves, gobbling up black bread soaked in yesterday's soup – to know all this is a young man's salvation.

PYTHIAS [*who has come out again in time to hear some of this*]: I'll see you suffer for these words, you rascal, and for what you've done too – you shan't get away with fooling us. [*Raising her voice but still ignoring* PARMENO] Heavens above, what a wicked deed! Oh the poor young man! Oh that vile Parmeno who brought him here!

PARMENO: What's that?

PYTHIAS: I'm sorry for him. . . . I couldn't bear it, I came out here so as not to see the cruel punishment they say he's going to suffer.

PARMENO: Good God, what's all this commotion? It can't mean trouble for me. . . . I'll ask her. What's the matter, Pythias? What are you saying? Who's going to be punished?

PYTHIAS: Need you ask, impudence? You brought a young man here instead of the eunuch; all you think about is tricking us, but you've been the death of *him*.

PARMENO: How? What happened? Go on.

PYTHIAS: I'll tell you. That girl who was given to Thais today – do you realize she's a free-born citizen? And has a brother in one of the best families?

PARMENO [*uncomfortably*]: I don't know, I'm sure.

PYTHIAS: Well, that's what's come out. Your wretched fellow assaulted her, and when her brother found out, in a proper fury –

PARMENO: What did he do?

PYTHIAS: First he tied him up in a shocking fashion –

PARMENO: Tied him up?

PYTHIAS: Yes, though Thais begged him not to.

PARMENO: Impossible!

PYTHIAS: And now he's threatening to deal with him as they do adulterers – a thing I've never seen and shouldn't want to see.[1]

PARMENO [*horrified*]: How could he dare to do such a monstrous thing!

PYTHIAS: Why monstrous?

PARMENO: Could it be worse? And whoever saw a man arrested for adultery in a house of this reputation?

PYTHIAS [*imitating him*]: I don't know, I'm sure.

PARMENO: But I'll have you all know this, Pythias – and be warned. I tell you this young man is my master's son.

PYTHIAS: Gracious, you don't say so!

PARMENO: Thais had better not let anything happen to him. I think I'd best go in myself. [*He moves towards* THAIS's *house.*]

PYTHIAS [*catching at him*]: Be careful what you're doing, Parmeno: you may do him no good and yourself a lot of harm. They think you were at the bottom of everything that happened.

PARMENO: What on earth am I to do then? Where am I to start? [*Looking along the street*] And now here's my old master coming back from the country. Shall I tell him or not? Better tell him – even if it means real trouble for me, I must help the boy.

PYTHIAS: You're right. I'm going in; you tell him the whole story from beginning to end.

[*She goes into the house as the young men's father,* DEMEA, *comes on left.*]

DEMEA: There's one advantage in having a country place so near town: I'm never bored in either place. When I've had

1. Terence typically leaves unnamed the penalty of castration for adulterers allowed by Greek and Roman law.

enough of one I can change to the other. But isn't that our man Parmeno? Yes, it is. Parmeno! Why are you standing outside this door? Who are you waiting for?

PARMENO [*jumps round*]: Who's that? Oh, sir, I'm glad to see you safely back.

DEMEA: Who is it you're waiting for?

PARMENO [*aside*]: Damn it, I'm struck dumb with fear.

DEMEA: Well, what is it? You're shaking – aren't you well? Speak up.

PARMENO: Sir, I'd like you first to know the facts; whatever's happened here, it wasn't my fault.

DEMEA: What did happen?

PARMENO: Quite right, sir, I should have told you that first. Phaedria bought a eunuch to give to – the lady here.

DEMEA: Who's she?

PARMENO: Thais.

DEMEA: He *bought* one? That'll finish me. How much?

PARMENO: Two thousand drachmas.

DEMEA: I'm ruined.

PARMENO: Then Chaerea's in love with a girl in this house –

DEMEA: *What*! Chaerea in love? What does he know about those women at his age? Is he in town? One calamity after another!

PARMENO: Don't look at me like that, sir, please; I didn't put him up to it.

DEMEA: Never mind about yourself. I'll see to *you*, you scoundrel, if this doesn't kill me. First you tell me what you're trying to say.

PARMENO: Chaerea was taken to Thais instead of that eunuch –

DEMEA: Instead of a *eunuch*?

PARMENO: Yes. And afterwards ... they arrested him as an adulterer and tied him up.

DEMEA: Oh no, no!

PARMENO: It just shows the impudence of these women, sir.

DEMEA [*after a shocked pause*]: Is there any other disaster or disgrace you haven't told me?

PARMENO: That's the lot, sir.

DEMEA: Then I shall go straight in. [*He rushes into* THAIS'*s house.*]

PARMENO: That spells trouble in plenty for me as well, no doubt about it. Well, it couldn't be helped, and anyway I'm glad I've made trouble for those bitches too. The old man has been looking for an excuse for ages to do something drastic to them, and now he's found one.

   [PYTHIAS *comes out, laughing.*]

PYTHIAS: That's the best thing I could have wanted to happen! Oh the way old Demea burst in on us, barking up the wrong tree! I'd the joke to myself – no one else knew what he dreaded to see.

PARMENO [*aside*]: *Now* what's happened?

PYTHIAS: Now I must find Parmeno! Where on earth is he?

PARMENO [*aside*]: It's me she wants.

PYTHIAS: There he is, I'll – [*goes on laughing*].

PARMENO: What's the matter, you fool? What do you want? What are you laughing about? Can't you stop?

PYTHIAS: This'll be the death of me! I've split my sides laughing at you.

PARMENO: Why?

PYTHIAS: Don't you know? A sillier man I've never seen and never shall see! Oh I can't tell you what fun you've given us indoors – and I used to think you such a smart clever fellow! Did you have to swallow whole the tale I just told you? You ought to feel ashamed of putting young Chaerea up to the shocking things he did, without giving the poor boy away to his father as well. What do you suppose he felt when his father saw him in those clothes? Well – now do you believe you're done for?

PARMENO: What's that you say, you wretched woman? Did you make up that tale? You're still laughing – damn it, do you find it funny to jeer at us?

PYTHIAS: Very funny [*laughs still more*].

PARMENO: If you get out of this for nothing –

PYTHIAS: Well?

PARMENO: I'll pay you back, I swear I will.

PYTHIAS: I don't doubt it, Parmeno, but maybe your threats'll have to wait awhile – you'll be the one to be strung up at once for ruining the character of a silly boy and then telling on him; father and son will both make an example of you.

PARMENO: It's the end for me.

PYTHIAS: It's your reward for faithful service. Good-bye. [*She goes in, laughing.*]

PARMENO: Damn it all, it's my own fault – betrayed like a mouse with my own squeaking.

[THRASO *and* GNATHO *come on from the right.*]

GNATHO: What are you proposing now, Thraso? What do you hope or plan to gain by coming back here? What are you trying to do?

THRASO [*impressively*]: I shall surrender myself to Thais and do her bidding.

GNATHO: What!

THRASO: Why not? Hercules turned slave to Omphale.[1]

GNATHO: Ah yes, a worthy precedent. [*Aside*] I hope I'll see her take a slipper to knock your head into shape. [*To* THRASO] I can hear her door opening.

1. Hercules was bound as a slave to the Lydian queen Omphale in expiation of a murder, and compelled by her to do women's work.

1045] THE EUNUCH 215

[CHAEREA *bursts out, in his own clothes, wildly excited;* THRASO *and* GNATHO *stand aside.*]

THRASO: Good God, more trouble! Who's this? I've never seen him in my life. Why's he rushing out in such a hurry?

CHAEREA: Good people all, is there a man alive as lucky as I am? No one, I'll swear. So much has turned out well for me so quickly, and all the powers of heaven are on my side!

PARMENO: Now why's he so pleased with himself?

CHAEREA [*seeing* PARMENO *and hugging him*]: Parmeno, dear man, author and instigator and perfecter of all my joys, do you know how happy I am? Do you know my Pamphila turns out to be a free citizen?

PARMENO: I'd heard that.

CHAEREA: And I'm going to marry her?

PARMENO: Bless me, *that* will be a deed well done.

GNATHO [*to* THRASO]: Did you hear that?

CHAEREA: And then I'm so happy for my brother – Phaedria's love affair has weathered its storms, and we're going to be one happy family. Thais has found favour with my father and has put herself under our patronage and protection.

PARMENO: So she's all your brother's?

CHAEREA: Of course.

PARMENO: Then there's another cause for rejoicing – that soldier will be kicked out.

CHAEREA [*shaking him*]: Quick, quick, find my brother and tell him at once.

PARMENO: I'll see if he's at home [*goes into* DEMEA'*s house*].

THRASO: Gnatho, I suppose there's no doubt this finishes me for good and all?

GNATHO: No doubt at all, I fancy.

CHAEREA: Where shall I begin? Who deserves most praise? Parmeno who gave me the idea, or myself who dared to carry it out? Or should it be Fortune who guided me and brought so many vital matters to a happy conclusion in a single day? Or my father for his kindness and good humour? All I pray is that heaven's blessing will continue!

[PHAEDRIA *hurries out of* DEMEA's *house.*]

PHAEDRIA: Good God, this is a fantastic story of Parmeno's! Where's my brother?

CHAEREA: Here he is.

PHAEDRIA: I'm delighted.

CHAEREA: I'm sure you are. No one deserves to be loved more than your Thais, Phaedria; she has done so much for all our family.

PHAEDRIA [*laughing*]: I don't need you to praise Thais!

THRASO: Damn it, the fainter my hopes the more I love her. Please, Gnatho, I pin all my hopes on you.

GNATHO: What do you want me to do?

THRASO: Beg him – or pay him – to let me keep on some sort of footing with Thais.

GNATHO: It won't be easy.

THRASO: If you really want something – I know you. Only manage this, and you can ask for any reward you like; you shall have it.

GNATHO: Do you mean that?

THRASO: I do.

GNATHO: If I succeed I'll ask for your house to be open to me whether you're at home or not, then I need never wait for an invitation and can always be sure of a place.

THRASO: I give you my word on that.

GNATHO: Then I'll prepare myself for battle. [*They move up to the others.*]

PHAEDRIA: Who's that? Oh, Thraso.

THRASO: Good evening to you both.

PHAEDRIA: Perhaps you don't know what's been happening here?

THRASO: I know.

PHAEDRIA: Then why do I see you around here at all?

THRASO: I was relying on you –

PHAEDRIA: Shall I tell you what you *can* rely on? Listen to me, my man; if I ever find you in this street again, even if you tell me you're looking for someone else and are just going this way – you're a dead man.

GNATHO: This is no way to talk!

PHAEDRIA: That's all I have to say.

THRASO: I can't understand your attitude –

PHAEDRIA: I mean it.

GNATHO: Let me say a few words first, and when you've heard me you can carry on as you like.

CHAEREA: Let's hear him.

GNATHO: Just move off a little way over there, Thraso. [*To the others*] Now first of all, I very much want you both to understand that all I'm doing is primarily in my own interests; but if it happens to benefit you too, it would be silly of you not to fall in with it.

PHAEDRIA: Well, what is it?

GNATHO: In my opinion you should accept Thraso as a rival.

PHAEDRIA: What! Accept him –

GNATHO: Now think, Phaedria; for you to go on enjoying life with Thais, living in the style you do, you must always be paying out to her, and you haven't really much to give. Thraso's the very man to provide for all the requirements of love without it costing you a penny – no one can be so useful. In the first place, he has the means and he's lavish with his money. Then he's a silly idiot, a lazy dim-wit who snores night and day; you need never fear any woman will fall for him, and you can easily throw him out when you like.

CHAEREA [*to* PHAEDRIA]: What shall we do?

GNATHO: Then there's what I consider more important than anything; no one entertains so well on the scale he does.

CHAEREA: It looks as though we need the man after all.

PHAEDRIA [*reluctantly*]: I suppose so.

GNATHO: Thank you. Now there's just one more thing – please let me into your circle. I've had uphill work long enough with that clod.[1]

PHAEDRIA: All right, we will.

CHAEREA: With pleasure.

GNATHO: In return I offer you both – Thraso: for the laughs and everything else you can get out of him.

CHAEREA: We'll take him.

PHAEDRIA: He deserves it.

GNATHO: Thraso, you can come here now.

THRASO [*coming across*]: For pity's sake, how are we getting on?

GNATHO [*airily*]: Oh they didn't know you; I only had to reveal your true character and praise you according to your deeds and merits, and it did the trick.

THRASO: Splendid. I'm most grateful. [*Recovering his complacency*] I must say I've always found myself exceedingly popular wherever I've been.

GNATHO [*to* PHAEDRIA *and* CHAEREA]: Perfect manners, as I told you!

PHAEDRIA [*laughing*]: Up to expectations anyway! This way, please. [*To the audience*] Farewell, and give us your applause.
[*They all go into* THAIS*'s house.*]

1. 'Stone' if we keep the reference (suggested by Donatus) to Sisyphus pushing his stone uphill, only to have it roll back.

PHORMIO

INTRODUCTORY NOTE

Phormio is aptly named after the character who dominates the play. There is no one quite of his stature in any other Roman comedy – he is the genuine adventurer who lives by his wits, a far more vigorous personality than any conventional sponger such as Gnatho in *The Eunuch*, whose sole aim is to wheedle his way into a comfortable life. Phormio is called in almost in a professional capacity (much as old Demipho brings in his legal advisers) to help the two young men out of their difficulties, and he applies his ingenuity to the task of extracting money from their fathers more for the pleasure of exercising his skill than for what he may hope to get out of it himself. As Gilbert Norwood remarks, 'To all seeming Phormio conducts and administers a swindle on the principle of "art for art's sake".'

This is pure comedy of intrigue, moving as lightly and rapidly as a French farce. Phormio is always on top of every situation, and we never doubt that he will succeed; thus we are left free to concentrate on the finesse of his movements. There is no place here for the romantic touch of *The Girl from Andros*, the greater seriousness of *The Self-Tormentor* and *The Mother-in-Law*, or the subtlety of *The Brothers*, but Terence's characters always behave consistently as human beings within the framework of comic conventions, and are more than character-types. The slave-dealer Dorio, for instance, is not abused and caricatured as he would be in a comedy by Plautus; like Sannio in *The Brothers* he plays a small but plausible part as a man-of-business who quite properly stands up for his legal rights. The two elderly brothers are neatly contrasted, Chremes with his anxiety to save his reputation at all costs, and Demipho, the more positive character. His meanness and obstinate determination not to part with his money cause most of the trouble, and, in the end, precipitate Phormio's disclosure about the one thing he and Chremes are trying to conceal.

Phormio was followed very closely by Molière in *Les Fourberies de Scapin*, and one way of appreciating how it was possible for Terence to be a creative writer while using Greek models is to compare this lively comedy in its French setting with the Latin original.

PRODUCTION NOTICE

PHORMIO by Terence: performed at the Roman Games[1] during the curule aedileship of Lucius Postumius Albinus and Lucius Cornelius Merula.

Produced by Lucius Ambivius Turpio and Lucius Atilius of Praeneste.

Music composed by Flaccus, slave of Claudius, for unmatched pipes throughout.

Greek original *The Claimant* by Apollodorus.[2]

The author's fourth play, written during the consulship of Gaius Fannius and Marcus Valerius.[3]

1. Held annually in September in honour of Jupiter.
2. Apollodorus of Carystus, a writer of New Comedy in the first half of the third century B.C.
3. i.e. 161 B.C.

SYNOPSIS

Demipho, brother of Chremes, went abroad, leaving his son Antipho in Athens. Chremes kept a wife and daughter secretly on Lemnos, and another wife in Athens, with his son (Phaedria), deeply in love with a lute-player. The wife on Lemnos came to Athens and died there, leaving her daughter (Phanium) to arrange her funeral alone (Chremes was away at the time). There Antipho saw her, fell in love and took her as his wife, with the aid of an adventurer (Phormio). His father and Chremes are furious on their return and give Phormio 3,000 drachmas to marry the girl himself; but this money is used to buy the lute-player for Phaedria. Antipho's wife is recognized by his uncle as his daughter, so he can keep her.

CHARACTERS

DEMIPHO	*an Athenian gentleman*
CHREMES	*his brother*
ANTIPHO	*his son, in love with Phanium*
PHAEDRIA	*Chremes' son, in love with Pamphila*
GETA	*a slave, Demipho's servant*
DAVOS	*a slave, Geta's friend*
PHORMIO	*an adventurer*
HEGIO	
CRATINUS	*Demipho's legal advisers*
CRITO	
DORIO	*a slave-dealer*
NAUSISTRATA	*Chremes' wife*
SOPHRONA	*nurse to Phanium, Chremes' daughter*

Phanium, Chremes' daughter by his bigamous marriage on Lemnos, and Pamphila, the music-girl belonging to Dorio, do not appear

*

The scene is laid in Athens in front of the houses of Demipho, Chremes and Dorio. To the audience's right the street leads to the centre of the town, to the left to the harbour

AUTHOR'S PROLOGUE TO
PHORMIO

SINCE the old playwright[1] cannot divert the poet from his calling and force him to retire, he is now trying to deter him from writing by use of slander. He goes on damning all his previous plays for feeble language and weak composition, simply because none of them describes a love-lorn youth who sees hounds pursuing a fleeing hind which begs and prays him to save her. But if he realized that on the occasion when *he* had a success with a new play the credit should really go to the producer, not himself, he would be a great deal more restrained in his insinuations than he is now. Some of you may be saying, or at least thinking, that if the old playwright had not launched the first attack, the young one would have had no one to abuse and so no material for a prologue. The answer to that is that the prize of victory is open to all dramatic poets. The old playwright set out to drive the other from his profession and leave him to starve. The young one intends this to be his answer, not a further challenge. Kind words would have been answered by kind words; as things are he must realize that he is only getting tit for tat. For my part I shall stop talking about him, although he puts no stop to his misdeeds.

Now please listen to what I have to say. I am presenting for the first time a comedy entitled *The Claimant* in Greek and *Phormio* in Latin, for the adventurer Phormio plays the leading part and directs most of the intrigue, as you will see if the author has your support. Pay attention, and give us a fair hearing in silence, so that we do not suffer the same fate as we

1. Luscius Lanuvinus.

did when the uproar drove our company from the stage.[1] Now we are here again, thanks to the courage of our producer and your own sense of fairness and goodwill.

1. The first production of *The Mother-in-Law* failed in 165 because of the rival attractions of boxers and tight-rope walkers. The second also failed in 160 at the prospect of a gladiators' show.

[*The slave* DAVOS *comes on from the right carrying a bag of money.*]

DAVOS: My great friend and ally Geta came to me yesterday with a small bill – a petty little sum outstanding on an old debt of mine. I was to find the money and I did. Here it is. I hear his master's son has got married, so I suppose he's scraping up something for a gift to the bride. Unfair I call it, the have-nots always obliged to give to the rich. Poor old Geta struggled to save this little by little from his rations, denying himself his pleasures, and now she'll make off with the lot, never stopping to think of the labour it cost him. Then he'll be stung for another present when she has a child, and after that there'll be birthdays and an initiation ceremony, all needing presents, and the mother takes all – the child is only an excuse for a present. But here *is* Geta.

[GETA, *a respectable middle-aged servant, comes out of his master* DEMIPHO'*s house talking to someone inside.*]

GETA: If a red-head comes asking for me –

DAVOS: All right, he's here.

GETA: Oh Davos, I was just going to look for you.

DAVOS [*handing him the money*]: There you are, take it. It's all good money and the right amount.

GETA: Thanks for remembering it. I'm most grateful.

DAVOS: So you should be, the way things are today. We've come to the point of being 'most grateful' if a man does no more than pay his debts. But you look gloomy. What's the matter?

GETA: Do I? You don't know our fears and the danger we're in!

DAVOS: What do you mean?

GETA: I'll tell you; but don't breathe a word about it.

DAVOS: Go on, you idiot. If you can see a man's honest over money do you hesitate to trust him with a secret? And what'd I gain by deceiving you?

GETA: Then listen.

DAVOS: I am listening.

GETA: You know Chremes, our old man's elder brother?

DAVOS: Of course I do.

GETA: And his son Phaedria?

DAVOS: As well as I know you.

GETA: Well, it happened that both the old men went abroad at the same time, Chremes to Lemnos and Demipho to an old friend in Cilicia who had lured him over with letters promising him pretty well mountains of gold.

DAVOS: And him with wealth enough and to spare?

GETA: Oh well, that's his nature.

DAVOS: I wish I'd been born a rich patron!

GETA: When they set off they both left me here as guardian to their sons.

DAVOS: That was a tough job.

GETA: So I found by experience. Looking back on it, I remember my luck was out from the day they left. I began by trying to stand up to the boys – well, all I need say is that loyalty to my master's wishes just about broke my back.

DAVOS: Just as I thought: 'It's folly to kick against the pricks.'

GETA: Then I took to doing anything to please them and fell in with all their wishes.

DAVOS: You know how to work the market!

GETA: Young Antipho gave no trouble at first, but Phaedria promptly picked up a girl, a lute-player, and fell head over ears in love with her. She was working for that dirty pimp [*pointing to* DORIO's *house*] and there wasn't a penny to pay for her; both fathers had seen to that. All he could do was feast his eyes on her, follow her around, take her to her music school and bring her back; I'd nothing to do so I gave him all my attention. Right opposite her school was a barber's shop where we generally waited for her to come out and go home. We were sitting there one day when a young man came in in tears. We were surprised, and asked him what was the matter. 'Never before,' said he, 'did I realize the sheer misery and burden of poverty. Round the corner I've just seen a young girl weeping piteously for her dead mother. The body was laid out facing the door, but there wasn't a single person, friend, acquaintance or neighbour, except one old woman to help with the funeral. It upset me terribly; and the girl's a real beauty.' To cut a long story short, we were all much touched by his story, and suddenly Antipho cried, 'I say, shall we go and see her?' Someone else said, 'Yes, let's, please take us.' We set out, arrived, and saw her. She was a lovely girl, and what was more she was beauty unadorned – hair loose, bare feet, weeping and generally dishevelled and dressed in mourning, all enough to hide her looks if she hadn't had the advantage of true natural beauty. Phaedria was taken up with his own girl, so all he said was 'Not bad.' But our Antipho –

DAVOS: I can guess; he fell for her.

GETA: Didn't he! Now mark what follows. Next day he goes straight to the old woman and begs her to introduce him. She refuses, says it wouldn't be right; the girl is an Attic citizen, honest daughter of honest parents. If he wants her for a wife he can marry her, all proper and legal. If it's anything else, no. Antipho couldn't think what to do. He was dying to marry her and at the same time terrified of his absent father.

DAVOS: Wouldn't his father have given permission on his return?

GETA: What, him? Permission for his son to marry a girl with no dowry and no family? Never!

DAVOS: So what happened in the end?

GETA: You may well ask. There's a fellow called Phormio, a real adventurer – devil take him for an impudent rascal.

DAVOS: What did he do?

GETA: He gave us this advice. 'The law says that female orphans must be married to their next-of-kin, and the same law puts the next-of-kin under obligation to marry them. I'll say you are her relative and I'll take out a summons against you. I'll pretend to be a friend of the girl's father. We'll go to court; who her father was and her mother, and how she's related to you I can easily make up in the way that suits me best. You won't contest anything, so I'm sure to win. Of course your father will come back and I'll be in trouble, but no matter. We shall have got the girl.'

DAVOS: What cheek!

GETA: Antipho agreed, and everything else followed: summons, case, defeat, marriage.

DAVOS: You don't say so!

GETA: Well, you heard me.

DAVOS: But what'll become of *you*, Geta?

GETA: I've no idea [*striking a heroic attitude*]. All I know is that I shall meet my fate with equanimity, come what may.

DAVOS: Splendid! There's heroism!

GETA: I can trust myself, none other.

DAVOS: Bravo!

GETA [*in his normal manner*]: And now I suppose I'd better find someone to plead my case thus: 'Let him off just this once, please, but if he's in trouble again he'll get no help from me.' Which amounts to saying 'As soon as I've gone you can hang him.'

DAVOS: What about the other fellow – the one who's playing escort to the lute-player? How's he getting on?

GETA: Phaedria? Not too well.

DAVOS: He hasn't much he can give, maybe?

GETA: Nothing at all but pure hope.

DAVOS: Is his father back yet or not?

GETA: Not yet.

DAVOS: And your old man, when do you expect him?

GETA: I don't really know, but I heard that a letter has just come from him and been handed in at the customs office. I'm going along to collect it now.

DAVOS: Nothing else I can do for you, is there?

GETA: No, no, look after yourself. [DAVOS *goes off right and* GETA *knocks at* DEMIPHO's *door*.] Here, boy! Is no one coming? [*A slave boy comes out and* GETA *gives him the money-bag*.] Take this and give it to my wife.

[*The boy goes in and* GETA *goes off left, to the harbour.* DEMIPHO's *door opens again and out come* ANTIPHO *and his cousin* PHAEDRIA, *both young men looking very gloomy and* ANTIPHO *in a great state of nerves.*]

ANTIPHO: Oh Phaedria, fancy things coming to this pass – I'm in terror of my father's return whenever I think of it! And yet he always had my best interests at heart, and if only I hadn't been so thoughtless I should have been expecting him in the right spirit.

PHAEDRIA [*wearily*]: What's the matter now?

ANTIPHO: You ought to know, as you had a hand in that mad venture. I wish Phormio'd never thought of suggesting it. I wish I'd never been so eager to be pushed into it and landed myself with all this trouble. I shouldn't have had *her* and it would have been hell, but only for a few days, not this daily worry which is getting me down –

PHAEDRIA: Quite so.

ANTIPHO: – while all the time I'm waiting for him to come
and take her away from me.

PHAEDRIA: Other people suffer through being *denied* what
they love, but here you are groaning away over having too
much of it. Yes, Antipho, you've got love and to spare –
anyone would beg and pray for a life like yours. Good God,
if I could enjoy my love as long, I'd be glad to die for it!
Just you tot up all I get out of my nothing and you from
your plenty, not counting the fact that without spending a
penny you've got a girl who is free and well-born *and* have
married her openly and honourably, just as you wanted.
You've got everything to make you happy except the sense
to take your life as it comes. If you had to deal with that
pimp as I do, you'd see! Most of us are like that I suppose,
each one discontented with his own lot

ANTIPHO: But you're the one I'd call fortunate, Phaedria.
You're still quite free to decide what you really want, to
keep her, love her or give her up. I'm in the unhappy position of knowing that the decision to keep her or not is out
of my hands. [*He looks down the street, left.*] Now what – isn't
that Geta I see running this way? Yes it is. Dear, dear, I'm
sadly afraid he's bringing me bad news.

[*They move back as* GETA *hurries on, talking to himself.*]

GETA: You're done for, Geta, unless you can think of something at once – there's a storm of trouble threatening to
break on you all unprepared for it. How to avoid or escape
it I just don't know; that crazy venture of ours can't be kept
secret much longer.

ANTIPHO: What's put him in such a state?

GETA: Besides, I've only a minute . . . master's here.

ANTIPHO: What's his trouble?

GETA: Once he's heard something, he'll be furious and what

shall I do? Tell him? It'll only infuriate him. Keep quiet?
It'll make things worse. Defend myself? Labour wasted. Oh
misery! I'm not only afraid for myself, I'm worried to death
for Antipho – he's the trouble and worry, he's what's keeping me here. But for him I'd have looked after myself and
got my own back on the old man for his temper: I'd have
packed up something and done a bolt.

ANTIPHO: Bolting? Thieving? What's the man thinking of?

GETA: Where *is* Antipho? [*Peering along the street*] Where am
I to start looking for him?

PHAEDRIA [*pushing* ANTIPHO *forward*]: It's you he wants.

ANTIPHO [*shrinking back*]: I'm sure he's got something awful
to tell me.

PHAEDRIA: Oh don't be a fool.

GETA: I'll go home, he's usually there.

PHAEDRIA: Let's call him back.

ANTIPHO: Stop!

GETA [*scarcely turning his head*]: What? Pretty free with your
orders aren't you, whoever you are.

ANTIPHO: Geta!

GETA [*coming back*]: Why it's you, sir, the very man I wanted.

ANTIPHO: Now then please, give me your news and be quick
about it.

GETA: All right.

ANTIPHO: Then tell me.

GETA: Just now at the harbour –

ANTIPHO: You saw my –

GETA: You've got it.

ANTIPHO: There, I'm finished.

PHAEDRIA: I say –

ANTIPHO: What shall I do?

PHAEDRIA: What's all this?

GETA [*to* PHAEDRIA]: I saw his father, your uncle.

ANTIPHO [*pacing about distractedly*]: Oh, what a disaster! How can I find a quick way out of it? If it's my fate to be torn from you, Phanium, no life's worth living.

GETA: Come, come, sir, as things are there's all the more reason for making an effort. Fortune favours the brave.

ANTIPHO: I'm not myself.

GETA: But this is the moment when you *must* be, sir. If your father sees you looking nervous he'll guess you've done something wrong.

PHAEDRIA: Geta's quite right.

ANTIPHO: No good, I can't change.

GETA: What if you had something even harder to face?

ANTIPHO: If I can't cope with this I'd find that even worse.

GETA: Oh he's hopeless, sir, leave him. Why waste more time on him? I'm going.

PHAEDRIA: So am I.

[*They start to move off when* ANTIPHO *catches at them.*]

ANTIPHO: No, please; what if I pretended – would that do?

GETA: Don't be silly.

ANTIPHO [*trying to look resolute*]: Look at my face, both of you. Is that all right?

GETA: No.

ANTIPHO: What about this?

GETA: Nearly.

ANTIPHO: Like this then?

GETA: That'll do. Now keep it up. Answer him word for word, give as good as you get, or he'll bowl you over in his savage bursts of fury.

ANTIPHO: I know.

GETA: Say you were forced into it against your will.

PHAEDRIA: By the law, by order of court.

GETA: Got it? Now who's that old man I can see at the end of the street? Yes, it's the master all right.

ANTIPHO [*his resolution rapidly leaving him*] : I can't stay –

GETA: Hi, what are you doing? Where are you going? Stop, sir, can't you –

ANTIPHO: I know myself and what I've done. I'm leaving Phanium in your hands – and my life. [*He disappears along the street right.*]

PHAEDRIA: What'll happen now, Geta?

GETA: You're in for a row, sir, and I'll be strung up and flogged unless I'm much mistaken. But our duty now is to follow the advice we gave Antipho.

PHAEDRIA: Never mind about duty, just tell me what to do.

GETA: Do you remember the tale you both originally decided to tell your uncle to excuse your conduct: that Phormio had right and justice on his side and was bound to win?

PHAEDRIA: I remember.

GETA: We'll have to use that now if we can't think of something better and cleverer.

PHAEDRIA: I'll do my best.

GETA [*who is watching* DEMIPHO'*s approach off-stage*] : Now you go in to attack while I lie in ambush as a reserve in case you have to give ground.

PHAEDRIA: Come on then.

[*They both stand back as* DEMIPHO *comes on left, tired after his journey and exasperated by the news which has already reached his ears.*]

DEMIPHO [*to himself*] : So that's it – my son has married without my permission! With no regard for my outraged feelings – let alone my authority – no sense of shame! A disgraceful piece of impudence! So much for Geta as a guardian!

GETA [*to* PHAEDRIA] : I wondered when he was coming to me.

DEMIPHO: What will they say to me – what excuse will they find? I wonder.

GETA: I'll find one, don't worry.

DEMIPHO: Perhaps he'll say, 'I didn't want to do it: the law compelled me.' Precisely, I grant that.

GETA: Good.

DEMIPHO: But did the law also compel him to throw up the case to the prosecution open-eyed, without saying a word?

PHAEDRIA: That's quite a problem.

GETA: Leave it to me, I'll solve it.

DEMIPHO: Now what am I to do? The whole thing is so unforeseen and unexpected, and I'm so angry I can't think straight. It just shows that when things look best it's the time for us all to be thinking how to bear the worst – dangers, losses and exile – and a man returning from abroad should always have in mind the common misfortunes which may be awaiting him, a son's misdeeds, death of a wife or sickness of a daughter; so that nothing takes him by surprise, and anything which betters his expectations can be counted pure gain.

GETA [*to* PHAEDRIA]: I could never have believed that I was wiser than my master, sir, but I've been thinking of all the misfortunes awaiting *me* when he returned, flogging, fetters, grinding at the mill and toiling at the farm. . . . None of this will take me by surprise, and anything which betters my expectations I'll count pure gain. But why don't you approach him, sir? Say something soothing for a start.

DEMIPHO: That's my nephew Phaedria I see coming to meet me.

[PHAEDRIA *comes forward and greets* DEMIPHO *effusively*.]

PHAEDRIA: Good morning, uncle.

DEMIPHO [*curtly*]: Good morning. Where is Antipho?

PHAEDRIA: I'm delighted to see you –

DEMIPHO: I don't doubt it. Answer my question

PHAEDRIA: He's well, he's somewhere around. . . . Is everything all right with you?

DEMIPHO: I only wish it were!

PHAEDRIA: What do you mean, uncle?

DEMIPHO: Don't ask silly questions, Phaedria. A fine marriage you people have arranged for him while I was away.

PHAEDRIA [*with a great show of astonishment*]: Is *that* why you're angry with him?

GETA [*aside*]: Oh, good show!

DEMIPHO: Is there any reason why I should *not* be angry? All I want is to have him here before me so that he can see how his conduct has changed his indulgent father into one of very different temper.

PHAEDRIA: But uncle, he hasn't done anything to make you angry.

DEMIPHO: There you are! All of a pattern, all the same. Know one, you know the lot.

PHAEDRIA: That's not true.

DEMIPHO: A's at fault, B's on the spot to defend him. Reverse them, and A's there to defend B. It's a mutual benefit society.

GETA [*aside*]: The old man's drawn them to the life if he did but know it.

DEMIPHO: If it weren't so, Phaedria, you wouldn't be taking his side.

PHAEDRIA [*virtuously*]: If Antipho has really done wrong, uncle, and been careless of his property and reputation, I'm not arguing against his getting what he deserves. But if some ill-natured person has successfully laid a trap for our inexperienced youth, is that our fault? Shouldn't you blame the courts, which often take from the rich in spite and give to the poor out of pity?

GETA [*aside*]: If I didn't know the facts I'd think he spoke the truth.

DEMIPHO: How can any court recognize rights if the defendant is as speechless as Antipho was?

PHAEDRIA: He behaved like the well-brought-up young man he is. Once in court he couldn't find words for his carefully prepared defence. He's naturally shy, and on this occasion was struck dumb with embarrassment.

GETA [aside]: He's doing well. This is where I come in. [Coming forward] Good morning, sir. I'm glad to see you safely back again.

DEMIPHO: Good morning, faithful guardian, prop and mainstay of my home, to whom I entrusted my son when I went abroad!

GETA: I've been listening for some time, sir, to your unjust charges against us all – including me who deserves them least of anybody. What did you want me to do for you in all this? The law doesn't permit a slave to plead in court and he isn't allowed to give evidence.

DEMIPHO: I know, I know. The boy's nervous and inexperienced and you're a slave, I grant that. But however closely the girl is supposed to be related to us, there was no need for him to *marry* her. You could have supplied the dowry the law demands and looked for another husband for her; instead of which he goes and brings home a penniless wife. What's the sense of it?

GETA: It wasn't sense we lacked, it was cash.

DEMIPHO: He could have borrowed it from somewhere.

GETA: Somewhere? Easily said.

DEMIPHO: On interest, if all else failed.

GETA: That's the best I've heard! Who'd give him credit while you're alive?

DEMIPHO: I won't have it, I tell you! It's impossible. I refuse to allow this marriage for another day. They deserve no indulgence. Now kindly point out that individual, or show me where he lives.

GETA: You mean Phormio?

DEMIPHO: I mean the man who acted for the girl.

GETA: I'll have him here in no time.

DEMIPHO: And now where's Antipho?

GETA: Gone out.

DEMIPHO: Phaedria, you go and find him and bring him here.

PHAEDRIA: All right uncle, I'll go straight – there [*with a wink at* GETA *and gesture at* DORIO's *house where* PAMPHILA *is; he then pretends to go off right but slips in unnoticed*].

GETA [*aside*]: I know, to Pamphila.
     [*He goes off, right.*]

DEMIPHO: I'm going in to give thanks to the gods for my return. Then I shall go into town to find some friends to support me in this matter. I must be ready for Phormio when he comes.
     [*He goes into his house. After a short interval, a smart and self-confident young man comes on jauntily from the right; here at last is* PHORMIO. *With him is* GETA.]

PHORMIO: You say he went off in a panic at the sight of his father?

GETA: Yes.

PHORMIO: Then Phanium's alone?

GETA: Yes.

PHORMIO: And the old man is furious?

GETA: He certainly is.

PHORMIO: Then it all devolves on you, Phormio. It's your cooking, you must eat it. Prepare for action!

GETA: Please –

PHORMIO [*ignoring him*]: Now if he asks –

GETA: You're our only hope –

PHORMIO [*still to himself*]: Look, suppose he replies . . .

GETA: It was you who pushed us into this —

PHORMIO: . . . That'll do, I think.

GETA: Please help us.

PHORMIO [*condescending to listen at last*]: Bring on the old man. Now all my plans are laid.

GETA: What'll you do?

PHORMIO: What do you want? Antipho rescued from this charge, Phanium to remain his wife, and the full flood of the old man's wrath to be diverted on to me?

GETA: You're a brave man, Phormio, and a good friend. All the same I often have my fears that this sort of bravery will end by landing you in jail.

PHORMIO: Nothing of the sort. I've tested the path and know where to put my feet. I've had men beaten up, foreigners and citizens too, nearly to death: do you know how many? The better I know my way, the more I've done this. Well, have you ever heard of my being charged with assault?

GETA: No. How do you manage it?

PHORMIO: The net isn't spread for harmful birds like the hawk or kite but for the harmless ones which are profitable to catch. The others are waste effort. There are all sorts of risks for people who can be fleeced, but everyone knows I've got nothing. You may say they'll get me convicted and take me off home, but who wants to feed an appetite like mine? So if they don't choose to repay villainy with a handsome reward, I'd say they're only showing sense.

GETA: My young master will never be able to repay you properly.

PHORMIO: Ah no, it's a man's patron who can never be repaid. *You* contribute nothing, but come to dinner washed and scented after a bath without a care in the world while *he* is harassed by worry and expense. Everything's done for your pleasure while he can only grin and bear it; you're the one who smiles, takes first seat and first drink. Then a – difficult sort of dinner is set before you.

GETA: What do you mean, difficult?

PHORMIO: Difficult to decide what you'll take first. And when you start reckoning how delicious and costly it all is, won't you look upon its provider as your guardian god?

GETA [looking down the street]: Here's old Demipho. Now look out – first clash is fiercest. If you can hold your ground now you can play with him afterwards as you please.

[DEMIPHO comes on right[1] with his three legal advisers; the others stand back.]

DEMIPHO: Did you ever hear of such an outrageous insult? Stand by me, please.

GETA [to PHORMIO]: He's in a temper.

PHORMIO: Now play up; I'm going to tease him. [Aloud, so that DEMIPHO can hear their pretended quarrel] Good God, does Demipho really deny the relationship? Does he actually deny that Phanium is related to him?

GETA: Yes, he does.

PHORMIO: And says he doesn't know who her father was?

GETA: That's right.

DEMIPHO [to his friends]: I believe that's the man. Follow me.

PHORMIO: Says he doesn't know who Stilpo is?

GETA: That's right.

PHORMIO: Just because that poor girl is left penniless, her father's disowned and she is cast off. See what avarice does!

---

1. As Demipho went into his house at l. 314, he must have gone out through his house to the back street and then to the forum. (In the Greek play an altar stood on the stage, so he could have offered his thanks to the gods without going indoors, where the Romans kept their Penates. See *The Girl from Andros* 726 and *The Eunuch* 845.)

GETA [*in mock defence*]: If you're out to charge my master with bad faith you'll only get yourself a bad name.

DEMIPHO: What impudence! I do believe he's going to turn the charge against me.

PHORMIO: Mind you, I've nothing against young Antipho if he didn't know him, for he was getting on in years and pretty hard up, worked for his living and spent nearly all his time in the country where he had a bit of land to farm from my father. He often used to tell me in those days how this relative of his ignored his existence; but what a man he was! One of the best I ever set eyes on.

GETA: Then you could see about being more like him – if we're to believe your tale.

PHORMIO: Oh go to hell! If I hadn't thought well of him should I be quarrelling like this with your household on behalf of his daughter – who is rejected by your master in this shabby fashion?

GETA: Will you kindly stop abusing him behind his back, you foul-mouthed brute?

PHORMIO: Abuse is just about what he deserves.

GETA [*threateningly*]: What's that you're saying, jail-bird?

DEMIPHO: Geta!

GETA: Extortioner! Twister!

DEMIPHO: Geta!

PHORMIO [*aside*]: Answer him.

GETA [*coming forward*]: Who's that? Oh it's you, sir.

DEMIPHO: Be quiet.

GETA: He's been carrying on behind your back all day, sir, with insults better suited to himself.

DEMIPHO: That will do. [*To* PHORMIO, *who comes forward*] By your leave, young man, perhaps you'll be so good as to answer me one question: who exactly was this man you say was your friend, and how did he say I was related to him?

PHORMIO [*insolently*]: Fishing for information, are you, as if you didn't know him?

DEMIPHO: *I* knew him?

PHORMIO: You knew him all right.

DEMIPHO: I deny it. But as you say I did, please refresh my memory.

PHORMIO: Why, don't you know your own cousin?

DEMIPHO: Stop this tomfoolery and tell me his name.

PHORMIO: His name? Certainly.

　　[*There is a pause.*]

DEMIPHO: Then why don't you say it?

PHORMIO: Dear me, I've forgotten it.

DEMIPHO: What's that?

PHORMIO [*aside*]: Geta, can you remember the name I used before? Whisper it. [*To* DEMIPHO] Well, I'm not saying it. You're up to some trick, pretending you don't know him.

DEMIPHO: What do you mean, up to some trick?

GETA [*in* PHORMIO'*s ear*]: Stilpo.

PHORMIO: Oh I might as well tell you. It's Stilpo.

DEMIPHO: Who did you say?

PHORMIO [*with exaggerated clarity*]: The – man – you – knew – was – Stilpo.

DEMIPHO: Never heard of him. No one of that name has ever been related to me.

PHORMIO: Really? You ought to be ashamed of yourself, before these gentlemen here. Of course if he'd left you a few thousands –

DEMIPHO: Damn you!

PHORMIO: – you'd be the first to trace your family tree in detail right back to your grandfather and great-grandfather.

DEMIPHO [*trying hard to keep his temper*]: Quite so. And if I had come before the court I should have said how the girl was supposed to be related to me. You do so now: come on, how is she my relative?

GETA: Well done, our side! [*To* PHORMIO] Now, look out.

PHORMIO: I made a clear statement in the proper place, in court. If it wasn't correct, why didn't your son refute it?

DEMIPHO: Don't talk to me of my son. When it comes to his stupidity, words fail me.

PHORMIO: Well, you're no fool. You go to the magistrates and ask for a new trial. You're top dog and the only person here likely to get the same case heard twice.

DEMIPHO: This is sheer victimization, but sooner than have to go to law – and listen to you – I'll assume she *is* my relative and give her the dowry the law prescribes. Here's five hundred drachmas, now get her out of my house.

PHORMIO [*laughing scornfully and waving the proffered money away*]: Very nice of you, I'm sure.

DEMIPHO: *Now* what? Isn't that a fair proposal? Am I even to be denied common justice?

PHORMIO: Do you really mean to tell me that this law exists to enable a man to pay off a kept woman and get rid of her when he's had his pleasure? Or was it to prevent any Athenian woman's having to disgrace herself through poverty that she was ordered by law to marry her nearest relative and live with him alone? This is what you are trying to prevent.

DEMIPHO: Yes, her nearest relative. But where do *we* come in? And why?

PHORMIO: Now, now; 'what's done can't be undone'.

DEMIPHO: Can't be undone? On the contrary, I shan't rest until I see that it is.

PHORMIO: Nonsense.

DEMIPHO: You wait and see.

PHORMIO: One last word, Demipho; we're not interested in

you. The court dealt with your son, not you. [*Rudely*] You're past the age of marrying.

DEMIPHO: You can take it that all I'm saying to you comes from him too. Otherwise I shall forbid him the house along with that wife of his.

GETA [*aside to* PHORMIO]: He's furious.

PHORMIO: You'd do better to keep out yourself.

DEMIPHO: Then you are prepared to oppose anything I do, you poor fool?

PHORMIO [*to* GETA]: He's afraid of us, however much he tries to hide it.

GETA [*to* PHORMIO]: You've made a jolly good start.

PHORMIO: Why can't you bow to the inevitable? Do what's worthy of you and let us be friends.

DEMIPHO: Do you expect *me* to seek *your* friendship? I never want to see or hear you again.

PHORMIO: If you could reconcile yourself to *her* you'd have someone to amuse you in your declining years. Think of your age.

DEMIPHO: You keep her then. *You* can be amused.

PHORMIO: Temper, temper!

DEMIPHO: Listen to me; we've said quite enough. If you don't hurry up and remove that woman from my house I shall throw her out. That's my last word, Phormio.

PHORMIO: She's a free citizen, and if you so much as lay a finger on her improperly I'll bring an action which will finish you. And that's *my* last word, Demipho. [*Beckoning to* GETA] If I'm wanted, I'm at home.

GETA: I see.

[PHORMIO *swaggers off right, pleased with himself.*]

DEMIPHO [*to himself*]: Oh the trouble and worry that boy has given me by entangling us both in this marriage! And he doesn't even show his face so that at least I could know what

he has to say for himself and what he thinks about it all.
Geta, go and see if he has come home yet or not.

GETA: Very good, sir.

[*He goes into* DEMIPHO's *house and* DEMIPHO *turns to his three friends who have been listening and perhaps taking a few notes.*]

DEMIPHO: You see the situation. What shall I do? You tell me, Hegio.

HEGIO: Me? I think Cratinus would be better, if you don't mind.

DEMIPHO: Then you, Cratinus.

CRATINUS: Me?

DEMIPHO: Yes, you.

CRATINUS [*after a lot of thought*]: I should like you to act in your best interests. In my view your son's actions during your absence should rightly and properly be rendered null and void: and you will succeed in this. That is my opinion.

DEMIPHO: Now Hegio.

HEGIO: I am sure Cratinus has delivered a carefully considered opinion. But the truth is, there are as many opinions as there are men to give them, no two think alike. I cannot agree that a legally pronounced judgement can be quashed; and it would be discreditable to attempt it.

DEMIPHO: Now you, Crito.

CRITO [*after a long pause*]: I must have further time to consider my opinion. It is a difficult case.

[*There is another long and embarrassing silence, broken by* CRATINUS *asking politely*:]

CRATINUS: Have you further need of us?

DEMIPHO: No, no, you have done very well. [*They go off right with dignity.*] I'm more undecided than ever.

[GETA *comes out of the house.*]

GETA: They say he's not back, sir.

DEMIPHO: I shall have to wait for my brother. He'll have some advice which I can follow. I'll go along to the harbour and find out when he's due.

[*He goes off left.*]

GETA: And I'll find Antipho and tell him what's been happening here. [*He sets off right and then stops.*] Good, here he is on his way back.

[ANTIPHO *comes on right, preoccupied with his troubles.*]

ANTIPHO: In fact, Antipho, you've mostly yourself and your lack of spirit to blame – dashing off like that and leaving your life in other folks' hands. Did you suppose they would look after your interests better than you could yourself? And quite apart from that, you should have given a thought to that girl who is in your house at the present moment, and not left her to come to harm through her misplaced trust in you. You're her only hope now, poor girl, she depends on you for everything.

GETA [*coming forward*]: Just what we've been saying, sir, all the time you were away. You ought never to have gone off like that.

ANTIPHO: Geta! I was looking for you.

GETA: Anyway, we didn't wait to do what we could for you.

ANTIPHO: Please tell me, how are things going? Any luck? Has my father suspected anything?

GETA: No . . . not yet.

ANTIPHO: Is there any hope then?

GETA: I can't really say.

ANTIPHO [*groans*]

GETA: But Phaedria's never stopped trying everything on your behalf.

ANTIPHO: He always does.

GETA: And Phormio's been playing the active friend, as usual.

ANTIPHO: What's he been doing?

GETA: Talking to the old man when he got worked up and calming him down.

ANTIPHO: Good old Phormio!

GETA [*modestly*]: *I*'ve done all I can too, sir.

ANTIPHO [*hugging him*]: Geta, dear man, thank you all.

GETA: The first round's over, as I say, and things are still quiet. Your father's going to wait until your uncle arrives.

ANTIPHO: What does he want out of him?

GETA: He said he wanted to follow his advice, at any rate in this matter.

ANTIPHO [*dashed again*]: Oh dear, Geta, how I dread seeing my uncle safe home again! I know he's only got to say the word and I'm dead – or alive!

GETA: Here comes Phaedria, sir.

ANTIPHO: Where?

GETA: Coming away from his private wrestling-ground.
      [PHAEDRIA *and the slave-dealer* DORIO *come out of* DORIO's *house, arguing.*]

PHAEDRIA: Dorio, do listen, please –

DORIO: I won't.

PHAEDRIA: Just a word –

DORIO: No. Leave me alone.

PHAEDRIA: Do listen to what I'm going to say.

DORIO: I'm sick of listening to you. It's the same thing all the time.

PHAEDRIA: But this time I'll say something you *want* to hear.

DORIO: All right, I'm listening.

PHAEDRIA: Can't I persuade you to wait – just for the next three days? [DORIO *makes a move towards his house.*] Now where are you going?

DORIO: I thought it was queer if you'd something new to tell me.

ANTIPHO: Geta, I'm afraid this man is –

GETA [*drily*]: Asking for trouble? Oh yes, I'm afraid of that too.

PHAEDRIA: Don't you trust me?

DORIO: However did you guess that?

PHAEDRIA: If I give you my word?

DORIO: Nonsense.

PHAEDRIA: You'll say your kindness was a good investment.

DORIO: Rubbish!

PHAEDRIA: Believe me, you'll be glad you did it. That's true, honest it is.

DORIO: Moonshine.

PHAEDRIA: Just *try*; it isn't for long.

DORIO: The same old story.

PHAEDRIA: I count you one of the family, a father, a real friend, a –

DORIO: Talk on, talk on.

PHAEDRIA: How can you be so stubborn and hard-hearted? You won't be softened by pity or prayers.

DORIO: How can *you* be so impudent and dim-witted? You think you can move me by fancy words and make off with a girl of mine for nothing.

ANTIPHO [*to* GETA]: That's his way of showing pity.

PHAEDRIA [*tearfully*]: True, I suppose; he's got me there.

GETA: How the pair of them run true to type!

PHAEDRIA: And the blow didn't fall when Antipho was having *his* bit of trouble. . . .

ANTIPHO [*coming forward*]: Whatever is the matter, Phaedria?

PHAEDRIA: Oh Antipho, you lucky, lucky man –

ANTIPHO: *Me* lucky?

PHAEDRIA: Yes. You've got the one you love at home. You've never known what it is to be battling against this sort of misfortune.

ANTIPHO: Got her at home? I'd say I've the proverbial wolf by the ears – can't let go and can't hold on.

DORIO: That's exactly how I am with him.

ANTIPHO [*to* DORIO]: Come, come, you should know your job. [*To* PHAEDRIA, *indicating* DORIO] Has he been up to anything?

PHAEDRIA: What do you think? This beastly brute has sold my Pamphila.

ANTIPHO: Sold her?

GETA: Did you say he'd *sold* her?

PHAEDRIA: Sold her.

DORIO: Can't a man sell a girl he bought and paid for? What's wrong in that?

PHAEDRIA: I can't persuade him to cancel his bargain with the other fellow and wait – just for the next three days until I can raise the money promised by my friends. [*To* DORIO] If I don't pay you then, you needn't wait another hour.

DORIO: Carry on, don't mind me.

ANTIPHO: He isn't asking for long. Come on, Dorio, say Yes. Do him this service and he'll repay it twice over.

DORIO: So you say.

ANTIPHO: Are you going to let Pamphila be sent away from Athens? Can you bear to see these two lovers torn apart like this?

DORIO: Well, neither of us can –

PHAEDRIA: Then I hope the gods will see you get your deserts!

DORIO: Look here, I've put up with you against my better judgement for a good many months, with your promises and tears and never a penny paid up. Now I've found the exact opposite: someone who'll pay – and no tears. You stand down for your betters.

ANTIPHO: Surely, if I remember rightly, there was a day fixed for you to pay him?

PHAEDRIA: Yes, there was.

DORIO: Am I denying it?

ANTIPHO: Is it past the date?

DORIO: No, but the new one's come first.

ANTIPHO: That's double-crossing. Aren't you ashamed?

DORIO: Not in the least, so long as I'm making something out of it.

GETA: You – you muck-heap!

PHAEDRIA: Dorio, seriously, ought you to behave like this?

DORIO [with a shrug]: It's how I am. If you like me, you'll find I have my uses.

ANTIPHO: Cheating Phaedria like this!

DORIO: Actually it's he who's cheating *me*, Antipho. He knew all along what I was like, but I thought he was quite different. He's deceived me, but I've been the same as I've always been. However, let it pass. This is what I'll do: the Captain promised to pay me the money tomorrow morning. If you can bring it before then, Phaedria, I'll stick to my rule of first pay first served. Good-bye.

[*He bows and goes into his house, slamming the door.*]

PHAEDRIA: Now what shall I do? Just my luck! Wherever can I find him the money so soon? I'm completely broke. If only I'd been able to get the three days out of him, I had it promised.

ANTIPHO: Geta, we can't leave him in his misery like this, when he was so good about helping me, so you told me. We simply must try to repay his kindness now he needs us.

GETA [*dubiously*]: I know that's the right thing to do.

ANTIPHO: Well, come on then, you're the only one who can save him.

GETA: What can *I* do?

ANTIPHO: Find the money.

GETA: Nothing I'd like better: but just you show me where.

ANTIPHO: My father's home again.

GETA: I know, but how does that help?

ANTIPHO: A word's enough for the wise . . .

GETA: You don't mean –

ANTIPHO: Yes, I do.

GETA: Very nice, sir, I'm sure. Oh get away with you! Isn't it triumph enough for me to have escaped trouble over your own wedding without being told now to stick my neck out for your cousin here?

ANTIPHO [*to* PHAEDRIA]: He's right, you know.

PHAEDRIA: What? Don't you count me one of the family, Geta?

GETA: I suppose I do. But the old man's mad enough with the lot of us as it is without us goading him on until we'll never be able to beg for mercy.

PHAEDRIA [*dramatically*]: Shall another man snatch her off to an unknown land before my very eyes? Ah, speak to me, Antipho, look on me here and now while you can, while you have me still with you –

ANTIPHO: What for? What are you going to do? Come on, tell us.

PHAEDRIA: Whatever part of the world shall be her destination I am determined to follow her – or die.

GETA: Heaven help your plans, sir, but not too quickly.

ANTIPHO [*to* GETA]: See if you can give him any help.

GETA: Any help? What help?

ANTIPHO: Do please *think* or he may do something we'll be sorry for later on.

GETA: I'm thinking . . . [*After a pause evidently an idea comes to him.*] He'll be all right, I do believe – but I'm afraid there'll be trouble.

ANTIPHO: Don't be afraid. We're all in this together, good or
bad, whatever happens.

GETA [*to* PHAEDRIA]: First tell me how much money you
need.

PHAEDRIA: Only three thousand drachmas.

GETA: Three thousand? Good gracious, she's very expensive,
sir.

PHAEDRIA [*indignantly*]: At that price she's cheap.

GETA: All right, all right, I'll see you have it.

PHAEDRIA [*hugging him*]: Geta, you're a darling!

GETA [*primly disengaging himself*]: That will do, sir.

PHAEDRIA: I must have it at once.

GETA: You *shall* have it at once; but I must have Phormio to
help me.

PHAEDRIA: He's here to help. Put any burden on him you
like and he'll shoulder it manfully. He's the only man who's
a friend to his friends.

GETA: Let's hurry then and find him.

ANTIPHO: Is there anything I can do for you?

GETA: Nothing. No, you go home and comfort your poor
Phanium, who must be waiting there half-dead with fright.
Hurry along now!

ANTIPHO: There's nothing I'd rather do.

[*He hurries into* DEMIPHO'*s house.*]

PHAEDRIA: How on earth are you going to manage this?

GETA: I'll tell you on the way. Come on, sir.

[*They go off right in search of* PHORMIO *and so miss* DEMI-
PHO *and his brother* CHREMES *who come on left, from the
harbour.*]

DEMIPHO: Now, Chremes, what about the purpose which
took you to Lemnos? Have you brought back your daughter?

CHREMES: No.

DEMIPHO: Why not?

CHREMES: Because her mother had already left to look for me – so I was told. She thought I was staying here too long, and the girl was growing up and couldn't wait while I neglected her, so she set out with all her household to join me.

DEMIPHO: Then why did you stay there so long when you heard this?

CHREMES: I was ill and couldn't get away.

DEMIPHO: What was the matter? Where did you catch it?

CHREMES: Never mind; it's illness enough to be old. But I heard they had arrived here safely from the sailor who brought them.

DEMIPHO: Have you heard what happened to my son while I was away?

CHREMES: Yes, I have, and it puts me in a quandary. If I try to make a match for the girl outside the family I shall have to give a proper account of how she comes to be my daughter. I knew my secret was as safe with you as with myself, but any outsider who wants to marry into my family will hold his tongue only so long as we are on good terms. If we fall out he'll soon find out more than he need know. I'm terrified too of my wife's getting to hear about this somehow – if that happens all I can do is to throw everything up and clear out; my person is the only thing in the house I can call my own.

DEMIPHO: I realize that, and the whole thing is a great worry to me. I shan't give up trying everything I can in the hope of carrying out our previous arrangement.

[*They move aside, still deep in conversation, and so do not see* GETA *hurrying on right.*]

GETA [*to himself*]: I've never seen a man so quick-witted as Phormio. I came to tell him we needed money and find out how we could get it. I'd scarcely said half before he'd got the point. He was delighted, congratulated me and asked to see the master. He thanked heaven for giving him the chance to show himself as much the friend of Phaedria as of Antipho. I told him to wait for me in the market-place and I'd bring the old man along. . . . But there he is – and who's that behind him? My God, it's Phaedria's father come home! Now you ass, no need to panic if you've got two to handle instead of one. It's better to have two strings to one's bow I suppose. I'll aim at the one I first had in mind. If he pays up that'll do. If there's nothing doing with him I'll tackle the new arrival.

[ANTIPHO *opens the door of* DEMIPHO's *house and stands listening.*]

ANTIPHO: I'll just wait for Geta – I wonder how soon he'll be back. Oh damn, there's my uncle with my father. I dread to think what effect his arrival will have.

GETA: Now for it. [*He approaches* CHREMES.] Oh sir –

CHREMES [*curtly*]: Well, Geta.

GETA: I'm delighted to see you safely back, sir.

CHREMES: Doubtless.

GETA [*nervously*]: How are things with you, sir? One always comes home to find a good many changes.

CHREMES: A *great* many changes.

GETA: Yes, sir. You've heard about your nephew Antipho?

CHREMES [*grimly*]: Yes. Everything.

GETA [*to* DEMIPHO]: Was it you who told him, sir? Shocking isn't it, to find what's done behind your back like this.

CHREMES: I was discussing it with my brother just now.

GETA [*catching at his opportunity*]: And I swear I've never stopped thinking about it too, sir, but now I do believe I've found a solution.

CHREMES: What is it?

DEMIPHO: What solution?

GETA: When I left you, sir, I ran into Phormio.

CHREMES: Who's Phormio?

GETA: The girl's –

CHREMES: I remember.

GETA: I thought I'd sound his opinion so I took him aside. 'Phormio,' I said, 'why don't you see that we settle this matter between us in a friendly spirit with no ill feeling? My master is generous and hates lawsuits, but the fact is that all his friends without exception have been telling him with one voice to throw the girl out of his house.'

ANTIPHO [*aside*]: What's he up to? What's his idea?

GETA: 'You may say he'll have the law after him if he turns her out, but that's all been worked out. *You*'ll be the one in trouble if you let yourself be involved with that man. You should hear his eloquence! Even supposing he loses, it isn't his life and liberty at stake, only his money.' I saw my words were beginning to have some effect on him, so I went on: 'We're alone here at the moment, so just you name the price you want in cash for my master to drop his present suit, the girl to take herself off, and you to stop making a nuisance of yourself.'

ANTIPHO: Has he gone off his head?

GETA: 'He's an honest gentleman,' I said, 'and I'm quite sure if there's anything fair and honest in the terms you offer it can all be settled at once between you in a couple of words.'

DEMIPHO [*coldly*]: And who gave you authority to talk like this?

CHREMES: No, no, he's right. It's the best way of getting what we want.

ANTIPHO: That finishes me!

DEMIPHO: Continue.

GETA: At first the man was furious.

CHREMES [*impatiently*]: How much did he want?

GETA: Far too much. The first sum which came into his head.

CHREMES: *Tell* me.

GETA: He talked of a good six thousand –

DEMIPHO: And he'll get something not so good. What impudence!

GETA: Just what I told him, sir. 'Good heavens,' I said. 'He might be marrying off his one and only daughter! He's not gained much by not bringing up a daughter of his own if someone else turns up demanding a dowry like that.' To cut a long story short and pass over his impertinence, this was his final proposal: 'I always wanted to do the right thing and marry my friend's daughter, and I kept thinking how she'd suffer for her poverty if she had to slave for a rich husband, but to be quite frank with you, I needed a wife who could bring me a bit to pay off my debts. Still, if Demipho is willing to give me as much as I'm getting from the girl who's now engaged to me, I'd rather have Phanium for a wife than anyone.'

ANTIPHO: Is this malice or sheer stupidity? Does the man know what he's doing or not? I've no idea.

DEMIPHO: What if he's up to the eyes in debt?

GETA: 'There's some land,' he said, 'mortgaged for a thousand.'

DEMIPHO: All right, all right, let him marry her at once. I'll pay that.

GETA: 'A small house too for another thousand.'

DEMIPHO: No, no. That's too much.

CHREMES: Don't fuss. You can have that thousand from me.

GETA: 'My wife must have a little maid, and we shall need a few sticks of furniture; then there's the expense of the wedding. You can reckon all this as another thousand.'

DEMIPHO: Well then, he can bring any number of actions

against me: I'm not paying a penny. Does the scoundrel think he can fool me?

CHREMES: Calm yourself, please; I'll pay. All you need do is see that your son marries the girl we intended for him.

ANTIPHO: Damn you, Geta, your tricks have been the death of me.

CHREMES: She's being turned out on my account, so it's only right that I should stand the loss.

GETA: 'Let me know as soon as possible,' he said, 'so that I can get rid of my present girl if they'll let me have the other one. I don't want things left in the air, as the other family has agreed to pay me the dowry at once.'

CHREMES [*eagerly*]: He shall have it at once, break it off with them and marry her.

DEMIPHO: And much good may it do him!

CHREMES: Luckily I've got money with me now, the rent from my wife's property in Lemnos. I'll take it from that and tell her you needed it.

[*They go into* CHREMES' *house without seeing* ANTIPHO, *who now steps forward.*]

ANTIPHO: Geta!

GETA: Yes, sir?

ANTIPHO: What *have* you been doing?

GETA [*well pleased with himself*]: Diddling the old men out of their money, sir.

ANTIPHO: Do you think you've done enough?

GETA: Damned if I know. It's all I was told to do.

ANTIPHO: You wretch, can't you answer my question?

GETA: What do you mean then?

ANTIPHO: I mean that the rope's round my neck and it's clear you put it there. May all the powers of heaven and hell condemn you to utter damnation! [*To the audience*] Look here, anything you want done just give it to *him* – if you

want a proper job made of it. [*To* GETA] What good could
it possibly do to touch on that sore spot and drag in my
wife's name? You've buoyed my father up with hopes of
getting her out of the house. And what's more: if Phormio
takes the dowry she'll have to marry *him*. What'll happen
then?

GETA: But he won't marry her.

ANTIPHO: Oh no, I daresay not. And when they want the
money back I suppose he'll choose to go to jail on our behalf.

GETA: Look here, sir, everything sounds worse if it's told all
wrong. You leave out all the good bits and only mention
the bad ones. Just you look at it this way. If he takes the
money he must marry her, as you say, and I admit this; but
there must be a little time for the wedding preparations,
sending out invitations and sacrificing to the gods. Meanwhile Phaedria's friends will give him what they promised
and Phormio'll pay it back out of that.

ANTIPHO: But why should he delay? What reason will he
give?

GETA: Well, if you must know, he could say: 'I've had so
many warnings since then – a strange black dog came into
my house, a snake fell from the tiles through the skylight, a
hen crowed, a soothsayer spoke against it and a diviner for-
bade it. Fancy starting on anything new before the shortest
day!' That's the best kind of excuse; and that's the sort of
thing he'll say.

ANTIPHO: Oh if only he will!

GETA: He will, trust me. Now here's your father coming out –
run along and tell Phaedria the money's there.

[ANTIPHO *hurries off right as* CHREMES *and* DEMIPHO
come out of CHREMES' *house with the promised money*.]

DEMIPHO: Don't worry, I tell you. I'll see he doesn't cheat us.

I'll take care not to hand over the cash except in the presence
of witnesses, and when I do so I shall state exactly what it's
for.

GETA [*aside*]: Cautious, isn't he, now there's no need.

CHREMES: That's the way to do it, but do hurry up before his
mood changes. If the other girl puts pressure on him it's
possible he may turn us down.

GETA [*aside*]: How right you are!

DEMIPHO: Geta! Take me to him.

GETA: I'm ready, sir.

CHREMES: When you've finished, come over to my wife and
ask her to see the girl before she leaves you, and tell her we're
arranging a marriage with Phormio and she's not to be
annoyed. He's more her sort and a better match for her, and
we've done our duty by her – he's having all the dowry he
asked for.

DEMIPHO [*exasperated*]: What the hell does this matter to you?

CHREMES: It matters a lot, Demipho. Doing your duty isn't
enough unless people know and approve, and I want
Phanium's consent to this so that she won't go around saying
she was turned out of your house.

DEMIPHO: I can do it just as well myself.

CHREMES: Women are better at handling women.

DEMIPHO: All right, I'll ask her.

[*He goes off right with* GETA.]

CHREMES: And now I'm wondering where I can find the
other two.[1]

[*The old nurse,* SOPHRONA, *comes out of* DEMIPHO'*s house
to give voice to her troubles, and moves to the front of the stage.*]

SOPHRONA: What shall I do? Oh dear, dear, where can I find
a friend? Where can I tell my tale and seek help? I'm so

―――――――――――――

1. i.e. his Lemnian wife and daughter.

afraid my mistress will be cruelly wronged – and all through taking my advice. It seems the young man's father is furious at what we've done.

CHREMES: Who on earth is this old woman bursting out of my brother's house in such a state?

SOPHRONA: It was our poverty which drove me to it. I knew this marriage wasn't secure but I had to provide for her welfare somehow while we waited –

CHREMES: Unless my eyes deceive me and my mind is giving way I do believe I see my daughter's nurse!

SOPHRONA: And now there's no trace –

CHREMES: What shall I do –

SOPHRONA: – of her father.

CHREMES: – go up to her or wait until she says something which makes more sense?

SOPHRONA: If only I could find him I'd have nothing to fear.

CHREMES: It *is* the nurse. I'll speak to her.

SOPHRONA [*aware at last that she is not alone*]: Who's that?

CHREMES: Sophrona!

SOPHRONA: And he knows my name!

CHREMES: Turn round.

SOPHRONA: Heavens above, it's Stilpo!

CHREMES: No, no.

SOPHRONA: Did you say No?

CHREMES [*nervously*]: Come over here, please Sophrona, a little further from the door, over there . . . Don't ever call me by that name again.

SOPHRONA: Why? Aren't you the man you always said you were?

CHREMES: Sh . . .

SOPHRONA: Why are you afraid of this door?

CHREMES: I've a wife behind it – a dangerous one. And that

was why I gave you a false name before, in case any of you were careless enough to let out the real one and somehow my wife found out.

SOPHRONA: So that's why we poor women could never find you here!

CHREMES [*anxious to change the subject*]: Now please tell me why you came out of that door. Do you know the family? And where are – the others?

SOPHRONA [*tearfully*]: Oh dear . . .

CHREMES: What's the matter? Are they alive?

SOPHRONA: The daughter is. The mother, poor soul, died of the distress you caused her.

CHREMES: That's bad. . . .

SOPHRONA: And I was abandoned here, a penniless old woman without a friend, but I did what I could. I married the girl to the young gentleman who is master of this house.

CHREMES: To Antipho?

SOPHRONA: Yes, to him.

CHREMES [*obtusely*]: What! Has he *two* wives?

SOPHRONA: Good heavens no, sir, he only has this one.

CHREMES: What about the other one who's called his relative?

SOPHRONA: That's her.

CHREMES: *What* do you say?

SOPHRONA: It was all a put-up job, sir, so that her lover could marry her without a dowry.

CHREMES: Ye gods, how often chance brings about more than we dare to hope! I've come back to find my daughter happily married to the man I wanted and the very way I wanted! He has achieved by his own unaided efforts – with no help from us – the very thing my brother and I were trying so hard to bring about.

SOPHRONA: Now think what we must do, sir; the young man's father is here and they say he's very much put out.

CHREMES: Oh, there's no danger there, but I'd move heaven
and earth to stop anyone knowing she's my daughter.

SOPHRONA: No one shall learn it from *me*.

CHREMES: Come with me: I'll tell you the rest of the story
indoors.

[*They go into* DEMIPHO's *house; soon after* DEMIPHO *and*
GETA *return, right.*]

DEMIPHO: Well, we've only ourselves to blame if we allow
dishonesty to pay by being too careful to preserve our own
reputation for generosity and fair dealing. We shouldn't
overshoot the mark, as the saying goes. It was bad enough
to have to swallow the man's insults without paying him
cash into the bargain. Now he's got something to live on
while he's plotting fresh wickedness.

GETA: Quite so, sir.

DEMIPHO: Nowadays the rewards go for putting the straight
crooked –

GETA: Too true.

DEMIPHO: – and we've been a pair of fools, the way we've
handled this affair.

GETA: Let's hope the plan comes off and he really does marry
her.

DEMIPHO: Why, is there any doubt about it?

GETA: Well, being the man he is, he might change his mind.

DEMIPHO: But surely he won't?

GETA: I don't know, sir, I only said he might.

DEMIPHO: I'll do as my brother advised and fetch his wife to
talk to the girl. Go on ahead, Geta, and tell her that Nausistrata is coming.

[*He goes into* CHREMES' *house to fetch her.*]

GETA: We've got the cash for Phaedria, and there's no word
of an action against us. For the moment Phanium won't
leave us, but what about the future? What'll happen?

You're stuck in the same mud, Geta; you'll have to repay a new loan. You can put off the evil day for a while, but look out – the blows are mounting up. Well, I'm off home to tell Phanium she needn't fear Phormio or anything he says.

[*He goes into* DEMIPHO's *house as* DEMIPHO *comes out of* CHREMES' *house with* NAUSISTRATA.]

DEMIPHO: Now, Nausistrata, use your powers of persuasion to make her agree to what we want, and accept of her own accord what has to be.

NAUSISTRATA: I will.

DEMIPHO: Your support can help me as much now as your money did before.

NAUSISTRATA: You're welcome, and if I can't do as much as I should it's all my husband's fault.

DEMIPHO: What do you mean?

NAUSISTRATA: Chremes is so careless in the way he handles my father's properties. *He* used to make twelve thousand drachmas regularly out of those estates. What a difference there is between one man and another!

DEMIPHO: Did you say twelve thousand?

NAUSISTRATA: Yes, twelve thousand, and prices were much lower then.

DEMIPHO [*indicates astonishment*]

NAUSISTRATA: What do you think of that?

DEMIPHO [*not listening*]: Yes, yes, of course.

NAUSISTRATA: I wish I'd been born a man: I'd have shown him –

DEMIPHO: I'm sure you would.

NAUSISTRATA: – just how –

DEMIPHO: Not now, please, save your strength for the girl, she's young and may tire you.

NAUSISTRATA: I'll do what you want. [*She turns to go as* CHREMES *comes out in a state of great excitement.*] Why, there's my husband coming out of your house.

CHREMES [*not seeing* NAUSISTRATA]: I say, Demipho, have you paid him the money yet?

DEMIPHO: Yes, I did it at once.

CHREMES: I wish you hadn't. [*Aside*] Dear me, there's my wife. I nearly said too much.

DEMIPHO: Why do you wish I hadn't?

CHREMES: It's all right now.

DEMIPHO: What about you? Have you said anything to the girl about why we're sending *her*? [*indicating* NAUSISTRATA]

CHREMES: It's all settled.

DEMIPHO: What does she say then?

CHREMES: The move's off.

DEMIPHO: Why ever?

CHREMES [*searching for a reason*]: Because . . . they're in love.

DEMIPHO: What's that got to do with us?

CHREMES: A lot. [*Trying not to let* NAUSISTRATA *hear*] Besides, I've discovered she *is* related to me.

DEMIPHO: What? You're crazy.

CHREMES: You'll see. I'm not just talking. I've remembered something.

DEMIPHO [*mystified*]: Are you in your right mind?

NAUSISTRATA [*equally at sea*]: Now don't you be wronging a relative!

DEMIPHO: She isn't one.

CHREMES: Don't be so sure. Her father's name was wrongly given and that misled you.

DEMIPHO: Doesn't she know her own father?

CHREMES: Of course she does.

DEMIPHO: Then why get his name wrong?

CHREMES [*in a frantic whisper*]: Will you please drop this at once and try to understand what I'm saying?

DEMIPHO: But you don't talk sense.

CHREMES: Oh, you'll be the death of me.

NAUSISTRATA: I wonder what this is all about!

DEMIPHO: I haven't a clue.

CHREMES [*still trying to take him aside*]: If you really want to know – God help me, there's no one so nearly related to her as we two are.

DEMIPHO: Then for Heaven's sake let's go and find the girl and all be present to see if you're right about this – or not.

CHREMES: Oh . . .

DEMIPHO: What?

CHREMES: To think you trust me so little!

DEMIPHO: You want me to take your word for it? And stop asking questions? Oh, all right. But what about the daughter of that friend of ours? What's to become of her?

CHREMES: That's all right.

DEMIPHO: Are we giving her up?

CHREMES: Yes, yes.

DEMIPHO: And the other one's to stay?

CHREMES: Yes.

DEMIPHO: Then we needn't keep you, Nausistrata.

NAUSISTRATA [*trying to conceal her incomprehension*]: I'm sure it's best for everyone that she should stay, after all. She seemed a very ladylike girl when I saw her.

[*She goes back into* CHREMES' *house.*]

DEMIPHO: *Now*, Chremes; what's all this about?

CHREMES: Has she shut the door?

DEMIPHO: Yes.

CHREMES [*relaxing*]: Praise Heaven, the gods are on our side! The girl your son married – I find she's my own daughter!

DEMIPHO: How could she be?

CHREMES: It isn't safe to tell you out here.

DEMIPHO: Well then, come indoors.

CHREMES: Listen, I don't want even our sons to know this. . . .

[*They go into* DEMIPHO's *house; soon after,* ANTIPHO *returns, right, from his meeting with* PHAEDRIA.]

ANTIPHO: No matter how things are with me, I'm glad my cousin has got what he wants. How sensible people are who set their hearts on things which can easily be put right if they go wrong! Phaedria had only to find the cash to be rid of his worries, but look at me – I can't see any way of extricating myself from my troubles. If the secret's kept I live on tenterhooks, and if it comes out I'm disgraced. I shouldn't be going home now if there weren't some hope I can keep my wife. . . . I wish I could find Geta, to ask what he thinks is the best moment to approach my father.

[PHORMIO *comes on right, voicing his satisfaction without seeing* ANTIPHO.]

PHORMIO: I got the money, paid off Dorio, removed the girl, and saw that Phaedria took her for his own now she's been freed. Now I've only one more thing to do – get rid of the old men and have some peace for a drink. I'm thinking of taking a few days off.

ANTIPHO [*coming to meet him*]: Why, it's Phormio. Tell me –

PHORMIO: Yes?

ANTIPHO: What's Phaedria going to do now? How does he propose to take his fill of his love?

PHORMIO: He's going to take a turn in your part –

ANTIPHO: Which one?

PHORMIO: – and hide from his father. He asks you to take over his, and plead his case, while he comes over to my house for a drink. I shall tell the old men I'm off to the fair at Sunium to buy the maid Geta spoke of just now, for if they don't see me around they'll imagine I'm running through their money. That sounded like your door.

ANTIPHO: See who it is.

PHORMIO: It's Geta.

[GETA *bursts out in a state of incoherent excitement.*]

GETA: O Fortune, lucky Fortune, what blessings you have heaped on my master Antipho, now, this very day, with your divine aid –

ANTIPHO: What on earth does he mean?

GETA: And rid us, his friends, of all our fears! Quick, make ready, be off to find him, tell him his good luck!

ANTIPHO: Do you understand what he's saying?

PHORMIO: Do you?

ANTIPHO: Not a word.

PHORMIO: No more do I.

GETA: I'll try Dorio's; they must be there [*setting off towards* DORIO'*s house*].

ANTIPHO: Hi, Geta!

GETA [*not looking back*]: There you are; the same old thing, called back as soon as you've set off.

ANTIPHO: Geta!

GETA: How that fellow carries on. A proper nuisance, but he won't stop *me*.

ANTIPHO: Please wait.

GETA: Go hang yourself!

ANTIPHO: Exactly what'll happen to you if you don't stop, you rascal.

GETA: He must be one of the family, threatening me like this. Can it be the man I'm looking for? I do believe it is. Quick, come here, sir.

ANTIPHO: What is it?

GETA [*ecstatically*]: O man most fortunate of all men alive! Beyond dispute, sir, you're the only beloved one of the gods!

ANTIPHO: I wish I were. And I wish someone would tell me how I'm to believe you.

GETA: Suppose I soak you through in delight? Would that satisfy you?

ANTIPHO: Oh, you make me tired!

PHORMIO: Never mind about promises, just give us the news.

GETA [*affecting surprise*]: You here too, Phormio?

PHORMIO: Yes. Hurry up.

GETA: All right, listen. When we'd met you in town and handed over the money we came straight back home. Presently my master sent me across to your wife.

ANTIPHO: What for?

GETA: I'm not going into that, sir, it's beside the point. I was just going into the women's quarters when the boy Mida ran up, caught hold of my cloak and pulled me back. I looked round and asked why he was stopping me. He said his orders were no admission to his mistress. Sophrona had just taken in the master's brother, Chremes, and he was still in there with them. When I heard this, I tiptoed softly to the door, reached it, stood close with my ear to the crack, holding my breath, and listened hard – like this – to catch what was said.

PHORMIO: Bravo, Geta!

GETA: This way I heard something simply wonderful, and very nearly cried out for joy.

ANTIPHO: What was it?

GETA: Can you guess?

ANTIPHO: I've no idea.

GETA: It's really marvellous. It's now known that your uncle is the father of your wife Phanium.

ANTIPHO: I don't believe you.

GETA: He had a secret affair with her mother years ago on Lemnos.

PHORMIO: Nonsense! How was it she didn't know her own father?

GETA: There's a reason for that, Phormio, believe me. Anyway, I was outside the door. Do you suppose I could follow every word they were saying inside?

ANTIPHO: Good heavens! I've heard something about that story too.

GETA: What's more, here's something to convince you. Presently your uncle came out here, and soon afterwards went in again with your father. Both of them said you could have her for your wife. And finally, I've been sent to find you and take you in.

ANTIPHO: Then hurry, can't you. What are you waiting for?

GETA [as he hustles him into DEMIPHO's house]: There you are!

ANTIPHO: Good-bye, Phormio!

PHORMIO: Good-bye, Antipho. Bless me, this is lovely; I'm delighted. [ANTIPHO and GETA go in.] What an unexpected stroke of good luck for those two! And a splendid opportunity for me to diddle the old men and rid Phaedria of his money worries before he has to go begging to his friends. The money's been paid over and it's his to keep, whether the old men like it or not; in fact I know how I can put pressure on them. Now I must play a new part: I'll just slip down the nearest side-street and appear when they come out. I can give up the idea of pretending to go to Sunium.

[He hurries off right, as CHREMES and DEMIPHO come out of the house.]

DEMIPHO: Well, brother, things have turned out well for us, thank God; I'm truly and properly grateful. Now we must find Phormio as quickly as possible, and recover our three thousand[1] before he squanders the lot.

1. The total asked for in ll. 666–7, and the sum needed for Phaedria to pay Dorio in l. 557.

PHORMIO [*reappearing*]: I'll just see if Demipho's at home, so
that —

DEMIPHO: Why, we were coming to see you, Phormio.

PHORMIO: On the same old errand, I suppose?

DEMIPHO: That's right.

PHORMIO: I thought as much. Now I wonder *why* you
wanted me?

DEMIPHO: Don't be silly.

PHORMIO: Were you afraid that I shouldn't carry out what
I'd undertaken? Kindly note that though my means may be
of the smallest, I have always endeavoured to be a man of
my word.

CHREMES [*sarcastically*]: Didn't I tell you he was the perfect
gentleman?

DEMIPHO: Quite so.

PHORMIO: I am on my way now, Demipho, to tell you I am
ready; you can hand my bride over any time you like. I
postponed all my personal affairs, as was only proper, when
I saw you were both so anxious for this marriage.

DEMIPHO: But my brother here has persuaded me not to give
her to you; he reminds me what people will say if I do: that
I didn't do so at the time when I could have done without
loss of reputation, and to turn her out of the house now
would create a scandal. In fact, his arguments are much the
same as the ones you used against me yourself earlier on.

PHORMIO: You can't make a fool of me in this high-handed
way!

DEMIPHO: What do you mean?

PHORMIO: You know very well I shan't be able to marry the
other girl either. I should never have the face to go back
after I treated her so badly.

CHREMES [*prompting* DEMIPHO]: Say 'And now I find that
Antipho is unwilling to part with her'.

DEMIPHO: And now I find my son is most unwilling to part with his wife. Please come across to the bank and have the money transferred back into my account.

PHORMIO: But I've already drawn it to pay my debts.

DEMIPHO [*at a loss*]: What are we to do then?

PHORMIO [*with injured dignity*]: If you intend to give me the bride you promised, Demipho, I will marry her; but if you really wish her to stay with you, the dowry stays with me. It is not right that I should be cheated on your account, gentlemen, especially as it was to safeguard your position that I broke with another girl who was going to bring me the same sum.

DEMIPHO: Go to hell with your high and mighty airs, you miserable creature! Do you imagine we don't know you and your doings?

PHORMIO: Don't provoke me.

DEMIPHO: Would you marry her if she were offered you?

PHORMIO: Try me!

DEMIPHO: This is all a plot between you and Antipho; he's going to live with her in your house!

PHORMIO: What *are* you talking about?

DEMIPHO: You hand over my money!

PHORMIO: No, you hand over my wife!

DEMIPHO [*seizing him*]: Then come to court –

PHORMIO [*disengaging himself*]: If you people continue to be so offensive –

DEMIPHO: What will you do?

PHORMIO [*meaningly*]: Aha! Maybe you think it's only penniless girls whose cause I champion. . . . Well, I'm interested in women of property too.

CHREMES: That's no concern of ours.

PHORMIO: No, none at all. [*Slowly*] I knew a lady here whose husband had –

CHREMES: What?

DEMIPHO: What's that?

PHORMIO: – another wife in Lemnos –

CHREMES [*aside*]: I'm done for.

PHORMIO: – by whom he had a daughter. He brought the girl up secretly. . . .

CHREMES [*aside*]: It's the end of me.

PHORMIO [*with relish*]: And that's the story I intend to tell to her [*indicating* CHREMES' *house*] in – all – its – details.

CHREMES: No, no, please don't.

PHORMIO: Well, well. Could you be that man?

DEMIPHO: He's only fooling.

CHREMES: We'll let you off.

PHORMIO: Rubbish!

CHREMES: What do you want for yourself? We'll make you a present of the money in your possession.

PHORMIO: And I'll accept your offer. What the devil do you mean, putting me off with all this shilly-shallying like a pair of stupid children? 'I won't, I will: then, I will, I won't; take it, give it back; take what's said as unsaid, cancel what was just agreed.'

[*He turns to go.*]

CHREMES [*to* DEMIPHO]: How did he find out? Who told him?

DEMIPHO: I've no idea. I only know I told no one.

CHREMES: Damn it all, it's uncanny.

PHORMIO [*aside*]: That's stung them.

DEMIPHO: But is this man to have the laugh on us quite openly and make off with all that cash? I'd rather die. Just you be a man and show some presence of mind. You can see your misdeeds are out and can't be kept from your wife; she's bound to hear the news from someone, and it would be easier to placate her if we told her ourselves. Then we can deal with this filthy brute in our own way.

PHORMIO [*aside*]: I'm caught if I don't look out. They'll round on me in desperation.

CHREMES: But I very much doubt if she *can* be placated.

DEMIPHO: Courage, Chremes. I'll see you're reconciled. After all, the girl's mother is out of the way.

PHORMIO [*coming back*]: Is this how you treat me? Artful pair, aren't you. My God, Demipho, you don't do your brother much good, trying my patience like this. Well, Chremes: you took your pleasure abroad, without scruple or thought for your excellent wife to restrain you from insulting her in this unheard-of fashion. Are you coming now with prayers on your lips to wash away your sins? I've something to tell her which will spark off such a blaze of fury that you'll never put it out, not even if you dissolve into tears.

DEMIPHO: May all the powers of heaven see him damned! I never heard of such colossal cheek. The law should have him deported – a desert island's the place for him.

CHREMES [*hopelessly*]: I'm reduced to such a state I can't think *what* to do with him.

DEMIPHO: I know; let's take him to court.

PHORMIO [*insolently*]: Certainly; set up court in there [*moving to* CHREMES' *house*].

CHREMES: After him, hold him, while I call out the servants!

DEMIPHO [*seizing* PHORMIO]: I can't by myself – quick, help me!

PHORMIO [*struggling*]: I'll have the law on you for assault!

DEMIPHO: All right, you can.

PHORMIO [*as* CHREMES *catches hold of him*]: And on you, Chremes.

CHREMES: Take him off –

PHORMIO: Oh, would you. Very well, I'll try shouting. Nausistrata! Come out!

CHREMES [*frantically*]: Shut your dirty mouth! Oh, how strong he is.

PHORMIO: Nausistrata!

DEMIPHO: Be quiet.

PHORMIO: Why should I?

DEMIPHO: If he won't come, punch him in the belly.

PHORMIO: Knock an eye out if you like. There's a proper punishment coming to you – both of you.

[*He struggles free as* NAUSISTRATA *comes out of* CHREMES' *house.*]

NAUSISTRATA: Who's calling me? Goodness me, Chremes, what's all this about?

PHORMIO [*triumphantly*]: Aha! Struck dumb now, are you?

NAUSISTRATA: Who's that man? Why don't you answer me?

PHORMIO: How can he answer you? He doesn't know where he is.

CHREMES [*his teeth chattering with fright*]: D–don't you b–believe a word he says.

PHORMIO: Go on, touch him. Strike me dead if you don't find him frozen stiff.

CHREMES [*trying to control himself*]: It's n–nothing.

NAUSISTRATA: Then what is it? What's he talking about?

PHORMIO: You'll soon know; just listen.

CHREMES: Must you believe him?

NAUSISTRATA: What's there to believe when he hasn't spoken yet?

PHORMIO: Poor creature, he's crazed with fear.

NAUSISTRATA: There must be something wrong, to frighten you like this.

CHREMES: Who says I'm frightened?

PHORMIO: That's a good one! No, you're not frightened, and there's nothing in what I say – so *you* tell her.

DEMIPHO: Not at your bidding, you scoundrel!

PHORMIO: Now, now, Demipho, you've done a good job for your brother.

NAUSISTRATA: Chremes, please won't you tell me?

CHREMES: But—

NAUSISTRATA: But what?

CHREMES: There's no need to tell.

PHORMIO: No need to tell *you*, maybe; but *she* should know. On Lemnos—

DEMIPHO: Look here—

CHREMES: Will you be quiet?

PHORMIO: —unknown to you—

CHREMES [*aside*]: O woe!

PHORMIO: —he married a wife.

NAUSISTRATA: My good man, you must be crazy.

PHORMIO: It's the truth.

NAUSISTRATA: No, no, that's too much.

PHORMIO: Then he had a daughter by her. All the time you slept soundly.

CHREMES: What are we to do?

NAUSISTRATA: Gracious heavens, what a monstrous, wicked thing!

PHORMIO [*to* CHREMES]: Do? Nothing. It's too late.

NAUSISTRATA: Could anything be more cruelly unfair? It's only when they're with their *wives* that men can remember their age. Demipho, I appeal to you; I'm too disgusted to speak to him. Is this the explanation of all those journeys and long visits to Lemnos? Are these the low prices which reduced my profits?

DEMIPHO [*uncomfortably*]: I'm not denying he's to blame in this, Nausistrata, but perhaps you should forgive him—

PHORMIO: And that's the last word on him!

DEMIPHO: He didn't do anything out of disregard or dislike

of you. It all happened about fifteen years ago, when he was drunk. ... He seduced this woman, and then the girl was born ... but he never touched her after that. Now she's dead, which takes away a lot of the difficulty, so I do beg you to show your usual good sense and take this calmly.

NAUSISTRATA: How can I take it calmly? I should like to see the end of my troubles in this sorry matter, but what hope have I of doing so? Are advancing years likely to improve his future behaviour? If old age makes men better behaved – well, he wasn't young *then*. Am I younger now and more attractive than I was? What reason can you give, Demipho, for me to have better hopes and expectations that this won't happen again?

PHORMIO [*loudly*]: All who should attend Chremes' funeral kindly note the time has come! Now then: anyone want to challenge Phormio? All right, let him come. I'll see he suffers the same misfortune as this man. [*In his normal voice*] Very well, restore him to favour; my vengeance is satisfied. His wife'll have something to whine about in his ear for the rest of his life.

NAUSISTRATA: I suppose he'll say I deserve this! Have I to start now, Demipho, and tell you in detail all I've been to him?

DEMIPHO: No, no, I know it all as well as you do.

NAUSISTRATA: And do you think I deserve this?

DEMIPHO: Certainly not. But you can't mend matters by this sort of accusation, so you'd best forgive him. He confesses, apologizes and begs for mercy. What more do you want?

PHORMIO [*aside*]: Quick, before she forgives him – I must look out for myself and Phaedria. [*Aloud*] Madam, before you give a hasty answer, please listen to me.

NAUSISTRATA: What is it?

PHORMIO [*with emphasis*]: I tricked your husband out of three thousand drachmas and gave them to your son. He's already paid them over to the dealer to buy the girl who's his mistress.

CHREMES: What's that you're saying?

NAUSISTRATA [icily]: Surely you can't blame your son who's a young man for keeping a single mistress when you have two wives? Oh, you're shameless! Have you really the face to rebuke him? Answer me.

DEMIPHO [hastily]: Chremes will do anything you like.

NAUSISTRATA: No; first you can hear what I have to say. I don't forgive you, Chremes, and I'm making no promises and giving no answers until I've seen Phaedria. Everything rests on his decision; I shall do what he advises.

PHORMIO: You're a wise woman, madam.

NAUSISTRATA: Does that satisfy you?

PHORMIO: Yes indeed. I'm getting off lightly, much better than I expected.

NAUSISTRATA: Please tell me your name.

PHORMIO: My name's Phormio: a good friend of the family, and a very good one to your son Phaedria.

NAUSISTRATA: Phormio, from now on I will say and do anything I can to further your wishes.

PHORMIO: You're very kind.

NAUSISTRATA: No more than you deserve.

PHORMIO: Would you like to begin today, madam, and do something which will be a pleasure to me – and a slap in the eye for your husband?

NAUSISTRATA: I certainly would.

PHORMIO: Then invite me to dinner.

NAUSISTRATA: Of course; I invite you now.

DEMIPHO: Let us go in then.

NAUSISTRATA: We're coming. But where's Phaedria? We await his opinion.

PHORMIO: I'll fetch him at once. [*To the audience*] Farewell, and give us your applause.

> [PHORMIO *goes off right, to his house, where* PHAEDRIA *is hiding;* DEMIPHO *escorts* NAUSISTRATA *into her house;* CHREMES, *quite ignored, slowly follows them.*]

THE MOTHER-IN-LAW

[HECYRA]

INTRODUCTORY NOTE

The Mother-in-Law is generally considered to be Terence's fifth play, though the first production notice says that its first failure was in 165 B.C., after *The Girl from Andros*, and its final successful production was after *The Brothers*. The two production notices and the discrepancy between Donatus and the production notice on the subject of its Greek model point to recollections of different productions. It must have been a play which Terence and his producer valued, or they would not have persisted in reviving it after two failures. It is certainly Terence's most original play, with its close-knit plot, absence of comic fooling, clearly defined characterization, and economy of dialogue pruned down to a mere 880 lines. It has generally won admiration, and critics have judged it to be the prototype of serious domestic comedy.

The problem is a common one: a marriage is breaking down and the two families involved are trying to save it. Everyone is acting for the best, but the comedy arises out of the fact that the truth of the situation is withheld even from the audience until the final scene. So the young man's harassed father vents his feelings on his wife, and she is prepared to leave home if it will help towards a reconciliation. The girl's mother stands by her daughter and adds to the confusion by trying to conceal things from her husband. The young wife, though never seen, becomes a personality through what different people say about her, and her young husband's character is sympathetically drawn in depth, his self-pity in his first scene being ousted by a new restraint and consideration for others along with increasing self-awareness when he is confronted by a real crisis. Throughout Terence observes people's reactions to an

unforeseen situation with a good deal of quiet humour –
the two fathers' delight in a grandchild and the new problem
presented to Pamphilus thereby, and Bacchis's calm mastery of
her scene with Laches contain some of the best passages he ever
wrote.

This is a play in which the women provide the chief interest
– the two mothers, the girl, and especially the courtesan
Bacchis, whose charm and dignity are shown by contrast with
Laches' clumsy approach and Pamphilus's youthful self-
centredness, as well as by the vulgarity of the pair in the opening scene who lead us to expect someone quite different.
Bacchis has no counterpart in literature, though according to
Livy (39.9–18) there was a fairly close parallel in history just
before Terence was born. Hispala Fecenna, the courtesan
freedwoman who gave evidence at the inquiry into the
Bacchanalian orgies in Rome in 189 B.C., had been genuinely
in love with her young neighbour Aebutius, had supported
him in the face of opposition from his family, and had made
him her heir.

PRODUCTION NOTICE I

THE MOTHER-IN-LAW by Terence: performed at the Megalensian Games during the curule aedileship of Sextus Julius Caesar and Gnaeus Cornelius Dolabella.[1]

Music composed by Flaccus, slave of Claudius, for equal pipes throughout.

Greek original by Menander.[2]

The author's fifth play.

First performance without a prologue.

Second performance during the consulship of Gnaeus Octavius and Titus Manlius, at the funeral games for Lucius Aemilius Paulus:[3] a failure.

Third performance during the curule aedileship of Quintus Fulvius and Lucius Marcius, produced by Lucius Ambivius and Lucius Sergius Turpio: a success.[4]

1. i.e. in April 165 B.C.
2. Both Donatus and Eugraphius say that Apollodorus of Carystus was the model for this play.
3. i.e. 160 B.C. L. Aemilius Paullus Macedonicus was the victor at the battle of Pydna; his younger son was adopted into the Scipio family and was Terence's patron. See Introduction, p. 14. The incorrect spelling appears in all the Production Notices.
4. Also in 160 B.C.

PRODUCTION NOTICE II

THE MOTHER-IN-LAW by Terence: performed at the Roman Games[1] during the curule aedileship of Sextus Julius Caesar and Gnaeus Cornelius, but withdrawn unfinished.

Music composed by Flaccus, slave of Claudius, for a pair of pipes throughout.

Second performance during the consulship of Gnaeus Octavius and Titus Manlius, at the funeral games for Lucius Aemilius Paulus.

Third performance during the curule aedileship of Quintus Fulvius and Lucius Martius.

1. Held annually in September in honour of Jupiter.

SYNOPSIS

Pamphilus marries Philumena, the girl he once assaulted, without knowing who she is and that it is her ring he took by force and gave to his mistress, the courtesan Bacchis. He then departs for Imbros without consummating the marriage. She is pregnant; her mother pretends she is ill and takes her home in order to conceal this from her mother-in-law. Pamphilus returns to find a baby born and keeps the secret, but refuses to take back his wife. His father accuses him of continuing his affair with Bacchis, but she refutes the charge. Meanwhile the girl's mother, Myrrina, happens to recognize the ring. Pamphilus then takes back his wife with their son.

CHARACTERS

LACHES
PHIDIPPUS } *elderly neighbours in Athens*

SOSTRATA *wife of Laches*

MYRRINA *wife of Phidippus*

PAMPHILUS *son of Laches and Sostrata, married to Philumena,*
daughter of Phidippus and Myrrina

SYRA *an old bawd*

PHILOTIS *a young prostitute*

BACCHIS *a courtesan, lately mistress of Pamphilus*

PARMENO *Laches' elderly house-slave*

SOSIA *slave of Laches*

Two other slaves

A nurse

Philumena does not appear

*

The scene is laid in Athens in front of the houses of Laches and
Phidippus. To the audience's right the street leads to the centre of
the town, to the left to the house of Bacchis and the harbour

AUTHOR'S PROLOGUE
TO THE SECOND PRODUCTION

THE title of this play is *The Mother-in-Law*. When it was first produced as a new play, it was interrupted by a novel form of mischance and disaster: it could neither be seen nor heard through the stupid whim of the public whose interest was taken up by a tight-rope walker. Today it is presented as a genuinely new play. The author had no intention of repeating the former production so that he could sell it a second time. You have known other plays by him, so please hear this one.

AUTHOR'S PROLOGUE
TO THE THIRD PRODUCTION

(Spoken by Lucius Ambivius Turpio)[1]

IN the guise of a prologue I stand before you to plead my case. Let me prevail on you to allow me in my old age to enjoy the just treatment I received in my youth; then I always managed to ensure the survival of plays whose novelty brought them failure at first, and so stopped an author's work from dying with him. When I first played in new plays by Caecilius,[2] I was sometimes hissed off the stage and sometimes I just managed to hold my ground. I realized the hazards of an actor's career and decided to set my uncertain hopes a definite task. I began to repeat the same plays, as a way of introducing new ones by the same author, always with the aim of not discouraging his efforts. I succeeded in putting these on the stage; once they were known they were a success. So I restored the poet to his proper position, after the ill-will of his enemies had almost driven him from his intentions, his profession and the whole art of drama. But if at the time I had poured scorn on his work and set out to discourage him, so that his activity dwindled to nothing, I could easily have deterred him from writing any new plays.

Now for my sake give a fair hearing to my plea. Once more I am presenting *The Mother-in-Law*, a play for which I have never been able to gain a hearing uninterrupted, so much has misfortune dogged its progress. You can remedy this by your understanding, if you will support our efforts. At the first

1. Terence's producer and leading actor.
2. Caecilius Statius, d. 168 B.C. See Introduction, p. 12, and Appendix A, p. 389.

production, much talk of some boxers, as well as the rumour that a tight-rope walker would appear, the mob of their supporters, shouting and women's screaming forced me off the stage before the end. I then decided to follow my old practice with this new play and try it out. I put it on a second time. The first part was doing well when news arrived that there was to be a gladiators' show. In surged the people, pushing, shouting, jostling for a place, leaving me powerless to hold my own.

Today there is no distraction, all is calm and peaceful; this is my chance to present the play and your opportunity to do honour to the stage. Do not be responsible for allowing the art of drama to sink into the hands of a few: make sure that your influence aids and supports my own. If I have never been greedy in putting a price on my profession, and have always held that my highest reward was to be wholly at your service, grant my plea on behalf of the author, who has entrusted his interests to my protection and his future to your own sense of honour. Do not let him be cheated and derided by unjust men. For my sake, give my plea a hearing, and listen in silence. Others will then feel encouraged to write, and it will be profitable for me in future to present new plays bought at my own expense.

[*The girl* PHILOTIS *and the elderly woman* SYRA *come on right, talking together.*]

PHILOTIS: Talking of lovers, Syra, precious few of them prove faithful to girls like me. Take Pamphilus for instance; he promised Bacchis no end of times that he'd never take a wife as long as she lived, swore it on oath so that anyone might have believed him. Now look at him – married.

SYRA: That's just why I'm always telling you not to be soft-hearted with anyone. You mark my words, catch whom you can, then rob him, fleece him, and skin him alive.

PHILOTIS: Can't there be exceptions?

SYRA: Certainly not. Nobody comes to you, you may be sure, who doesn't intend to wheedle you into letting him have his pleasure as cheaply as he can. You'd better see about setting your traps to get your own back, my girl.

PHILOTIS: All the same, it seems wrong to treat all men alike.

SYRA: Wrong to get your own back on your enemies? Wrong to trip them up like they'd trip you? Goodness me, I wish I were your age and had your looks, or else you had my sense.

[PARMENO, *an elderly slave, comes out of* LACHES' *house talking to someone inside.*]

PARMENO: If the old man asks for me, say I've just gone down to the harbour to find out when Pamphilus is expected. Are you listening, boy? Only if he *asks*, mind; if he doesn't ask, say nothing, and the excuse can keep for another time. Why, here's little Philotis! Where's she sprung from? How are you, my dear?

PHILOTIS: How are you, Parmeno?

SYRA: Good morning, Parmeno.

PARMENO: Good morning to you, Syra. [*Gallantly*] Well, well, Philotis, where have you been having fun all this time?

PHILOTIS: Having fun? Far from it! A brute of a soldier took me off to Corinth, and there I've had two years' continuous hell.

PARMENO: I'm sure you missed Athens, my pet, and cursed the day you thought of leaving us!

PHILOTIS: I've been longing to come back, I can't tell you how much, dying to get away from *him* and see you all again, and be with you all free and easy like we always were. There I couldn't say a word without being told first what *he* wanted.

PARMENO: I should like to see the soldier who could stop *you* talking, my dear.

PHILOTIS: I've just been to see Bacchis – what's all this she told me? I could never have believed your master would take it into his head to marry while she was alive.

PARMENO: Marry, did you say?

PHILOTIS: Well, isn't he married?

PARMENO: I suppose he is, but it's a broken-down sort of marriage, if you ask me.

PHILOTIS: I hope to God it is, if that will help Bacchis. But tell me why I'm to believe that, Parmeno.

PARMENO: It's not a story to spread around, so you needn't ask.

PHILOTIS: I suppose you're afraid it'll become public property, but I swear to heaven I'm not asking you because I want to spread it around – I only want to enjoy it myself. I shan't say a word.

PARMENO: Well said, but you'll never catch me risking my skin on *your* word of honour.

PHILOTIS: Come off it, Parmeno. You know you're as keen to tell me as I am to hear – and more so.

PARMENO [*aside*]: She's got me there. It's my worst fault. [*Aloud*] If you promise not to breathe a word, I'll tell you.

PHILOTIS: That's more like you! I promise: go on.

PARMENO: Listen.

PHILOTIS: I *am* listening.

PARMENO: Pamphilus was just as much in love with Bacchis as ever when his father began to beg him to take a wife. The old man used the same arguments as all fathers do – he was getting on, he only had one son, and he wanted security for his old age. The boy refused flat at first, but when his father pressed him still harder he began to waver between his duty to his parents and his love. In the end he got fed up with being pestered, and let the old man have his way and fix up a marriage with the daughter of our next-door neighbour here. Pamphilus didn't really take it seriously till the actual day of the wedding when he saw all the preparations made and realized it couldn't be put off. Then it came home to him at last and his misery would have won sympathy from Bacchis herself, had she been there. He would steal off by himself whenever he could, and talk to me alone. 'Parmeno, I'm lost!' he would cry; 'What have I done? What a mess I've got myself into . . . I can't bear it. Oh, Parmeno, I'm so miserable!'

PHILOTIS: To hell with that interfering old fool Laches!

PARMENO: To cut it short, he married the girl and took her home, but he never touched her that night nor the night after.

PHILOTIS: You aren't telling me that a young man could spend a night with a girl after a few drinks and keep off her? A likely story! I don't believe it.

PARMENO: I don't suppose you do, seeing that it's only desire that brings men to you; but this was an unwilling bride-groom.

PHILOTIS: Well, what happened next?

PARMENO: A few days later Pamphilus took me out of the house and told me that the girl was still a virgin and that before he married her he was hopeful that he could become reconciled to the marriage. 'But now I've decided that I just can't live with her any longer, it seems neither honest on my part nor good for the girl to carry on with this farce and not return her to her parents in the state I received her.'

PHILOTIS: He sounds a decent fellow with the right sort of ideas.

PARMENO: 'On the other hand it won't do me any good to publish the facts,' he said; 'it would only be an insult to return a bride to her father when there's nothing against her. What I'm hoping is that when she finds I'm impossible to live with she'll end by going away herself.'

PHILOTIS: Meanwhile what about Bacchis? Did he go on seeing her?

PARMENO: Every day. But naturally when she saw he was no longer all her own she became much more demanding and grudging of her favours.

PHILOTIS: Not surprising.

PARMENO: But what really broke things up between them was when Pamphilus began to have a better understanding of himself, Bacchis, and the wife he had at home, and started to think about the characters of the two women and the example they set him. His wife was modest and retiring, as a lady ought to be; she bore with all her husband's unkind-ness and unfair treatment, and said nothing of his insults. His heart was won, partly through pity for his wife and partly because his mistress's unkindness wore him down, until he gradually drifted from Bacchis and transferred his love to the one whose disposition he found more like his own. Meanwhile an elderly relative died in Imbros, leaving the family his legal heirs. Pamphilus was packed off there by his father, protesting and in love, and left his wife here with his mother, Sostrata. His old father has buried himself in the country and rarely comes to town.

PHILOTIS [*bored*]: Are we ever coming to the breakdown of this marriage?

PARMENO: I'm coming to it now. For the first few days the women got on well enough together, but all the time the girl was developing an extraordinary dislike for her mother-in-law, not that there was any quarrelling or complaint from either of them.

PHILOTIS: What then?

PARMENO: If Sostrata ever came to her for a chat, she'd disappear at once and refuse to see her, and in the end when she couldn't stand it any longer, she pretended her own mother wanted her for some religious ceremony and went off. She stayed away several days and then Sostrata sent for her, but she made some excuse. Sostrata sent again; no one brought her back. After repeated summons, the excuse came that she was ill. Thereupon my mistress went to visit her and was refused admittance. When the master heard of it he came back from the country, yesterday that was, and met Philumena's father at once. I haven't heard yet what passed between them, but I can't wait to know how it will all end. That's the whole story. I'll be on my way.

PHILOTIS: Me too; I've got a date booked with a friend from abroad.

PARMENO: Good luck to you then.

PHILOTIS: Bye-bye, Parmeno.

PARMENO: Good-bye to you, my dear.

[*He goes off left and* SYRA *and she go off in the other direction.*

Almost immediately LACHES *bursts out of his house in a fury,
followed by* SOSTRATA *in tears.*]

LACHES: Heaven and earth, what a tribe they are! In league
the lot of them. Every blessed woman with the same likes
and dislikes as all the others, and not a single one can you
find who'll show up a different mentality from the rest!
Mothers-in-law and daughters-in-law, they're all of one
mind – in hating each other. And they're all of a piece, too,
in setting themselves against their men-folk, the same
damned obstinacy in every one. I'd say they'd all learned
their cussedness at the same school, and if there *is* such a
school I can tell you who's head-mistress: my wife.

SOSTRATA: Oh dear, what am I accused of now? I can't
think.

LACHES: Can't you?

SOSTRATA: I can't, Laches, heaven help me and spare us to
live together in peace.

LACHES: Heaven forbid!

SOSTRATA: Some day you'll find how unjustly I'm accused.

LACHES: Unjustly? You? Is there any word to fit your conduct? You're bringing disgrace on yourself and me and the
family and grief to your son – making enemies out of his
new relatives who were our friends and had thought our son
was a fit person to receive their child. You stand out as a
trouble-maker, you and your shameless behaviour!

SOSTRATA: *I*?

LACHES: Yes, you, woman. Do you suppose I've no feelings?
Am I not flesh and blood? Because I'm mostly at the farm,
do you women think I don't know how each one of you is
spending her time? I'm much more alive to the goings-on
here than to what happens where I usually am, and shall I
tell you why? My reputation abroad depends on how you
behave at home. I heard long ago that Philumena had taken

242] THE MOTHER-IN-LAW 301

a dislike to you, and no wonder; I'd have wondered if she hadn't. But I didn't believe she could extend her dislike to the whole household – if I'd known that, she should have stayed here, and you could have taken yourself off. [*Softening a little*] Sostrata, can't you see how little I deserve this distress you cause me? I went to live at the farm out of consideration for you, to look after our affairs so that our income could meet the expenses of a comfortable life for you and the boy; I'm always working, harder than is right and proper for my age. In return, you might have thought of trying to save me from worry.

SOSTRATA [*sobbing*]: It's not my doing, it's not my fault this has happened.

LACHES: But that's exactly what it was, Sostrata; you were here alone, and it can only be all your fault. I relieved you of all the other responsibilities, and you should be responsible for things here. A woman of your age ought to be ashamed of starting a quarrel with a girl! Or will you say it was her fault?

SOSTRATA: No, my dear Laches, I don't say that.

LACHES: Thank heaven for that, for my son's sake. I fancy *you*'ve no reputation to lose whatever wrong you do.

SOSTRATA: How do you know she didn't pretend to dislike me so that she could be more with her mother?

LACHES: Nonsense; surely it's proof enough that when you wanted to call on her yesterday no one would let you in.

SOSTRATA: Not necessarily. They said she was very tired at the time, and that was why I couldn't come in.

LACHES: It was something in *you* which made her ill, nothing else I'm sure, and no wonder; all you women want your sons to marry, and only the matches you fancy are arranged; then when you've pushed them into taking wives it's you who push them into getting rid of them.

302 THE MOTHER-IN-LAW [243

[PHIDIPPUS *comes out of his house speaking to* PHILUMENA *indoors.*]

PHIDIPPUS: I know I have the right to compel you to obey my orders, Philumena, but I'm too soft-hearted a father and always give in. All right, have it your own way.

LACHES [*aside*]: Good, here's Phidippus. Now I'll learn the truth. [*Stiffly, as* PHIDIPPUS *comes forward*] Phidippus, I know I may be indulgent to an extreme towards all the members of my family, but not to the extent of allowing my compliance to ruin their character. If you were to follow my example, it would be in your own interests as well as in ours. As things are, I see your women have you under their thumb.

PHIDIPPUS [*indignantly*]: Indeed!

LACHES: Yesterday I called on you for information about your daughter: you sent me away no wiser than I came. If you wish this connection between our families to continue, it is most unbecoming conduct on your part to leave your resentment unexplained. If there has been any fault on our side, kindly name it; we can then disprove it or apologize and make such amends to your family as you think suitable. But if your reason for detaining your daughter is that she is ill, and you fear she will not be sufficiently well cared for in my house, I take it as a personal insult. Heaven be my witness, I cannot allow that you care more for her welfare, though you are her father, than I do myself; what is more, I do so on my son's behalf, knowing as I do that he values her more highly than his own life. I am only too well aware how seriously he will take this if he comes to hear of it; that is why I am anxious for her to come back to us before he returns home.

PHIDIPPUS: Laches, I know the care and kindness to be found in your home, and I am ready to believe that everything you say is as you say. Please believe me now when I say that I am anxious for her to return to you if I can prevail on her in any way.

LACHES: What is stopping you? You don't mean she has anything against her husband?

PHIDIPPUS: No, no. When I pressed her and tried to compel her to return she swore on oath she could not endure living in your home while Pamphilus was away. I suppose we all have our own faults, and I know I've always been a mild sort of man and simply can't set myself against my family.

LACHES: Well, Sostrata?

SOSTRATA [*with renewed tears*]: Oh I'm so unhappy!

LACHES [*to* PHIDIPPUS]: That's definite on your side?

PHIDIPPUS: For the moment it looks as if it is. And now, if you'll excuse me, I have business in town.

LACHES: I'll go with you.

[*They go off right together.*]

SOSTRATA: There's no justice in the way our men detest all women alike, simply on account of a few wives whose behaviour brings disgrace on us all. I swear to heaven I'm innocent of what my husband accuses me – but it's no easy matter to clear myself when they've got it into their heads that all mothers-in-law are unkind. I *know* I'm not: I've always treated the girl as my own daughter, and I just can't think how this could happen to me. All I can do is wait and hope for my son's return.

[*She goes back into her house. After a pause* PAMPHILUS *comes on left, talking to* PARMENO.]

PAMPHILUS: I don't believe there was ever a man who suffered so much in love as I do. Just my luck! Is this the life I've tried not to throw away? Was this the reason why I was so keen to be home again? I'd far rather live in any hole than come back here and find things in this state. Oh misery! If there's trouble ahead for any of us, all the time spent before it's known is that much gained.

PARMENO: Maybe; but this way you're more likely to find a quicker way out of your troubles. If you hadn't come, this resentment would have gone on mounting; as it is, I fancy your arrival will make both of them reflect. You can learn the facts, settle their differences, and restore good humour all round. You're making far too much of trifles.

PAMPHILUS [*gloomily*]: You needn't try cheering me up. I tell you no one has such wretched luck. Before I married I lost my heart in another affair, but I never dared refuse the wife my father thrust on me. Anyone can see without being told what a rotten situation *that* was for me. I had scarcely broken with her and freed myself from this entanglement – and I'd just begun to transfer my affections to my wife – when something new happened to take me away from *her*. Now I suppose I'll find either my mother or my wife's to blame, and doesn't that mean further misery? I ought to bear with my mother's faults as her son, but then I owe something to my wife; she's been patient with me from the beginning, and never breathed a word anywhere about all she had to put up with from me. But whatever happened, Parmeno, it must have been something serious to stir up ill-feeling between them which has lasted so long.

PARMENO: Nonsense, it's nothing. If you'll only think it over properly you'll see that the worst quarrels don't always mean the biggest wrongs; for it often happens that one man may find nothing to irritate him in a situation which would turn a more irascible type into your worst enemy. Children lose their tempers over little things simply because they have so little self-control, and these women are like children – no sound sense at all. It may have taken no more than a word to start this quarrel.

PAMPHILUS: Go in then, Parmeno, and tell them I'm here.
[*Noises inside* PHIDIPPUS'*s house.*]

PARMENO: What on earth's that?

PAMPHILUS: Shh. . . . I can hear hurrying and running to and fro.

PARMENO: Just let me get nearer the door. Did you hear that?

PAMPHILUS: Shut up. God, I heard a scream.

PARMENO: Shut up yourself, if I must.

MYRRINA [*inside*]: Hush, please hush, my dear.

PAMPHILUS: That sounded like Philumena's mother. Oh, this is too much!

PARMENO: Why?

PAMPHILUS: I can't bear it!

PARMENO: Can't bear what?

PAMPHILUS: I'm sure it's something awful which they're keeping from me.

PARMENO: They did say something about your wife having shivering fits. . . . It might be that. I don't know.

PAMPHILUS: No, no, not that! Why didn't you tell me?

PARMENO [*sulkily*]: I can't be telling everything at once.

PAMPHILUS: What's wrong with her?

PARMENO: Don't know.

PAMPHILUS: Hasn't anyone called in a doctor?

PARMENO: Don't know.

PAMPHILUS: I'm going in straightaway to get to the bottom of this. Philumena, my darling, how shall I find you? If you're in danger, I can only die with you. [*He hurries into the house.*]

PARMENO: No good now my following him in; they hate the whole lot of us I think – yesterday they refused to let my mistress in. If this is some serious illness (though I hope not for the young master's sake) they'll say at once one of Sostrata's servants has been in the house, and then they'll

cook up a tale of something brought in to endanger the
health and life of the whole damn lot of them. Then more
blame for my mistress and a pack of trouble for me.

[SOSTRATA *comes out of her house.*]

SOSTRATA: I'm so worried by the noises I keep hearing next
door – I can't help fearing Philumena's illness has taken a
turn for the worse. Gods of healing,[1] I pray this may not be.
. . . Now I *must* see her.

PARMENO: Madam –

SOSTRATA: Who's that?

PARMENO: – you'll find the door slammed again.

SOSTRATA: Oh, Parmeno, is that you? This is terrible; what
can I do? Mayn't I visit my son's wife when she's lying ill
next door?

PARMENO: Better not – nor send round anyone else, I'd say.
Love in return for hatred is double stupidity: useless effort
on your part and a bore to the other. Besides, your son's
here and went in at once to find out what's up.

SOSTRATA: What did you say? Is Pamphilus back?

PARMENO: Yes.

SOSTRATA: Thank God for that! This puts heart in me and
takes a load off my mind.

PARMENO: And that's the real reason why I don't want you to
go in just now. If Philumena feels a little better, as soon as
they are alone together I'm sure she'll tell him the whole
story of what came between you and how this ill-feeling
started. But here he is coming out again – *and* looking
ghastly.

[PAMPHILUS *comes out of the house, obviously much
shocked.*]

SOSTRATA: My son!

1. She calls on Aesculapius, Greek Asclepios, the god of healing, and
Salus, a personification of welfare and a purely Roman deity.

PAMPHILUS: Mother!

SOSTRATA: Oh, I'm glad to see you safely home. Is Philumena all right?

PAMPHILUS [*with difficulty*]: A bit better.

SOSTRATA: God help her. . . . But why are you in tears? What has upset you so?

PAMPHILUS: It's all right, mother.

SOSTRATA: What was the noise? Please tell me; was it a sudden attack of pain?

PAMPHILUS: That's right.

SOSTRATA: What exactly is the matter with her?

PAMPHILUS: A fever.

SOSTRATA: The recurrent kind?

PAMPHILUS: So they say. Please go in, mother, I'll join you soon.

SOSTRATA: Very well. [*She goes in.*]

PAMPHILUS: Parmeno, run and meet the boys and help them with the luggage.

PARMENO: Why? Don't they know their own way home?

PAMPHILUS [*at the end of his tether*]: Clear off!

　　[PARMENO *goes off left.*]

PAMPHILUS: I don't know where to begin – it's all so unexpected: where can I start on all I've seen and heard? I had to get out of the house. . . . I'm just about dead. It seems only a minute since I hurried in full of fears, expecting to see my wife suffering from something quite different from what I found. Ah! [*he groans*]. The maids saw me coming and all cried out for joy as I took them by surprise: 'He's come!' Next moment I saw their faces all change because I'd chanced to come at such a bad time. One of them hurried on ahead to say I was there, and I followed hard after, all eagerness to see my wife. I saw what was wrong with her the minute I was in her room – more's the pity – there

wasn't time to cover it up and in her condition she couldn't
control her cries. I took one look, shouted something at her
for her wickedness, and fled in tears, shocked and stunned
by the incredible truth. Her mother ran after me, caught me
up at the door, and fell on her knees, weeping, poor soul. I
was touched; the fact is, I think, all of us are proud or
humble only as circumstances permit. Then she began to
speak: 'Oh my dear Pamphilus, now you see why she left
your house. She was assaulted before you married her – we
don't know the brute's name. She took refuge here to hide
the birth of the child from you and the neighbours.' The
very thought of her words sets my tears flowing again.
'Whatever chance brought you here to us today,' she went
on, 'in the name of Fortune we both beseech you, if the
laws of god and man permit, to keep her misfortune untold
and hidden from the world. Oh Pamphilus, if you have ever
known her love for you, she begs you now to grant her this
favour in return; it will cost you nothing. As for taking her
back, you must do what suits you best. No one but you
knows she's in labour and this baby isn't yours; at least I
presume it can't be, for I'm told it was two months before
she slept with you and it's the seventh month now since she
came to you. I can see you know what the situation is. What
I'm hoping and trying to do now, if it's at all possible, is to
keep the birth secret from her father and all the neighbours.
If it can't be kept from them, I shall have to say the baby is
premature. I don't believe anyone will suspect anything else
when there's no reason to doubt you are its true father. I
shall expose the baby at once; then it shan't be any trouble
to you, and you will have concealed the wrong done to my
poor undeserving child.' Well, I gave my promise and I'm
determined to keep my word. But to take her back! It's all
wrong and I can't do it, however strong the pull of our

companionship and love. . . . These tears spring at the thought of my life in future and my loneliness. . . . Ah, fickle fortune! But I ought to have learned from experience with my old love, which I had to stifle deliberately; now I must do the same again. . . . Here's Parmeno with the boys. He must be kept out of this at all costs, for he's the only person I trusted to know that for the first weeks of marriage I never slept with my wife. If he hears her repeated cries I'm afraid he must guess she is in labour. I'll send him off somewhere until it's all over.

[*He moves back as* PARMENO *and* SOSIA *come on left with slaves carrying luggage.*]

PARMENO: You were saying it was an awful crossing?

SOSIA: Damn me if I can tell you in words just how awful it is on board ship.

PARMENO: Really?

SOSIA: You lucky devil, you don't know what you've escaped by never going to sea. Cut out all the other miseries and take this one – all the thirty days and more I was aboard never a day passed when I wasn't in terror of death. That's the sort of foul weather we were having.

PARMENO: Horrible!

SOSIA: Don't I know it. I'd clear off rather than come home if I thought I had to go back there.

PARMENO: It never took much to make you do what you're threatening now, Sosia. But look, there's Pamphilus outside the house. Go in, all of you, while I see if he wants me. [*To* PAMPHILUS] Still standing around, sir?

PAMPHILUS: I was waiting for you.

PARMENO: What for, sir?

PAMPHILUS: Someone must run up to the acropolis.

PARMENO: Who must?

PAMPHILUS: You.

PARMENO: Up there? Why ever?

PAMPHILUS: Find Callidemides, the man I stayed with on Myconos, who was on the ship with me.

PARMENO [*aside*]: That's the end! The man must have taken a vow that if he ever got home he'd burst my guts with running his errands.

PAMPHILUS: Hurry along now.

PARMENO: What am I to say to him? Or am I just to *find* him?

PAMPHILUS: You're to say I can't keep my engagement to meet him today, so he needn't wait. Be quick.

PARMENO: But I don't know what the man looks like.

PAMPHILUS [*distractedly*]: I'll tell you – a big man, red face, curly hair, fat belly, green eyes – and a face like a corpse.

PARMENO: To hell with him! Suppose he doesn't turn up? Am I to hang around all day?

PAMPHILUS: Yes. Now *run*.

PARMENO [*sulkily*]: I can't run. I'm tired. [*He trails off, right.*]

PAMPHILUS: Now I'm rid of him, but what on earth am I to do? How to conceal this baby's birth I can't think, much as I'd like to do what Myrrina asked; I'm sorry for the poor woman. I'll do what I can, short of disloyalty to my mother, for I must defer to her rather than to my love for Philumena. [*He looks down the street.*] That looks like Phidippus and my father, and they're coming this way ... and I still don't know what to say to them.

[PHIDIPPUS *and* LACHES *come back from the town.*]

LACHES: Do I understand you to say she was waiting for my son's return?

PHIDIPPUS: That's right.

LACHES: I'm told he is here now, so she can come back.

PAMPHILUS [*aside*]: Now what reason can I give my father for not taking her back?

LACHES: Who's that speaking?

PAMPHILUS [*aside*]: I've chosen my road; no turning back now.

LACHES: Why here he is!

PAMPHILUS [*coming forward*]: How are you, father?

LACHES: Welcome back, my son.

PHIDIPPUS: It's good to have you back, Pamphilus, and best of all to see you safe and well.

PAMPHILUS: Thank you, sir.

LACHES: Have you just arrived?

PAMPHILUS: Only a minute ago.

LACHES: Tell me, how much did our cousin Phania leave?

PAMPHILUS: Well, he was obviously a fellow who thought a lot of his pleasures in life, and his type don't do much for their heirs. The best that can be said of their sort of life is 'a good one while it lasted'.

LACHES: So that sentiment is all you've brought back?

PAMPHILUS: And the bit he did leave, which is your gain.

LACHES: Or rather my loss; for I'd rather have him alive and well.

PAMPHILUS [*aside*]: No harm in wishing that when he can't come back to life again, but I fancy I know your real wishes.

LACHES: Yesterday Philumena's father sent for her. [*Nudging him*] Say you sent for her.

PHIDIPPUS: Don't prod me. Yes, I did.

LACHES: Now he'll send her back to us.

PHIDIPPUS: Of course.

PAMPHILUS: I know the whole story. I was told as soon as I landed.

LACHES: Confound all mischief-makers who go out of their way to spread news like that!

PAMPHILUS [*full of injured dignity*]: Phidippus, I am satisfied that I have always been careful not to deserve reproach from your family, and if I wished to recount here and now my fidelity, affection, and sympathy towards your daughter, I could certainly do so, did I not prefer you to hear it from her own lips. The best way of restoring your confidence in my character is for my wife who wrongs me now to do me justice. Heaven is my witness that this separation has come about through no fault of mine. But evidently she thinks it beneath her dignity to give way to my mother and respect her ways with proper deference, and it appears impossible for good relations to be restored between them; so I must choose whether to be separated from my mother or my wife. My sense of duty bids me put the interests of my mother first.

LACHES: Pamphilus, I confess it is good to hear this from you, and to know how you value your mother above everything; but are you sure resentment against your wife is not driving you to take up a wrong attitude?

PAMPHILUS [with emotion]: What resentment could drive me to be unjust to her, father? She has never done anything I could dislike to me personally, and often did all I could wish. I have nothing but love and praise for her, and I long for her return knowing what her feelings once were for me. But since fate has snatched her from me, I hope and pray that she will spend the rest of her life with a husband who will be more fortunate than I.

PHIDIPPUS: It is in your power to prevent this.

LACHES: Of course, if you had some sense! Have her back.

PAMPHILUS: That is not my intention, father. I shall devote myself to my mother's happiness.

LACHES: Where are you going? Wait a minute, please. Where—

[PAMPHILUS goes into LACHES' house.]

PHIDIPPUS: How can he be so obstinate?

LACHES: Didn't I tell you he would take it badly? That was why I begged you to return your daughter.

PHIDIPPUS [*exasperated*]: Frankly I never believed he could be so pig-headed. Now does he expect me to go down on bended knees? If he wants to take his wife back he can have her; if he has other ideas he must return her dowry and clear off.

LACHES: Here's another unreasonable person losing his temper!

PHIDIPPUS [*shouting after* PAMPHILUS]: Coming back in this state, you stubborn fool!

LACHES: He's got good reason to be annoyed, but he'll get over it.

PHIDIPPUS: Just because you people have come into a bit of money you're getting above yourselves!

LACHES: Are you trying to quarrel with me too?

PHIDIPPUS: He can think it over and let me know before the end of the day whether he wants her or not. If he doesn't, someone else shall have her. [*He marches into his house.*]

LACHES: Phidippus, wait, one word – he's gone. I don't care, after all, they can settle it themselves as they like. Neither he nor my son pays any attention to me or takes any notice of what I say. I'll take this quarrel in to my wife – she's at the bottom of everything and I can vent my spleen on her.

[*He goes in, and soon after* MYRRINA *comes out of* PHIDIPPUS's *house.*]

MYRRINA: Oh I'm distracted, I don't know which way to turn; whatever can I say to my husband? I'm sure he heard the baby cry – the way he dashed into our daughter's room without a word to me. Once he finds out she's given birth, what reason can I give him for having kept it all secret? Heavens, I can't think. Now there's the door – it must be him coming out. I'm lost.

PHIDIPPUS [*hurrying out of the house*]: My wife ran out when she saw me going in to Philumena. There she is, I see her. I say, Myrrina! Here, Myrrina, I'm speaking to you!

MYRRINA [*nervously*]: To me, husband?

PHIDIPPUS: Your husband, am I? I wasn't sure you credited me with human feelings at all. If you'd ever thought of me as a husband, or even as a human being, woman, you wouldn't have made a fool of me with your goings-on.

MYRRINA: What have I done?

PHIDIPPUS: Can you ask? Our daughter has had a baby. Well, have you nothing to say? Who's the father?

MYRRINA: Is that a proper question for her father to ask? Gracious me, who on earth do you think but her own husband?

PHIDIPPUS: I suppose so; as her father I can hardly think otherwise. What I can't understand is why you should have been so anxious to conceal this birth from us all, especially when the birth was normal and at the right time. [*A sudden thought strikes him.*] Good heavens, can you be so perverse? Could you prefer the death of the baby which would strengthen the tie between the two households to seeing your daughter settled with a husband who may not have been your choice? And I had thought all this was *their* fault! I see now it is yours.

MYRRINA [*in tears*]: I'm so unhappy!

PHIDIPPUS: I only wish I could be sure about this. But I've just remembered your words at the time we accepted him as a son-in-law; you said you couldn't bear to see your daughter married to a man who kept a mistress and spent his nights away from home.

MYRRINA [*aside*]: Better any reason for his suspicions than the true one!

PHIDIPPUS: I knew long before you did that he had a mistress, Myrrina, but I never considered it a vice in a young man: it's only natural. The time will soon come when he will even hate himself for it. But you have never changed the attitude you took up at first, in the hopes of getting your daughter away from him and breaking the agreement I made. Today's events prove your intentions.

MYRRINA [*stung*]: Do you really believe me so perverse? I'm her mother. Should I really behave like this to my own daughter if this marriage were for the good of us all?

PHIDIPPUS: And have you the foresight or judgement to know what will benefit us? Perhaps you heard someone say he had been seen going in and out of his mistress's house. What of it? If his visits were discreet and not too frequent, surely it would be more reasonable on our part to turn a blind eye to them, rather than to ferret out the facts and thereby set him against us. And in any case, if he could break off relations immediately with a woman he had known for so many years, I should think poorly of him as a man, and certainly doubt his constancy as a husband for my daughter.

MYRRINA: For pity's sake stop! Let's have no more of the young man and my so-called misdeeds. You go and find him alone, ask him whether he wants his wife or not; if he says he does, give her back, and if he doesn't – then I think I've done the right thing for my own daughter.

PHIDIPPUS: If the unwillingness *is* on his side and you realized this fault in him, Myrrina, I was there and should have been allowed to use my own judgement in this. What makes me angry is that you dared to carry out your scheme without instructions from me. I forbid you to move the baby anywhere out of the house. [*As he turns to go*] But I'm the bigger fool to expect her to obey my orders – I'll go in and tell the servants not to let it be taken out. [*He goes in.*]

MYRRINA: Was ever woman more unfortunate? If he discovers the truth it's clear to me how he'll take it, when a much smaller thing can make him lose his temper like this, and how to make him change his mind I've no idea. On top of all these miseries it will be the last straw if he forces me to bring up a child whose father we don't know. The night Philumena was assaulted it was too dark for her to recognize the man, and she failed to seize anything of his so that he could be afterwards identified, though in the struggle he went off with the ring from her finger. And when Pamphilus finds out that another man's child is being brought up as his, I'm so afraid he'll feel he can't keep our secret any longer. [*She goes in. After a short pause* SOSTRATA *and* PAMPHILUS *come out of* LACHES' *house.*]

SOSTRATA: I know very well, my son, that I'm under suspicion, however much you try to hide it, and you think your wife left us because of something in me. But God be my witness and grant what I hope for from you! I swear I have never consciously done anything to deserve her hatred. I knew before that you loved me, and now you have given me proof of it, for your father has just been in to tell me how you have put my interests before those of the woman you love. That has decided me to make you due return and assure you that in my heart a son's affection has its proper reward. My dear Pamphilus, I think this plan will be best for my reputation and for you two: I have made up my mind to go away and live at the farm with your father. Thus I shall rid you of my presence and remove any reason which remains to prevent Philumena's returning to you.

PAMPHILUS: What on earth put that idea into your head? Is her stupidity to drive you from town to bury yourself in the country? Certainly not. Besides, I'm not having any ill-wisher suggesting you went because of my obstinacy and not through your own unselfishness. I've no intention of letting you give up your friends and family and the festivals you enjoy, all because of me.

SOSTRATA: But I don't really get much pleasure out of the things you mean. I had plenty of them when I was younger, and by now I'm tired of them. My chief concern is not to be a nuisance in my old age and not to feel people are waiting for my death. I can see that I'm disliked here, through no fault of mine, so it's time for me to go. I'm sure it's the best way to cut short all this argument on both sides, clear me of suspicion, and comply with the wishes of our neighbours next door. Please let me be exempt from this universal slander of my sex.

PAMPHILUS: How lucky I am in all but one thing – with a mother like you, but what a wife!

SOSTRATA: Come, my boy, can't you make up your mind to put up with just one unpleasantness, whatever it is? If everything else is as you want it and as I take it to be, do this one thing for me: take her back.

PAMPHILUS: I'm so unhappy, mother.

SOSTRATA: So am I, my son. This distresses me as much as it does you.

[LACHES *has come out of the house during this and been standing unseen.*]

LACHES: My dear, I was standing within earshot and overheard your conversation. Now that is really sensible, to adapt yourself to what is necessary and do now what you might perhaps have to do later.

SOSTRATA: I hope to heaven it is.

LACHES: Off you go then to the farm, and there I'll bear with you and you with me.

SOSTRATA: I trust we shall.

LACHES: Go in then, and gather up the things you want to take with you; that's all I want to say.

SOSTRATA: I will. [*She goes in.*]

PAMPHILUS: Father –

LACHES: What is it, Pamphilus?

PAMPHILUS: My mother shan't go away!

LACHES: What do you mean?

PAMPHILUS: I haven't made up my mind yet what to do about my wife.

LACHES: What? What can you intend to do but take her back?

PAMPHILUS [*aside*]: I do want her – I can scarcely hold myself back – but I shall stick to my resolve. [*Aloud*] I must do what's best, and I think the women are more likely to be reconciled if I don't take her back.

LACHES: You can't tell; but what they do once your mother has gone is no concern of yours. Young folks never really like people of our age, and it's better for us to slip away. You'll see us ending up like the old couple[1] in the fairytale! But here's Phidippus, just when we want him. Come and talk to him.

[PHIDIPPUS *comes out talking to* PHILUMENA *inside.*]

PHIDIPPUS: I'm angry with you too, Philumena, really very angry; you've behaved extremely badly, though I suppose you have some excuse when you were put up to this by your mother. There's no excuse for *her*.

LACHES: Ah, Phidippus, you've come at the right moment.

PHIDIPPUS: What is it?

PAMPHILUS [*aside*]: What shall I say to them? How shall I explain this?

1. The reference is unknown. 'Darby and Joan' would be an equivalent.

LACHES: Tell your daughter that Sostrata is leaving for the country, so she needn't be afraid now to return home.

PHIDIPPUS: But it's not your wife who's in any way to blame for this, but mine; it was really all due to Myrrina.

PAMPHILUS [aside]: The tables turned!

PHIDIPPUS: It's she who stirs up all this trouble between us, Laches.

PAMPHILUS [aside]: So long as I don't have to take her back, they can go on having all the trouble they like.

PHIDIPPUS: For my part, Pamphilus, I should like our family connection to continue unbroken, if possible; but if you cannot feel the same, at least you must please take the child.

PAMPHILUS: Damn it all, he's found out!

LACHES: Child? What child?

PHIDIPPUS: We have a grandson, Laches. My daughter was expecting a baby when she was obliged to leave your house, though I never knew of it until today.

LACHES: Bless me, that's good news! I'm delighted. A grandson, and your daughter safe and well! But what sort of woman can your wife be? What a way to behave, keeping us all in the dark so long! Most improper – I can't say so too strongly.

PHIDIPPUS: I disapprove as much as you do, Laches.

PAMPHILUS [aside]: Whatever doubts I had before I've none now, if she's bringing with her another man's child.

LACHES [genuinely delighted]: This should end all your indecision, Pamphilus!

PAMPHILUS: Oh it's too much!

LACHES: This is the day we have often longed for, the day when you have a son to call you father. Thank God that day has come!

PAMPHILUS [groaning]: I'm finished.

LACHES: Take back your wife, and no more argument.

PAMPHILUS: Father, if she had really wanted to have children by me or to remain my wife, I feel positive she would not have kept from me what I now know she concealed. I can't help thinking that her feeling for me has changed. I don't believe we can ever live happily together after all this; so is there any reason why I should take her back?

LACHES: Your wife is young, and only did what her mother told her. There's nothing surprising about that. Do you imagine you can find a woman who will be a blameless wife? What about husbands – haven't they their faults?

PHIDIPPUS: Settle it between yourselves, you two, whether you want to have her back or leave her with me. There'll be no difficulties on my side, either way. What she does as a wife is out of my hands; but what shall we do about the child?

LACHES: Need you ask? Whatever happens, of course you must hand his child over to Pamphilus for us to bring up: it is ours.

PAMPHILUS [aside]: Its own father hasn't taken much interest – why should I bring it up?

LACHES [catching the last words]: What did you say, Pamphilus? What! Not bring it up? Are you suggesting we should abandon it? You must be crazy. My God, I can't hold my tongue any longer. You force me to speak of things I'd prefer left unsaid in the presence of your father-in-law. Do you imagine I don't know about your weeping and whining and why you're in this state of distraction? At first the excuse you gave for not keeping her as your wife was your mother; so she promised to leave home. Now you see that you've lost that pretext, you've found another – you weren't informed of the birth of this child. If you think I can't see what's in your mind you're much mistaken. How long did I give you to carry on an affair with a mistress so that one

day you would apply your mind to matrimony? Did I ever
grumble at the bills I paid for what she cost you? I only
begged and prayed you to marry and told you it was high
time you did, and in the end I persuaded you. You did the
right thing then in complying with my wishes; but now
you've gone back to your mistress and she has put you up to
this unjust treatment of your wife. I can see you've slipped
back into your old life.

PAMPHILUS: You think that of me?

LACHES: Yes I do. And I tell you it is an insult to your wife,
trumping up false pretexts for breaking with her so that you
can live with that woman without her there to witness your
conduct. Yes, and your wife knew it. What other reason
could there be for her leaving you?

PHIDIPPUS: Good guesswork. That's quite right.

PAMPHILUS: I swear on oath that none of what you say about
me is true.

LACHES: Then take back your wife, or give us a reason why
you can't.

PAMPHILUS: It's the wrong moment –

LACHES: At least you can take the child: it is not to blame. I'll
see about the mother later.

PAMPHILUS [breaking away from them]: Nothing can be worse
than this; I'm at my wit's end. My father has me cornered
at every point, damn it all! I'll go, I'm doing no good by
staying here. I can't believe they'll acknowledge the child
without my consent, especially as my mother-in-law will
back me up. [He slips away, right.]

LACHES: Hi, are you running off without giving me a proper
answer? Do you think he's in his right mind? We shall have
to let him go. Give me the baby, Phidippus. I'll bring it up.

PHIDIPPUS: Very good. No wonder my wife was in such a
state; women are bitter about these things and find them

hard to take. This was at the bottom of all the trouble, my wife told me so herself, but I didn't want to mention it while your son was here. As a matter of fact I didn't believe her at first, but now all is clear and I can see that he's temperamentally quite unsuited to married life.

LACHES: What do you think I should do, Phidippus? Have you any advice?

PHIDIPPUS: Let me see. . . . I think we should first approach this woman, with pleas and accusations or even a pretty stiff threat, if she has continued relations with him since his marriage.

LACHES: I'll do that. [*He opens the door of his house and calls inside*] Boy! Run over to our neighbour Bacchis and say I should like her to come here. [*The servant comes out and hurries off left.*] I hope you'll stay to support me, Phidippus.

PHIDIPPUS: Ah, Laches, I said before and I say again that I want the connection between our families to continue, if it is at all possible, and I hope it will be. But do you really want me to be present at this interview?

LACHES: Perhaps not, after all. You go and find a nurse for the baby.

[PHIDIPPUS *goes off right and* LACHES *goes into his house. After an interval,* BACCHIS *comes along the street left, accompanied by two maids. She is a woman of mature charm and dignity, a complete contrast with* PHILOTIS *in the first scene.*]

BACCHIS: There's some good reason why Laches asks me to meet him, and unless I'm much mistaken I can guess what he wants.

LACHES [*coming out, in a great state of nerves*]: I must be careful not to show anger or I shan't get as much out of her as I might. And I must do nothing I might afterwards regret. Now for it. . . . Good evening, Bacchis.

BACCHIS: Good evening, Laches.

LACHES [*increasingly nervous*]: I – I expect you must be wondering, Bacchis, why I sent the boy to fetch you here.

BACCHIS [*with composure*]: I'm a little nervous myself, Laches, when I think of who I am, lest the name of my profession may prejudice you against me; I can answer for my conduct.

LACHES: If that's so, you're in no danger from me, my good woman. I've reached the age when a lapse isn't so easily forgiven, and I can't be too careful to watch my step and do nothing rash. So long as you behave or intend to behave as an honest woman should, it would be unjust of me to offer you a clumsy insult you have done nothing to deserve.

BACCHIS [*amused*]: Thank you, Laches. I can't be too grateful to you. I sometimes receive an apology *after* the sort of insult you refer to, but it doesn't help me much. And now, what can I do for you?

LACHES: You are in the habit of receiving my son Pamphilus.
[BACCHIS *makes a deprecating interruption.*]

LACHES: Please let me speak. Before he married I condoned this liaison – no, wait please. I haven't said yet what I meant to say. Now that my son has a wife, please find yourself a more permanent lover while you can look to your own interests, for his feelings will not stay the same for ever, any more than your present age will remain unchanged.

BACCHIS [*ignoring this offensive remark*]: Who says that?

LACHES: His mother-in-law.

BACCHIS: About me?

LACHES: Certainly: you. Moreover, she has removed her daughter, and because of this she planned to destroy secretly the child which has been born.

BACCHIS: I swear to you on oath, Laches, and I only wish I knew something stronger to make you believe me: I have had no relations with Pamphilus since the day he married.

LACHES [*after a pause*]: That is very good of you. . . . May I tell you, please, what I would like you to do now?

BACCHIS: What is it? Tell me.

LACHES: Go in to the women indoors and swear the same oath to them; satisfy their minds and clear yourself of this charge.

BACCHIS: Very well, though I doubt if any other woman of my profession would do the same, and show herself to a married woman for such a reason. But I don't want your son to rest under a false suspicion, and certainly you, as his parents, are the last people who should have the unjust idea that he's irresponsible. In fact, to do him justice, he should have all the help I can give him.

LACHES: Your words have won me over, Bacchis; I can truly say I wish you well. The women were not the only ones who thought this of him – I believed it too. . . . [*Stiffening again*] Now that I find you to be quite different from what we expected, I trust you will continue as you are, and then our friendship shall be at your disposal. Should you change – but no, I will say nothing you would not like to hear. I will only ask you to accept one piece of advice: try me, and what I can do for you, not as your enemy but as your friend.

[*PHIDIPPUS returns with the nurse.*]

PHIDIPPUS: I'll see you want for nothing in my house; there'll be plenty of everything you need, as long as when you've had all you can eat and drink you'll make sure my grandson is satisfied.

[*She goes into his house.*]

LACHES: Here comes our father-in-law with a nurse for the child. Phidippus, Bacchis has taken a solemn oath –

PHIDIPPUS: Is that her?

LACHES: Yes.

PHIDIPPUS: Her sort don't fear the gods, and I don't suppose the gods pay much regard to them.

BACCHIS: Take my servants – you have my leave to question them, under any torture you like. Our immediate concern is for me to make Pamphilus's wife return to him. If I am successful, I need not be ashamed when people say I was the only woman of my profession to do what the others avoid.

LACHES: Phidippus, we have proof that we wrongly suspected our wives; now let us see if Bacchis can help. If your wife finds that her suspicions were groundless, she will cease to be angry, and if my son is angry only because his wife had a baby without telling him, why, that's nothing – he'll soon get over it. There is nothing at all here which could justify a divorce.

PHIDIPPUS: I only hope you're right.

LACHES: Ask Bacchis, she's here. She'll settle your doubts herself.

PHIDIPPUS: Why say all this to me? Didn't you hear me tell you before what *my* feelings were? It's the women you two must satisfy.

LACHES: Please, Bacchis, keep the promise you made me.

BACCHIS: You really want me to go in to them about this matter?

LACHES: Yes, please go; put their minds at rest and make them believe you.

BACCHIS: Very well, I'll go, though I know they'll hate the sight of me. Once a wife is set aside by her husband she becomes the natural enemy of a woman like me.

LACHES: But they'll be friendly when they know why you have come.

PHIDIPPUS: I promise you they will be friendly when they have heard everything. And if you put an end to their misunderstanding you will clear yourself of suspicion.

BACCHIS: Oh, this is hard. . . . I'm ashamed to meet Philumena. [*To the maids*] Follow me in, you two. [*She goes into* PHIDIPPUS'*s house.*]

LACHES: The best bit of luck I could ever hope for! Here's Bacchis doing me a service *and* making herself liked without any cost to herself! If it's really true she has broken off relations with Pamphilus, she must know it'll bring her honour and fortune and glory too; she'll do him a good turn and make us all her friends.

[*He and* PHIDIPPUS *go into their houses. After a short pause* PARMENO *trudges on right, back from the town.*]

PARMENO: I wonder what the hell the master thinks I'm for, sending me off on a fool's errand like this. I've wasted a whole day hanging around the acropolis waiting for that fellow from Myconos. There I stuck all day like a prize fool, going up to every passer-by. 'Please, sir, are you from Myconos?' 'No.' 'Aren't you Callidemides?' 'No.' 'You haven't got a friend here called Pamphilus?' It was No all the time. I bet the man doesn't exist. I got fed up in the end, damn it, and cleared off. Why, there's Bacchis coming out of our in-laws'. What can she be doing there?

BACCHIS [*hurrying out*]: Parmeno, you're the very person I want. Quick, run and find Pamphilus.

PARMENO [*sulkily*]: What for?

BACCHIS: Tell him I ask him to come here.

PARMENO: To *you*?

BACCHIS: No, no, it's for Philumena.

PARMENO: Hey, what's up?

BACCHIS: Nothing to do with you, so never mind.

PARMENO: Anything else I'm to say?

BACCHIS: Yes, tell him Myrrina has recognized the ring he once gave me. It's her daughter's.

PARMENO: I see. Is that all?

BACCHIS: That's all. He'll be here at once when he's heard that. Only do stop dawdling!

PARMENO: I like that! What chance have I had of dawdling? I've done nothing but walk and run the whole blessed day. [*He goes off right.*]

BACCHIS: What happiness I have given Pamphilus by coming here today! I've brought him so many blessings and removed so many worries. I have saved his son for him, whom he nearly lost through his own fault and the women here; I've given him back the wife with whom he believed he would never live again, and I've removed the suspicions of his father and Phidippus. And all this train of discovery was set off by a ring! I remember it must have been about nine months ago when he came running in to me soon after dark, alone, rather drunk, panting for breath, and clutching this ring. I was alarmed: 'Pamphilus, my darling,' I cried, 'how on earth have you got into this state? And where did you get that ring? You must tell me.' He pretended he hadn't heard me, but I soon saw through this and began to be still more suspicious; then I made him tell me. He confessed he had assaulted a girl in the street, he couldn't say who, and had pulled the ring off in the struggle. This is the ring Myrrina recognized on my finger. She asked where it came from and I told her the whole story; then it all came out that Philumena was the girl he attacked, and so her child is his own son. I'm glad he has found so much happiness through me, though I suppose other women of my sort wouldn't agree – it isn't really in our interests for a lover to be happily married, but all the same, I can't bring myself to act unkindly for what I might make out of it. . . . So long as it could last, he was always a kind and generous and charming lover. His marriage hurt me, I don't deny, but thank God I can feel that I did nothing to deserve it. . . . Where men are concerned you must take the rough with the smooth.

[PARMENO *returns with* PAMPHILUS.]

PAMPHILUS: Are you absolutely certain, Parmeno, that what you say is positively true? I don't want you to lead me on to a moment's false happiness.

PARMENO: I'm certain, sir.

PAMPHILUS: Absolutely certain?

PARMENO: Absolutely, sir.

PAMPHILUS: I'm in heaven if this is really true.

PARMENO: You'll find it true all right. [*He starts to move off.*]

PAMPHILUS: Just wait a minute please – I'm afraid I may have misunderstood what you said.

PARMENO: I'm waiting.

PAMPHILUS: I think you said that Myrrina has seen her ring on Bacchis's finger?

PARMENO: That's right.

PAMPHILUS: The ring which I once gave Bacchis? And it was Bacchis who told you to tell me – is that right?

PARMENO: Right again.

PAMPHILUS: Oh I'm the most fortunate of men! No one could be so lucky in love! Now what reward can I give you in return for this message? Tell me – I can't think.

PARMENO: *I* can.

PAMPHILUS: What then?

PARMENO: Nothing. I can't see what good you've got from the message, or from me either.

PAMPHILUS: You have restored me to life and rescued me from hell![1] Shall I let you go without a gift? You must think me very ungrateful! But look, there's Bacchis standing by our door, waiting for me, I think. I must speak to her.

1. Orcus, the underworld abode of the dead.

[BACCHIS *comes forward to meet him.*]

BACCHIS: Well, Pamphilus!

PAMPHILUS [*eagerly*]: Oh, Bacchis, my own Bacchis, my saviour!

BACCHIS [*gently*]: It's all right; it was a pleasure.

PAMPHILUS: I shall have to believe you. . . . Oh, you still have all your old charm – it is always a joy to meet you, hear your voice, and see you come, wherever you are.

BACCHIS [*laughing*]: My dear, *you* are still your old self with the old ways. . . . There's not a man alive who can win hearts like you.

PAMPHILUS [*laughing nervously*]: Can you still say that to me?

BACCHIS [*suddenly serious*]: You did right, Pamphilus, to fall in love with your wife. I had never seen her to know her until today. She is what I would call a true lady.

PAMPHILUS: Do you mean that?

BACCHIS: I swear before heaven I do, my dear.

PAMPHILUS: Tell me, did you say anything about all this to my father?

BACCHIS: No.

PAMPHILUS: Then we needn't breathe a word. I'd rather this weren't like the comedies, where everyone ends by knowing everything.[1] In our case, the ones who ought to know know already; and the others who don't need to know shan't be told or know a thing.

BACCHIS: Yes, and I can tell you something to make it easier for you to believe that the secret will be kept. Myrrina has told Phidippus that she believes what I said under oath; so you are cleared of everything in her eyes.

PAMPHILUS: Perfect! And now I hope everything will go well for us all.

1. Terence's ironic comment on the comic convention is neatly inserted in this unconventional comedy.

[PARMENO *attracts his attention so that he never notices that* BACCHIS *walks quietly off down the street, left, pausing to look back at him affectionately.*]

PARMENO: Please, sir, can you tell me what exactly I'm supposed to have done for you today? And what you two were talking about?

PAMPHILUS: I can't tell you, Parmeno.

PARMENO: I might guess though. . . . But 'rescued you from hell' – how did I?

PAMPHILUS: You've no idea how much you've done for me today, and what misery you've saved me from.

PARMENO: Oh, but I *do* know, sir, and I knew what I was doing.

PAMPHILUS [*humouring him*]: I'm sure you did.

PARMENO: Would Parmeno ever miss a chance of doing what was wanted?

PAMPHILUS: Come in with me now, Parmeno.

PARMENO: I'm coming, sir. [*To the audience*] It seems I did more good today without knowing it than I've ever knowingly done before. So give us your applause!

[*They go into* LACHES' *house.*]

THE BROTHERS

[ADELPHOE]

INTRODUCTORY NOTE

The Brothers has always provoked discussion and is essentially
a problem comedy, looking into the relations between fathers
and sons, and setting out the conflict between the rival educa-
tional policies which in Rome were represented by the strict
discipline of Cato versus the new liberal Hellenism. This is a
question which every generation must try to answer – shall
youth be guided by rules of conduct or allowed to have its
fling? Both systems have had bad effects on the young brothers
of the play: Aeschinus has been spoilt by Micio and is thoughtless and irresponsible, and Ctesipho lacks self-confidence and
deceives his strict father Demea, though we feel Micio is right
in insisting that they are both good at heart. Both the elder
brothers are complex characters subtly drawn. For all his
worldly wisdom, Micio worries about Aeschinus and has mis-
givings about having allowed him so much freedom; he pulls
Aeschinus up sharply when the boy apparently intends to
shirk the consequences of his folly. In the end Demea proves
to him that a lot of his theorizing was no more than taking the
line of least resistance. Demea is repressive and fussy, and at
first may seem a conventional killjoy until we realize that he
has a sardonic sense of humour, and can thoroughly enjoy
putting on an act to teach Micio a lesson. The sudden ironic
end to the play has been variously assessed, but whether it is to
be found in Menander's original or is Terence's own solution,
it is surely not to be taken as a true change of heart on Demea's
part – he may end more willing to allow some concessions to
Ctesipho, but his principles are unshaken and he never does
more than play a part. Micio does not seem so harshly treated
if we remember that Pamphila's mother is not necessarily

unattractive, and is certainly not likely to be the 'decrepit old hag' of Micio's exaggerated outburst. No doubt he will adapt himself to a different way of living with his usual ironic detachment.

The minor characters are well drawn – Hegio, the old family friend, Geta the excitable family retainer, and Syrus with his quick wits and ready tongue which recall Phormio in an earlier play. Syrus and his like were excluded from *The Mother-in-Law*, where Parmeno's part is cut to a minimum, and perhaps Terence brought them back into his last play to ensure its success with a popular audience. The episode with Sannio the slave-dealer, which Terence took from a second source, has been skilfully integrated into the play so that it provides much more than a comic scene. It serves to bring out Aeschinus's high-handedness in dealing with an inferior, and Ctesipho's nervous apprehensions about his father's knowing what he has been doing.

Terence provides no ready answer to the problems which engage him and which continue to be discussed today, and *The Brothers* is his last word before he met his unexplained end. It is a mature achievement and a unique contribution to classical literature. It has had many imitators and translators, and was the model for Molière's *L'École des maris*.

PRODUCTION NOTICE

THE BROTHERS by Terence: performed at the funeral games for Lucius Aemilius Paulus held by Quintus Fabius Maximus and Publius Cornelius Africanus.[1]

Produced by Lucius Ambivius Turpio and Lucius Hatilius (*or* Atilius) of Praeneste.

Music composed by Flaccus, slave of Claudius, for Sarranian[2] pipes throughout.

Greek original by Menander.

The author's sixth play, written during the consulship of Marcus Cornelius Cethegus and Lucius Anicius Gallus.[3]

1. The sons of Aemilius Paullus, both aediles in the year of his death (160 B.C.). The younger was already adopted into the Scipio family and is better known as Scipio Aemilianus Africanus Numantinus (see Introduction, p. 14).

2. According to Servius (on *Georgics* 2. 506) these are equal pipes, called after the old Latin name for Tyre.

3. i.e. in 160 B.C.

SYNOPSIS

Demea has two young sons. He gives Aeschinus to his
brother Micio for adoption and keeps Ctesipho. The latter
is captivated by the charms of a lute-player while under his
stern father's strict authority; his brother Aeschinus keeps
the secret, takes on himself the scandal and intrigue of the
affair, and ends by abducting the girl from a slave-dealer.
Aeschinus has also seduced an Athenian citizen, a girl in
humble circumstances, and promised to make her his wife.
Demea grumbles and scolds; but soon the truth is revealed,
Aeschinus marries the girl he wronged, and Ctesipho is
allowed to have his lute-player.

CHARACTERS

DEMEA	⎱ elderly brothers. Micio lives in Athens and
MICIO	⎰ Demea farms just outside
AESCHINUS	⎱ Demea's sons. Aeschinus has been adopted as his
CTESIPHO	⎰ son by Micio
SYRUS	a slave, Micio's head servant
DROMO	⎱ two of Micio's house slaves
STEPHANIO	⎰
PARMENO	Aeschinus's personal slave
SOSTRATA	a widow, Micio's next-door neighbour
PAMPHILA	her daughter
CANTHARA	her old nurse
GETA	her slave and house servant
HEGIO	a neighbour and friend of her late husband
SANNIO	a slave-dealer
BACCHIS	a music-girl

*

The scene is laid in Athens in front of the houses of Micio and Sostrata. To the audience's right the street leads to the centre of the town and the harbour, to the left to the country

AUTHOR'S PROLOGUE TO
THE BROTHERS

THE poet is well aware that his writing is scrutinized by unfair critics, and that his enemies are out to depreciate the play
we are about to present; he therefore intends to state the
charge against himself in person, and you shall judge whether
his conduct deserves praise or blame. *Joined in Death* is a
comedy by Diphilus:[1] Plautus made a Latin play out of it with
the same name. In the beginning of the Greek play there is a
young man who abducts a girl from a slave-dealer. Plautus
left out this incident altogether, so the present author took it
for his *Brothers* and translated it word for word. This is the
new play we are going to act; watch carefully and see if you
think the scene is a plagiarism or the restoration of a passage
which had been carelessly omitted.

As to the spiteful accusation that eminent persons[2] assist the
author and collaborate closely with him: his accusers may
think it a grave imputation, but he takes it as a high compliment if he can win the approval of men who themselves find
favour with you all and with the general public, men whose
services in war, in peace, and in your private affairs, are given
at the right moment, without ostentation, to be available for
each one of you.

After this, you must not expect an outline of the plot – the
old men who come on first will explain part of it, and the rest
will be clear during the action of the play. Make sure that your
goodwill gives the author fresh enthusiasm for his work.

1. Diphilus of Sinope, a New Comedy poet of the later fourth century B.C. About sixty titles of his plays are known, and Plautus used him
as a model, though this title does not appear in any list of Plautus's plays.

2. The 'Scipionic circle'; see Introduction, p. 13–14.

[MICIO *comes out of his house calling to the servants within;* *as there is no answer he comes forward, and is revealed as a* *dapper middle-aged bachelor.*]

MICIO: Boy! ... Then Aeschinus didn't come home last night from that dinner-party, nor any of the servants he took with him. It's true what they say: you may have stayed away from home or be late coming back, but you'll have a better reception from your angry wife for all her hard words and suspicions than you'll get from your loving parents. Suppose you're late; your wife merely imagines you're in love or someone loves you, or you are drinking and enjoying yourself and like to go off alone while she mopes by herself. Now look at me when my son hasn't returned, full of fancies and forebodings. The boy may have caught a chill or fallen down and broken a leg. . . . Why on earth should a man take it into his head to get himself something to be dearer to him than his own self? It's not as if he's my own son – he's my brother's, and my brother and I have had quite different tastes since boyhood. I've always chosen an easy life, stayed in town and enjoyed my leisure; and my married friends count me lucky never to have taken a wife. My brother's the opposite in every way – lived in the country, always saved, and chose the hard way; he married and had two sons, then I adopted the elder and brought him up from boyhood, and regarded him as my own. I've loved him like my own son: he has been my joy and sole delight. And I do all I can to ensure that he returns my affection. I give him money, turn a blind eye, don't feel called on to exercise my authority in everything; in fact, I've brought him up not to hide from me those youthful misdeeds which other sons conceal from their fathers. For a young man who has acquired the habit of telling lies and deceiving his father, and has the effrontery to do so, will do this all the more to everyone else. A gentleman's children should be treated honourably and like gentlemen. They can be restrained better that way, I believe, than through fear. But none of this suits my brother – he has different ideas. He keeps coming to me crying 'What are you doing, Micio? Why are you ruining our boy? Why do you let him drink and go after women, pay his bills for all this, and give him so much to spend on clothes? You've no sense.' Well, *he* has no feeling. It's beyond all right and reason, and it's quite wrong (in my view, at any rate) to hold that there's more weight and stability in authority imposed by force than in one which rests on affection. This is my system and the theory I have evolved; if the threat of punishment alone drives a man to do his duty, he'll be careful only so long as he thinks he may be detected: once he hopes not to be found out, he falls back into his old ways. But a man won by kindness is sincere in his behaviour, eager to make you a return, and stays the same whether he's with you or not. A father's duty then is to train his son to choose the right course of his own free will, not from fear of another; this marks the difference between a father and a tyrant in the home. If he fails to do this, he should admit he doesn't know how to manage his children.... But I do believe that's the man himself.... Yes it is, and I can see something has made him cross; I suppose I'm in for a scolding as usual. [DEMEA *comes on right from the town: shabby and workworn, he looks older than his years.*] Glad to see you well, Demea.

DEMEA: Good, I was looking for you.

MICIO: You look put out. Why?

DEMEA: Put out indeed! Can you ask me why, with a son like Aeschinus on our hands?

MICIO [*aside*]: I told you so. [*Aloud*] What has he done?

DEMEA: Done? He has neither shame nor scruple nor fear of the law! Never mind his past deeds; look at his latest exploit!

MICIO: Well, what *is* it?

DEMEA: Breaking open a door, bursting into someone else's house, beating the master and the entire household pretty well to death, and making off with the girl he's carrying on with. The scandal's all over the town. I can't tell you, Micio, how many people came up to tell me; everyone's talking about it. Good heavens, if he needs an example, why on earth can't he look at his brother, thrifty, sober, living in the country, and managing his affairs in very different style? I'm talking of Aeschinus, but it's you I mean, Micio; you have let him go astray.

MICIO: Is anything as unjust as a narrow-minded man! He can only see right in what he has done himself.

DEMEA: What do you mean?

MICIO: Simply that you are all wrong, Demea. It's no crime, believe me, for a young man to enjoy wine and women; no, and neither is it to break open a door. If you and I didn't do these things it was only because we hadn't the money. Are you claiming credit now for your conduct when it was only restricted by poverty? How unfair! If we had had the means, we should have done the same. As for that boy of yours, if you had any humanity you would let him behave as a young man should, here and now; if not, he will only wait to bundle your corpse out of the house before carrying on just the same when he's past the right age.

DEMEA: Good heavens, man, you drive me mad! No crime for a young man –

MICIO: Now listen to me, instead of going on and on about this. You gave me your son to adopt; he's my son now. If he does wrong, it's my affair, Demea; I meet most of the bills. He dines and wines and reeks of scent: I pay for it all. He keeps a mistress: I shall pay up as long as it suits me, and when it doesn't, maybe she will shut her door on him. He has broken a door-lock; I'll have it mended. He has torn someone's clothes; they can be repaired. Thank God I have the means to do so, and so far it hasn't worried me. Once and for all, either shut up or name anyone you like to judge between us; I'll prove it's you who are more in the wrong.

DEMEA: Damn it all, why not learn how to be a father from others who really know!

MICIO: You may be his natural father, but morally he is my son.

DEMEA: You? A moral father?

MICIO: Oh, if you are going on, I'm off.

DEMEA: Leaving me like this?

MICIO: Why should I listen to the same tale again and again?

DEMEA [*after a pause*]: I'm worried, Micio.

MICIO: So am I worried, Demea, but we must stick to our own worries. You look after one boy and I the other. If you worry about both, it's as good as demanding back the son you gave me.

DEMEA: No, no, Micio.

MICIO: Well, that's how it seems to me.

DEMEA: All right, have it your own way. . . . Let him squander his money, ruin others and himself; it's no concern of mine. And if ever again a single word –

MICIO: Temper again, Demea?

DEMEA: Don't you believe me? But am I asking for him back? All the same, it's hard: he's my flesh and blood. . . . If I oppose – All right, I've done. You want me to look after one son, and so I do. Thank heaven he's a boy after my own heart. The one you've got will learn some day – but I won't be too hard on him. [*He goes off right towards the town.*]

MICIO: There's something in what he says, but it's not the whole story. I don't really like it, but I wasn't going to show him I was upset. However much I try to placate him, I only start arguing and put him off; he's that sort of man. He's being unreasonable, and if I were to add to his fury or even try to share it, I should soon be as crazy as he is. All the same, Aeschinus has treated me pretty badly over this. He has been the round of the whores, and they've all cost money; then only the other day he got sick of them, I suppose, and announced his intention of marrying. I hoped he was growing up and settling down, and I was delighted. Now it's all starting again! But in any case I must know the facts and find the boy if he's still in town. [*He goes off towards the town.*]

[*The young man,* AESCHINUS, *comes on from the other direction with the music-girl,* BACCHIS, *and his slave,* PARMENO, *followed by the slave-dealer,* SANNIO.]

SANNIO: Help, help, everyone, help a poor innocent man! I need your help!

AESCHINUS [*to the girl*]: Don't worry, now just stand here. Don't look round, there's no danger, he shan't touch you while I'm here.

SANNIO: I'll have her in spite of all –

AESCHINUS: He's a scoundrel but he won't want to risk a second thrashing today.

SANNIO: Aeschinus, listen; you can't say you don't know my character. I'm a slave-dealer –

AESCHINUS: I know.

SANNIO: – but as honest a man as ever was. You may apologize afterwards and say you meant me no harm, but I shan't give that [*snapping fingers*] for it. Take it from me, I'll have my rights, and you'll pay with more than words for what you've done to me. I know what you'll say: 'I'm sorry, I'm willing to swear you were attacked without provocation.' Meanwhile the way I've been treated is a disgrace.

AESCHINUS [*to* PARMENO]: Go on, get a move on and open the door.

SANNIO: You aren't listening to what I say?

AESCHINUS [*to the girl*]: Quick, go inside.

SANNIO: No you don't!

AESCHINUS: Stand over him, Parmeno, you're too far off; here, close up to him; that's right. Now watch, don't take your eyes off mine, and when I give the wink, be quick and plant your fist straight in his jaw.

SANNIO: Just let him try!

AESCHINUS: Now look out! [*With a look at* PARMENO, *who gives* SANNIO *a violent blow.*] Let go that girl!

SANNIO: It's monstrous!

AESCHINUS: He'll give you another if you don't watch out! [*He does.*]

SANNIO: Oh, oh!

AESCHINUS: I didn't wink, but it's a fault on the right side. [*To the girl*] Now go in.

[PARMENO *takes the girl into* MICIO's *house.*]

SANNIO: What's all this? Are you king here, Aeschinus?

AESCHINUS: If I were I'd see you got the reward you merit.

SANNIO: What do you want with me?

AESCHINUS: Nothing.

SANNIO: Do you know the sort of man I am?

AESCHINUS: I don't want to.

SANNIO: Have I ever touched anything of yours?

AESCHINUS: If you had, you'd suffer for it.

SANNIO: The girl's mine; I paid cash for her. What right have you to detain her? Answer me that.

AESCHINUS: You'd do better to stop this row outside my house. And if you go on making a nuisance of yourself, you'll find yourself *inside* being whipped within an inch of your life.

SANNIO: I'm a free man – you can't whip me.

AESCHINUS: Can't I!

SANNIO: You brute! Is this where all free men are supposed to be equal?

AESCHINUS: If you've quite finished making a scene, you pimp, be so good as to listen to me.

SANNIO: Who's making a scene? I or you?

AESCHINUS: Drop it. Talk business.

SANNIO: What business? What talk?

AESCHINUS: Are you ready now to hear something to your advantage?

SANNIO: I'm all ears, as long as it's a fair deal.

AESCHINUS: Bah! Now a pimp wants me to stick to fair dealing!

SANNIO: I know I'm a pimp, the bane of youth, a plague and a liar, but I never did any harm to *you*.

AESCHINUS: No, that's the only thing to come.

SANNIO: Go back to where you began, please, Aeschinus.

AESCHINUS: You paid two thousand drachmas for that girl, and much good may it do you! I'll pay you the same.

SANNIO: What if I refuse to sell? Will you use force?

AESCHINUS: No –

SANNIO: Good; I was afraid you would.

AESCHINUS: The girl is free-born and shouldn't be sold at all. That's my view and I'm laying hands on her to set her free.

Now make up your mind, take the money or get up a case.
You can be thinking it over till I come back: you pimp. [*He
goes into* MICIO's *house.*]

SANNIO: Gods above, I don't wonder folk go mad with the
injustice done them! That fellow has dragged me out of my
house, beaten me, carried off my girl under my nose, rained
blows galore on my wretched back, and on top of all he has
done insists I hand her over at cost price. Supposing it's a
fair offer, and he's demanding his rights. Well, I'm willing,
as long as he pays up. But I can predict just what'll happen;
once I agree to sell for a price he'll have witnesses on the
spot to prove I *have* sold her. As for the money – moonshine. 'Soon,' he'll say: 'come back tomorrow.' I can put
up with that too, so long as he pays up in the end, although
it's a swindle. But I have to face facts: when you follow my
profession you must put up with insults from these young
men and keep your mouth shut. Well, nobody's going to
pay me here. I'm only wasting time totting up accounts like
this.

[SYRUS *comes out of* MICIO's *house, talking to* AESCHINUS
within: he is a smart middle-aged manservant.]

SYRUS: All right, sir, I'll see the man myself. He'll be only too
keen to take the money when I've dealt with him, and think
himself well treated into the bargain. [*Coming forward*]
What's this I hear, Sannio? Have you been having a scrap
with my master?

SANNIO: Scrap? I never saw a fight on worse terms than the
one we've just had. He dealt all the blows and I took them
till we're both worn out.

SYRUS: It was your own fault.

SANNIO: What should I have done?

SYRUS: Humoured him: he's young.

SANNIO: What else did I do? I let him punch me on the jaw.

SYRUS: Come, you know what I mean. Forget money on occasion; that's sometimes the best way to make it. If you were afraid that if you gave up a fraction of your rights and humoured the young man you wouldn't get your cash back – and with interest – you really are a prize fool.

SANNIO [*sulkily*]: I don't pay down cash for expectations.

SYRUS: You'll never make your fortune, Sannio; you've no idea how to set your traps.

SANNIO: Maybe your way's best, but I'm not sharp enough. I've always liked to make what I could on the spot.

SYRUS: Go on, I know you. It's well worth two thousand to you to keep on the right side of my young master; and besides, I'm told you are off to Cyprus and [*ignoring* SANNIO'*s interruption*] you've made all your purchases to take there and hired a boat. I know you can't give your mind to this now, but once you're back again you'll fix things up with him all right.

SANNIO: I'm not going anywhere! [*Aside*] Damn it: that's what set them on to this.

SYRUS [*aside*]: That stung him; he's afraid.

SANNIO [*aside*]: Curse him, look what a moment for a hold-up! All those women and other things are bought ready to take over to Cyprus. If I miss the market there, it's a hell of a loss. If I drop this matter now and take it up when I'm back again – no go, it'll have gone stale and all I'll get will be 'Why come now? Why did you allow it? Where have you been?' It would be better to cut my losses than go on waiting here now or bring a case later on.

SYRUS: Have you finished working out what you stand to gain?

SANNIO: Is this the right way for him to behave? Should Aeschinus set about getting the girl away from me by force?

SYRUS [*aside*]: He's wavering: one word more. See if you like this better, Sannio. Rather than risk saving or losing the whole sum, halve it. He'll scrape up a thousand from somewhere.

SANNIO: No, no! Now can't a poor man be sure of his capital? Has your master no shame? Thanks to him every tooth in my head is loose and my skull is one great bump with his blows. Now he wants to cheat me, does he? I'm not going.

SYRUS: As you please. Anything more, or can *I* go?

SANNIO: No, damn it, please listen, Syrus. Never mind how I've been treated, sooner than go to law just let me have back the money I paid for her. Up to now I know you've had no proof of my friendship, Syrus, but you'll see I'll be grateful and remember you.

SYRUS [*accepting the proffered bribe*]: I'll do my best. Look, here comes Ctesipho, all smiles about his mistress.

SANNIO: Now what about my request?

SYRUS: Wait a minute.

[*Enter* CTESIPHO *from the town, right, a volatile young man in high spirits.*]

CTESIPHO [*not seeing the others*]: Any man's welcome in time of need, but the real joy comes when your helper is the very man you want! Aeschinus my brother, how can I find words to praise you? At least I'm sure that nothing I can say will be too good for you, and I know, too, that no one alive has what I possess – a brother who stands first among men in every virtue!

SYRUS: Sir –

CTESIPHO: Oh Syrus, where is Aeschinus?

SYRUS: In there, at home, waiting for you.

CTESIPHO [*in raptures*]: Ah!

SYRUS: What do you mean by that?

CTESIPHO: What indeed! It's all his doing, Syrus, that I can live today! The splendid fellow! He put my interests before all his own, took on himself all the hard words and gossip, my own trouble and misdeeds; no one could do more. Who's that at the door?

SYRUS: Wait, it's your brother coming out.

[AESCHINUS *comes out of the house.*]

AESCHINUS: Where's that dirty liar?

SANNIO [*aside*]: That's me he wants. Anything in his hand? Damn it, nothing.

AESCHINUS: Ah, good, I was looking for you, Ctesipho. How are you? Everything's settled now, so you can cheer up.

CTESIPHO: I can indeed, with a brother like you, Aeschinus, my own dear Aeschinus! I daren't praise you more to your face, or you might take it for flattery rather than true gratitude.

AESCHINUS: Come, come, you idiot, surely we know each other well enough by now. . . . I'm only sorry we heard of it so late and had almost reached the point of finding it impossible for anyone to help you, though we all wanted to.

CTESIPHO: I was ashamed –

AESCHINUS: Not ashamed but stupid, to let a little thing like that nearly drive you out of the country. It doesn't bear speaking of. God forbid such a thing!

CTESIPHO: I'm sorry.

AESCHINUS [*to* SYRUS]: And now what has Sannio to say?

SYRUS: Oh, he's calmed down.

AESCHINUS: I'm going to town to settle up with him. You go in to her, Ctesipho.

SANNIO [*to* SYRUS]: Try now, Syrus. [CTESIPHO *goes in.*]

SYRUS [*to* AESCHINUS]: Let's go, sir. This chap's in a hurry to be off to Cyprus.

SANNIO: Not so much hurry as you'd like! I've got time, and here I'll wait.

SYRUS: You'll be paid, don't worry.

SANNIO: But will he pay in full?

SYRUS: He will. Now shut up and come along.

SANNIO: I'm coming.

[AESCHINUS *and* SANNIO *go off right;* SYRUS *is following when* CTESIPHO *reappears.*]

CTESIPHO: Hi, Syrus!

SYRUS: Well, what is it?

CTESIPHO: Do please pay that horrible man as soon as you can. If he carries on worse than this it may reach my father's ears, and that'll be the death of me – for ever.

SYRUS: I'll see it shan't. [*With growing self-importance*] Now, courage, sir; enjoy yourself with your lady indoors, and have dinner laid and all ready for us. I'll see this business settled and then come home with the fish.

CTESIPHO: Yes, do. Everything's so marvellous we must celebrate today.

[*He goes back into* MICIO'*s house and* SYRUS *goes off after the others. After a short pause* SOSTRATA *comes out of her house, followed by the nurse,* CANTHARA.]

SOSTRATA: Please, nurse, how is my daughter? How are things going?

CANTHARA: How are things? All right, I hope, ma'am. My poor dear, your pains are only just beginning. . . . You're not worrying already, as if you'd never seen a birth nor had a baby yourself?

SOSTRATA: Alas, I'm friendless, we are two women alone – even Geta isn't here and I've no one to send for the midwife or to fetch Aeschinus.

CANTHARA: Bless you, he'll soon be here; he never lets a day pass without coming, whatever happens.

SOSTRATA: He's my sole comfort in my woes.

CANTHARA: And you couldn't have done better, ma'am, as it turns out, once the damage was done, at least as regards him – such a nice young man, well-born and good-hearted, coming from a grand home like his!

SOSTRATA: Yes, you're right; heaven keep him safe for us.

[SOSTRATA's *elderly slave*, GETA, *rushes on right in a state of great agitation, without seeing the women.*]

GETA: Here's a state of affairs! O world, unite, take counsel, seek a remedy, but what good will it do – such trouble as I'm in, and my mistress and her daughter too! O misery! Beset on all sides and no way out! Violence, destitution, injustice, desertion, disgrace! What times! What crimes! O wicked world, O vile wretch!

SOSTRATA: Heavens, why is Geta running about in such a state?

GETA: Honour, his promised word, pity, nothing could hold him back and turn him from his purpose – nor the thought that the poor girl he vilely seduced was just about to bear his child!

SOSTRATA: What *is* he saying? I still can't understand.

CANTHARA: Let's go nearer, ma'am, please.

GETA [*dancing about*]: O woe! I'm nearly out of my mind with fury. I'd like nothing better than to see that household in front of me – I'd vent my rage on the lot while my blood is roused! I'd have vengeance enough if I could wreak it on them! First I'd choke the life out of that old villain who brought up this monster, then that Syrus who put him up to this, how I'd smash him up! I'd grab him by the waist and fling him up, I'd dash his head on the ground and spatter his brains in the street! I'd take that young man and gouge out his eyes and pitch him headlong! As for the rest of them, I'd rush and knock them out, hit and hammer and stamp them underfoot! [*Pausing to get his breath back*] ... Now I'd best hurry and tell the mistress what's gone wrong. [*He moves towards the house.*]

SOSTRATA: Let's call him. Geta!

GETA: Don't bother me, whoever you are.

SOSTRATA: It's me, Sostrata.

GETA: Where? I was looking for you, madam.

SOSTRATA: And I was waiting for you. You're back in the nick of time.

GETA: Madam –

SOSTRATA: What is it? You're trembling.

GETA: Oh –

CANTHARA: What's the hurry, Geta? Get your breath back.

GETA: We are quite –

SOSTRATA: Quite what?

GETA: Done for. Ruined.

SOSTRATA: For heaven's sake, explain.

GETA: Now –

SOSTRATA: Now what, Geta?

GETA: Aeschinus –

SOSTRATA: What has he done?

GETA: He's broken away from us all.

SOSTRATA: No, it can't be. ... But *why*?

GETA: He has found a new girl –

SOSTRATA: O heaven help me!

GETA: And he makes no secret of it. He carried her off quite openly from the pimp.

SOSTRATA: Are you quite sure?

GETA: Quite, madam. I saw it with my own eyes.

SOSTRATA: Oh no, no. What can one believe? Who can be trusted? Our Aeschinus, the life of us all, in whom we put all our hopes and everything, who swore he could not live a day without her! And he promised he would put the baby in its grandfather's arms and beg the old man's leave to marry her!

GETA: Madam, try to stop crying and think of the future; what ought we to do? Put up with it and say nothing, or tell someone?

CANTHARA: Heavens, man, are you crazy? Do you think this the sort of news to spread around?

GETA: No, I don't. First, the facts show he cares nothing for us. If we make this public now, he'll deny it, I'm sure, and we'll risk your reputation, madam, and your daughter's life. And then, however much he might admit this is his doing, as he loves someone else it won't help your daughter to be married to him. So whichever way you look at it, best keep it quiet.

SOSTRATA [*after a pause for thought*]: No, not for the world! I won't.

GETA: What will you do then?

SOSTRATA: I'll tell everything.

CANTHARA: Oh my dear lady, think what you are doing.

SOSTRATA: Things couldn't be worse than they are now. In the first place she has no dowry, and then she's lost the next best thing – her reputation is ruined and she can't be married without one. There's just one thing we can do; if he denies it, I've got proof in the ring he sent her. Finally, my conscience is clear; no money, nothing unworthy of her or me has passed between us. I shall take him to court.

GETA [*dubiously*]: Very well, I suppose you're right.

SOSTRATA: Geta, you be off as fast as you can to her relative Hegio and tell him the whole story. He was my husband's dearest friend and has always looked after us.

GETA: Just as well, for no one else will. [*He goes off right.*]

SOSTRATA: You hurry too, Canthara, run and fetch the midwife; she mustn't keep us waiting when she's needed.

[CANTHARA *goes off to the town, right, and* SOSTRATA *into her house. After a short pause* DEMEA *comes back from the town.*]

DEMEA: I'm finished. Ctesipho, my own son, was with Aeschinus, they say, and had a hand in this abduction. This is the last straw, if the one who's still some good can be led astray by the other. Where am I to look for the boy? In some low dive I suppose, taken by that dissolute brother of his, you may be sure. [*Looking down the street, right*] Now here comes Syrus: he'll know where he is, but he's one of the gang and if he guesses I'm trying to find him he'll never say a word, the brute! I won't let him see that's what I want.

[SYRUS *comes back from the town with a basket of fish, pretending not to see* DEMEA.]

SYRUS [*aside*]: Well, we told the whole tale to our old man, just as it happened, and I never saw anyone better pleased.

DEMEA: Ye gods, the stupidity of the man!

SYRUS: He congratulated his son and thanked me for the advice I gave him. . . .

DEMEA: I shall explode!

SYRUS: He counted out the cash on the spot, and then gave me something to spend – which I've done to my liking [*looking in the basket*].

DEMEA: Here's the fellow for your orders if you want the job well done!

SYRUS: Why, sir, I didn't see you. What's the matter?

DEMEA: Matter? I never cease to marvel at the way you people behave.

SYRUS: Silly I know, in fact to be honest it's ridiculous. [*Calls indoors as he hands in the basket*] Gut all these fish, Dromo, except that biggest conger. Let it swim in water for a bit and it can be filleted when I come back, not before.

DEMEA: It's a scandal!

SYRUS [*virtuously*]: I don't like it either, sir, I often protest. [*Calls indoors*] This salt fish, Stephanio, see it's properly soaked.

DEMEA: Heavens above, does the man do it deliberately, or think he'll gain merit if he ruins my son? Damn it, I can see the day when that young man will have to leave home penniless and serve overseas.

SYRUS: Ah, sir, you can look to the future as well as seeing what's under your nose: that's true wisdom.

DEMEA: Tell me, is that girl still in your house?

SYRUS: She's there, indoors.

DEMEA: And she'll be kept there?

SYRUS: I suppose so; your son's crazy about her.

DEMEA: Impossible!

SYRUS: It's his father's foolish weakness, sir. He spoils him dreadfully.

DEMEA: I'm sick and tired of the man!

SYRUS: Ah, there's a world of difference between you and him, sir, and I don't say this just to your face. You're all wisdom, from top to toe; he's nothing but notions. Now *you* wouldn't have let your son carry on like this.

DEMEA: Of course not. I should have got wind of it at least six months before it all began.

SYRUS: No need to tell *me*, sir, how watchful you'd be.

DEMEA: So long as Ctesipho stays as he is, that's all I want.

SYRUS: Like father, like son, that's all we want.

DEMEA: What about him? Have you seen him today?

SYRUS: Ctesipho? [*Aside*] I'll pack this one off to the country. [*Aloud*] He's been up at the farm for some time I believe.

DEMEA: Are you quite sure?

SYRUS: Oh yes, sir, I went along with him myself.

DEMEA: Splendid. I was afraid he was hanging around here.

SYRUS: And what a temper he was in!

DEMEA: What about?

SYRUS: Oh, he'd had a row in town with his brother over that girl.

DEMEA: Really?

SYRUS: Yes, he spoke out all right. Just as the money was being counted out, up he came unexpectedly: 'Oh, Aeschinus!' he cried, 'Fancy you doing this! Think of the disgrace to the family!'

DEMEA: I could weep for joy.

SYRUS: 'It's not just money you are wasting, it's your life.'

DEMEA: Bless him, he's a chip off the old block; I have hopes of him.

[SYRUS *shrugs his shoulders expressively*.]

DEMEA [*ignoring this*]: He's full of maxims like that.

SYRUS: Naturally; he could learn them all at home.

DEMEA: I spare no pains, let slip no chance, and give him a sound training; in fact I'm always telling him to look at other men's lives as in a mirror, and choose from them an example for himself. 'Do this' I say –

SYRUS: And quite right too.

DEMEA: 'Avoid that' –

SYRUS: Splendid.

DEMEA: 'This does you credit' –

SYRUS: That's the way.

DEMEA: 'There you'll be wrong' –

SYRUS: Perfect.

DEMEA: 'And then' –

SYRUS: Excuse me, sir, I haven't time at the moment to listen to you. I've got just the fish I wanted and I must see they're not spoiled. It's as bad a fault in us servants not to see to such things as it is in you and yours, sir, not to do what you've just been saying, and as far as I can I train the other servants on the same lines as you. 'This is too salt,' I say, 'this is burnt to a cinder, this is not cleaned properly; but that's just right, remember to do that next time.' I spare no pains to give all the advice I can, as I understand it, and I end up by telling them to look in the pans like a mirror, sir, while I tell them what they ought to do. All this sounds silly I know, but what would you have us do? You have to take men as they are. . . . Anything else you want, sir?

DEMEA [*angrily*]: Only that you all had more sense.

SYRUS: You're off to the country now?

DEMEA: At once.

SYRUS [*blandly*]: Well, if no one takes your good advice, you're not really doing much good here, are you, sir? [*He goes into* MICIO'*s house.*]

DEMEA: Off to the country then, as the boy I wanted here is there already. He belongs to me, and he's the one to worry about. As for the other one, Micio can see to him, as that's what he wants. Now who can I see coming? My comrade Hegio I do believe, if my eyes don't deceive me, my old boyhood friend, a man of worth and honour of the good old sort, and heaven knows we've all too few citizens like him! It will be a long day before the country suffers anything from *him*. I *am* pleased; as long as I can still set eyes on one of his kind, life's worth living. I'll wait here to greet him and have a word with him.

[GETA *returns right, talking to* HEGIO, *and not seeing* DEMEA.]

HEGIO: Good heavens, Geta, what a monstrous story. Can it be true?

GETA: It's a fact, sir.

HEGIO: Such ungentlemanly conduct in a member of that family! Aeschinus, this is not like your father's son!

DEMEA [*aside*]: He must have heard about that girl. *He* can

feel it, though it's not his son, while the boy's own father
thinks nothing of it. Damn it, I wish Micio were here to
listen to him!

HEGIO: They must do the right thing; they shan't get away
with this.

GETA: We pin all our hopes on you, sir: you're all we have
and we all look to you as our father and protector. Our old
master entrusted us to you with his dying words, and if you
abandon us we're lost.

HEGIO: Never: don't talk like that. I can't do enough when
duty calls me.

DEMEA: I'll meet him. [*Coming forward*] Hegio, I hope with all
my heart I see you well.

HEGIO [*coldly*]: Oh, I was looking for you. The same to you,
Demea.

DEMEA: You wanted me?

HEGIO: Yes. Your elder son Aeschinus, the one you gave to
your brother to adopt, has shown himself neither an honest
man nor a gentleman.

DEMEA: What do you mean?

HEGIO: You knew our old friend Simulus –

DEMEA: Of course I did.

HEGIO: Your son has seduced his daughter.

DEMEA: Oh no!

HEGIO: Wait, Demea; you haven't heard the worst.

DEMEA: Can anything be worse?

HEGIO: Yes indeed. This could have been borne somehow –
there were excuses: darkness, passion, drink, and youth; it
is human nature. When he realized what he had done, he
went of his own accord to the mother, weeping, begging,
praying, promising, and swearing to marry the girl. He was
forgiven and trusted, and the matter was hushed up. The
girl was pregnant, and today her time is near. Now our fine

gentleman has bought himself another girl to live with, a music-girl, heaven help us, and the other is abandoned.

DEMEA: Are you sure this is true?

HEGIO: The girl is here and her mother too, and the facts are obvious; then there's Geta, an honest man as slaves go, and an active one – he's the prop and mainstay of the whole household. Take him, tie him up, get the truth out of him!

GETA: Put me on the rack, sir, if that's not the truth. Besides, the boy won't deny it; bring him face to face with me.

DEMEA [aside]: I'm ashamed. I can't think what to do or say to him.

PAMPHILA [from inside the house]: Ah, the pain! Juno Lucina, help me, save me, save me!

HEGIO: What, has her labour started?

GETA: It must have, sir.

HEGIO: Now you can hear her calling on the honour of your family, Demea. Do what you must do, and let it be of your own good will. I pray heaven you will take the proper course, but if your intentions are otherwise, I warn you I shall defend this girl and her dead father with all my power. He was my relative, and we were brought up together from our earliest childhood; we stood together in peace and war, and together we faced the hardships of poverty to the end. Hence I shall make every effort, do all I can, go to law if need be, lay down my life in fact, before I fail these women. . . . What is your answer?

DEMEA [at a loss]: I'll find my brother, Hegio, and do what he advises.

HEGIO: But bear this in mind, Demea. The more easy your life, the higher you people rise in power, wealth, good fortune and rank, the more you must judge rightly what is right and fair, if you want to be known as honest men. [He turns away.]

DEMEA: Just a moment; everything proper shall be done.

HEGIO: That is no more than your duty. Geta, take me in to Sostrata.

[*They go into* SOSTRATA'*s house.*]

DEMEA: I warned him this would happen. I only hope it will end here! But indulgence carried so far is bound to end in disaster of some sort. I'll go and find my brother and pour out the whole story. [*He goes off right.*]

HEGIO [*coming out of the house*]: Bear up, Sostrata, and do what you can to comfort her. I'll find Micio, if he's in town, and tell him exactly what has happened. If he intends to do his duty, let him do it. But if he has other ideas, he must give me an answer so that I know at once what steps to take.

[*He goes off, right, towards the town. Almost immediately* CTESIPHO *and* SYRUS *come out of* MICIO'*s house.*]

CTESIPHO: Do you really mean my father's gone off to the country?

SYRUS: Yes, some time ago.

CTESIPHO: Go on, please, tell me about it.

SYRUS: He's at the farm, busy with something at this very moment, I expect.

CTESIPHO: I hope he is! And so long as he doesn't kill himself, I wish he'd end up so tired that for the next three days he'd be unable to get out of bed!

SYRUS: Hear, hear; or something even better.

CTESIPHO: Agreed. I do so much want to spend this whole day as happily as I began. There's only one thing I don't like about our farm – it's too near. If it were farther off he couldn't be back before dark. As it is, I know what'll happen: he won't find me there, so he'll come running back here to ask me where I've been. 'I haven't seen you all day.' What's the answer to that?

SYRUS: Can't you think of anything?

CTESIPHO: Nothing at all.

SYRUS: The more fool you. Haven't you a dependant, a companion, or a friend?

CTESIPHO: Yes I have. What then?

SYRUS: You could have been doing business with them.

CTESIPHO: But I wasn't. I can't say that.

SYRUS: Yes you can.

CTESIPHO [*dubiously*]: That might account for the day. . . . If I spend the night here, what excuse have I then?

SYRUS: Oh, if only people made a habit of doing business with their friends by night as well! Never mind, don't worry, I know him and his ways. Let him seethe with fury, but I'll soon have him as quiet as a lamb.

CTESIPHO: How?

SYRUS: He likes to hear the best of you. I can sing your praises to heaven and go through the list of all your virtues.

CTESIPHO: *My* virtues?

SYRUS: Yours all right. I can have the old man crying like a child for joy. Now look out!

CTESIPHO: What is it?

SYRUS: Talk of the devil. . . .[1]

CTESIPHO: Is it my father?

SYRUS: His very self.

CTESIPHO: Oh, Syrus, what are we to do?

SYRUS: Quick, go in. I'll see to it.

CTESIPHO: If he wants me you haven't seen me, do you hear?

SYRUS: You shut up!

[*He pushes* CTESIPHO *into the house and stands back, by the door.* DEMEA *returns from the town.*]

DEMEA: Just my luck! First I can't find my brother anywhere; then while I'm looking for him I run into one of the farm

1. Literally, 'the wolf in the fable', a popular expression.

hands and he tells me Ctesipho is *not* at the farm. Now I don't know what to do.

CTESIPHO [*putting his head out*]: Syrus!

SYRUS: What?

CTESIPHO: Is it me he wants?

SYRUS: Yes.

CTESIPHO: Then I'm done for.

SYRUS: Bear up.

DEMEA [*still talking to himself*]: Nothing but bad luck . . . what the devil does it mean? I can't make it out. Maybe I'm to believe I was born for nothing but misery. I was the first to guess our troubles, the first to find everything out, the first to give the bad news. Whatever happens, I'm the one who suffers.

SYRUS [*aside*]: He makes me laugh. The first to know! He's the only one who hasn't a clue.

DEMEA: Now I'm back to see if Micio's home again.

CTESIPHO [*peeping out*]: Syrus! For heaven's sake don't let him in here.

SYRUS: Be quiet, can't you? I'll do my best.

CTESIPHO: Yes, I dare say, but I just can't trust you. I'll find a room and lock myself in with her, that'll be safest.

SYRUS: All right. I'll move him on, anyway.

DEMEA: There's that scoundrel Syrus.

SYRUS [*aloud, pretending not to see* DEMEA]: How the devil can anyone carry on here at this rate! I should just like to know how many masters I'm supposed to have. It's a dog's life!

DEMEA: What's all this whining about? What can he want? Now then, my man, is my brother at home?

SYRUS: Why the hell do you call me your man? I'm finished.

DEMEA: What's the matter with you?

SYRUS: Matter? Ctesipho's pretty well pummelled me to death, and that girl too.

DEMEA: What's that you say?

SYRUS: Just you take a look at the way he's split my lip.

DEMEA: Why was that?

SYRUS: He says it was all my doing that the girl was bought.

DEMEA: I thought you said just now that you'd gone with him to the farm.

SYRUS: So I did, but he came back in a towering rage. He spared nothing. Fancy not being ashamed to beat an old man like me! Why it seems only yesterday I held him in my arms and he was only *so* high.

DEMEA: Splendid! You're your father's son, Ctesipho! Why, you're a man at last!

SYRUS: Splendid indeed! If he's any sense he'll keep his fists to himself in future.

DEMEA: Well done!

SYRUS: Oh very, beating up a wretched girl and a poor slave who didn't dare hit back. Oh yes, well done!

DEMEA: Couldn't be better. He sees as I do that you're at the bottom of all this. Now, is my brother at home?

SYRUS [*sulkily*]: No he isn't.

DEMEA: I wonder where I can find him.

SYRUS: I know all right, but I'm certainly not telling you.

DEMEA: You say that?

SYRUS: Yes, I do.

DEMEA: Then I'll knock your head off here and now.

SYRUS: Well, there's a man. . . . I don't know his name, but I know where to find him.

DEMEA: Tell me then.

SYRUS: You know this colonnade near the meat market, down that way?

DEMEA: Of course I do.

SYRUS: Go straight up the street past it. Then there's a turning going downhill; go straight down and you'll see a chapel on this side and next to it that alley –

DEMEA: Which one?

SYRUS: Where there's a big fig-tree.

DEMEA: I know.

SYRUS: Go on through it.

DEMEA [*after some thought*]: That alley hasn't *got* a way through.

SYRUS: So it hasn't. What a fool I am! My mistake. Go back to the colonnade. Yes, this is a much shorter way and less chance of going wrong. Do you know Cratinus's house, that rich fellow's?

DEMEA: Yes.

SYRUS [*rapidly*]: Go past it, turn left, straight up the street, come to the Temple of Diana, then turn right and before you come to the town gate just by the pond there's a small flour mill and a workshop opposite. . . . That's where he is.

DEMEA [*suspiciously*]: What's he doing there?

SYRUS [*airily*]: Oh, giving orders for some seats . . . for sitting in the sun . . . to be made with oak legs.

DEMEA: For one of your drinking-parties I suppose. Very nice too! I'll be off. [*He goes off to the town, right.*]

SYRUS: That's right, go; and today I've given you the marching orders you deserve, old drybones. Well, Aeschinus is horribly late, lunch is spoiling, and Ctesipho – all *he* wants is love. That gives me time for myself. I'll go and have a sip of the wine and a pick at all the best bits . . . a nice easy way to spin out a day like this.

[*He goes into the house.* MICIO *and* HEGIO: *ome on right together from the town.*]

MICIO: I really can't see I deserve your praise for this, Hegio. The offence was on our side, and it is no more than my duty to put things right. I know there are men who see a wanton insult in any criticism of their conduct and deliberately turn the attack on their critics, but did you think I was one of them? Are you thanking me for being different?

HEGIO: No, no, of course not. I never thought you other than you are, Micio. But now please come with me to the girl's mother and tell her in person all you've said to me, that all her suspicions of Aeschinus were on account of his brother and that music-girl.

MICIO: Let us go in then, if we must and you think it's the right thing.

HEGIO: That's good of you. She's wearing herself out with grief and worry, and you can take this weight off her mind. It will be a duty well done. But if you prefer, I can tell her what you've said to me.

MICIO: No, I'll go.

HEGIO: It really is good of you. People who are not so lucky in life somehow always tend to be a bit suspicious and ready to take offence at everything; I suppose their poverty makes them feel inadequate. If you can explain to her yourself she'll take it better.

MICIO: True: how right you are.

HEGIO: Come in with me then.

MICIO: Certainly.

[*They go into* SOSTRATA's *house; there is a short pause, then* AESCHINUS *hurries on right and paces about distractedly*.]

AESCHINUS: This is sheer torture! I never thought to receive such a cruel blow. I just can't think what I'm to do with myself or what to do at all. I'm numb with terror, dazed with fear, robbed of reasoning power! How can I find a way out of this confusion? This awful suspicion – it all

seemed so natural! Sostrata is convinced I bought this girl
for myself – so I discovered from the old woman when I
caught sight of her on her way to fetch the midwife; I ran
up and asked her how Pamphila was, whether labour had
started and the midwife had been sent for. 'Get out!' was
all she said. 'Clear off, Aeschinus, we've had enough of your
lying words and your broken promises!' 'What on earth do
you mean by that?' I said. 'Good-bye, you can keep the girl
you've chosen.' I guessed at once what they suspected, but
held my tongue – one word about my brother to that old
gossip and all would be out.

Now what can I do? Say the girl is my brother's? But this
mustn't get abroad at all costs. I can't let it out if it's still
possible to keep the secret. . . . Besides, I doubt if they would
believe me: it all hangs together and sounds likely enough.
It was I who carried off the girl and I who paid the money,
and our house she was brought to. This at least was all my
doing, I admit. If only I'd told it all to my father however
I'd managed it! I could have persuaded him to let me marry
Pamphila. . . . [*After a pause*] Here I am, still putting things
off! Now's the time, Aeschinus, to pull yourself together!
And first of all I'll go to the women and clear myself. [*He
moves towards* SOSTRATA's *house.*] Here's the door. . . . No,
I can't face it. . . . I'm a poor thing, I can never raise a hand
to this door without a shudder. . . . [*He makes a tremendous
effort and knocks loudly*] Anyone there? It's Aeschinus. Open
the door, somebody, at once! Someone's coming out; I'll
stay over here.

[MICIO *comes out of* SOSTRATA's *house speaking back to
her.*]

MICIO: Do as I say, Sostrata, both of you, while I find
Aeschinus and tell him our arrangements. [*Coming forward*]
Someone knocked – who was it?

AESCHINUS [*aside*]: Heavens, it's my father; I'm done for!

MICIO: Aeschinus!

AESCHINUS [*aside*]: What can he want?

MICIO: Was it you who knocked? [*Aside*] No reply; I think I must tease him a bit – he deserves it for never wanting to trust me over this. [*Aloud*] Can't you answer me?

AESCHINUS [*in confusion*]: I didn't knock – at least I don't think I did.

MICIO: No? I was just wondering what you were doing here. [*Aside*] He's blushing: all's well.

AESCHINUS: Excuse me, father, but what took you there? [*pointing to* SOSTRATA's *house*].

MICIO: No business of mine. A friend brought me here just now – to act as a witness.

AESCHINUS: Witness for what?

MICIO [*watching him closely*]: I'll tell you. There are some women living here, in a poor way. I don't think you know them, in fact I am sure you can't, for they have not been here long.

AESCHINUS: Well, what then?

MICIO: There is a girl with her mother –

AESCHINUS: Go on –

MICIO: The girl has lost her father, and this friend of mine is her next-of-kin; so he must marry her. That's the law [1]

AESCHINUS [*aside*]: No – I can't bear it.

MICIO: What was that?

AESCHINUS: Nothing: it's all right: go on.

MICIO: He has come to take her away to Miletus – where he lives.

AESCHINUS: What, to take the girl away with him?

MICIO: That's right.

1. The provision of Attic law which is the basis of the plot in *Phormio*, set out there in ll. 125 ff.

AESCHINUS: All the way to Miletus did you say?

MICIO: I did.

AESCHINUS [aside]: Oh my head reels! [Aloud] But the women – what do they say?

MICIO: What do you expect? Nothing, in fact. The mother has a trumped-up story about the girl having a baby by another man, whom she won't name. He came first, she says, so the girl ought not to be married to my friend.

AESCHINUS: Then don't you think that's right?

MICIO: No, I don't.

AESCHINUS: You don't? And will he really take her away, father?

MICIO: Why on earth shouldn't he?

AESCHINUS [in a passionate outburst]: It was cruel of you both, it was heartless, and if I must speak plainly, father, it was – it was – downright dishonourable!

MICIO: But why?

AESCHINUS: You ask me why? What about the unhappy man who first loved her and for all I know, poor wretch, still loves her desperately? What do you suppose he will feel when he sees her torn from his arms and carried off before his very eyes? I tell you, father, it's a sin and a scandal!

MICIO: How do you make that out? Who promised this girl in marriage and who gave her away? Who was the bridegroom and when was the wedding? Who witnessed it? She was meant for another – why did this man take her?

AESCHINUS: Then was this girl to sit at home, at her age, waiting for a relative to turn up from heaven knows where? You could have said that, father, and stuck to it.

MICIO: Nonsense! I had come to help a friend; was I to turn against him? In any case, Aeschinus, the girl is no concern of ours. Why should we bother about them? Let us go. . . . But what's the matter? Why are you crying?

AESCHINUS: Father, please listen. . . .

MICIO [*gently*]: My son, I have heard the whole story; I understand, for I love you, so all you do touches my heart.

AESCHINUS: Then I'll try to deserve your love in future all your life, father – I feel so guilty and ashamed of what I've done that I can't look you in the face.

MICIO: I believe you; I know you are honourable at heart. But I worry about you and your heedless ways. What sort of a country do you think you live in? You seduced a girl you should never have touched. That was your first fault, and quite bad enough, though no more than human: honest men have done the same before you. But afterwards, tell me, did you give it a thought? Or did you look ahead at all and think what you should do and how to do it? If you were ashamed to confess to me yourself, how was I to find out? You delayed and did nothing while nine months went by. This was the greatest wrong you could do, to yourself, to that poor girl, and the child. Well: did you think you could leave everything to the gods and go on dreaming? And that she would be brought to you as a bride without your lifting a finger? I trust you are not so thoughtless in all your personal affairs. [*Changing his tone, after a pause*] Cheer up, you shall marry her.

AESCHINUS: What?

MICIO: I said, Cheer up.

AESCHINUS: Father, for pity's sake, are you making fun of me now?

MICIO: No, I'm not. Why should I?

AESCHINUS: I don't know, except that I'm so desperately anxious for this to be true that I'm afraid it isn't.

MICIO: Go indoors, and pray the gods to help you bring home your wife. Off with you.

AESCHINUS: What? My wife? Will it be soon?

MICIO: Yes.

AESCHINUS: How soon?

MICIO: As soon as possible.

AESCHINUS [*hugging him*]: Damn me, father, if I don't love you more than my own eyes!

MICIO [*gently disengaging himself*]: What, more than – her?

AESCHINUS: Well, just as much.

MICIO [*ironically*]: Very kind of you.

AESCHINUS [*suddenly remembering*]: But where's that man from Miletus?

MICIO [*airily*]: Lost, gone, on board his ship. . . . *Now* what's stopping you?

AESCHINUS: Father, you go, you pray to the gods. They'll be more likely to listen to you, I know; you're so much better than I.

MICIO: I *am* going in: there are preparations to be made. You be sensible and do what I say. [*He goes into* MICIO's *house.*]

AESCHINUS [*coming forward*]: What do you think of that? Is this what it means to be a father or a son? A brother or a friend couldn't do more for me. Oh, he's a man to love and cherish in one's heart! Wonderful! If he can be so kind I'll be sure never to be foolish again or do anything he doesn't like. This lesson will be a warning. But I must hurry indoors or I shall delay my own wedding!

[*He goes into* MICIO's *house, and almost at once* DEMEA *comes on wearily, back from his search.*]

DEMEA: I've walked and walked till I'm worn out. Curse you, Syrus, and your directions! I trailed all over the town, to the gate and the pool and everywhere, and found no sign of a workshop at all nor a soul who said he'd seen my brother. Well, my mind is made up: I'm sitting down here outside his house to wait till he comes back.

[MICIO *comes out of his house talking to* AESCHINUS *inside.*]

MICIO: I'll go across and tell them we are all ready now.

DEMEA: Here he is. I've been looking for you for hours, Micio.

MICIO: What for?

DEMEA: I've more news for you: more wicked deeds of that good young man of yours.

MICIO: What, again!

DEMEA: Unheard-of crimes, appalling ones!

MICIO [*impatiently*]: That'll do.

DEMEA: You've no idea of what he is –

MICIO: Yes I have.

DEMEA [*in a fury*]: You fool, you imagine I'm talking about that music-girl: this time it's an honest girl who is Athenian born.

MICIO [*quietly*]: I know.

DEMEA: You *know*? And you allow it?

MICIO: Why shouldn't I?

DEMEA: How can you be so calm? Aren't you furious?

MICIO: No. It's true I should prefer –

DEMEA: And now there's a child.

MICIO [*sincerely*]: Heaven bless it!

DEMEA: The girl has nothing –

MICIO: So I heard.

DEMEA: She'll have to be married without a dowry –

MICIO: Evidently.

DEMEA: What's to be done now?

MICIO: What the situation requires. She shall be moved from that house to this [*pointing to* SOSTRATA'*s house and his own*].

DEMEA: Good God! Is that the proper thing to do?

MICIO: What more *can* I do?

DEMEA: What indeed! If you really have no feelings about all this, it would surely be only human to *pretend* you have.

MICIO: But I've arranged for him to marry the girl; every-thing is settled and the wedding is on the way; I've removed all their fears; that is what seems to me only human.

DEMEA [*thoughtfully, after a pause*]: But are you really pleased, Micio, with what you've done?

MICIO: If I could alter the situation – no. But as things are, I can't; so I must accept it quietly. Life is like a game of dice; if you don't get the throw you need most, you must use skill to make the best of what turns up.

DEMEA [*furious again*]: Make the best indeed! And this skill of yours has thrown away two thousand drachmas on that music-girl! Now she'll have to be sold for what she'll fetch, or given away if no one makes an offer.

MICIO: No; I have no intention of selling her.

DEMEA: Then what *do* you propose to do?

MICIO: She shall stay with us.

DEMEA: Heavens above, is he going to keep a mistress in the same house as his wife?

MICIO: Why not?

DEMEA: Are you really in your right mind?

MICIO: *I* think so.

DEMEA [*with heavy sarcasm*]: God help me, all this tomfoolery makes me wonder if your idea is to have this girl to partner your own singing.

MICIO: Perhaps it is.

DEMEA: And the new bride to join in!

MICIO: Of course.

DEMEA: The three of you dancing hand-in-hand –

MICIO: Certainly.

DEMEA: Certainly?

MICIO [*seizing him by the hand*]: With you to make a fourth if we want one!

DEMEA [*shaking himself free with a cry of disgust*]: Have you no sense of shame?[1]

MICIO [*suddenly serious*]: Now then, Demea, that's enough of your ill-temper. Your son is to be married; can't you behave properly? Try to be pleased and look happy. I'm going to call them; then I'll be back. [*He goes into* SOSTRATA's *house.*]

DEMEA: Ye gods, what a life! what morals! what madness! Here's a bride coming without a penny, and a girl in the house! Too much money in the home, a young man ruined by indulgence, and the old one off his head! Salvation herself might intervene, but this household's beyond saving!

[SYRUS *staggers out of* MICIO's *house, drunk and self-satisfied. He does not see* DEMEA.]

SYRUS: Well, Syrus my lad, you've done yourself proud! Done your duty handsome-ly. [*Hiccups*] That's better. I've had all I can take *inside*, so I just took a fancy to stretch my legs out here. . . .

DEMEA: Now look at that! A fine example of discipline in the home!

SYRUS [*lurching towards him*]: Why, here's our old man! How do? Feeling glum?

DEMEA: Scoundrel!

SYRUS: Now, now; you spouting here now, Father Wisdom?

DEMEA: If you were in my service –

SYRUS: You'd be a rich man to be sure! You'd have a fortune on a *firm* footing – [*staggers*].

DEMEA: – I would make an example of you to all.

SYRUS: Why? What have *I* done?

1. Demea's sense of outrage at the head of a household dancing and singing can hardly have been in the original, as it shows Roman, not Greek prejudice.

DEMEA: Done? Here's all this trouble and dreadful wrong-doing, and nothing properly settled yet, and all you can do is drink, you wretch, as if there was something to celebrate.

SYRUS [*somewhat dashed*]: Sorry now I came out. . . .

[DROMO *opens the door of* MICIO's *house to call* SYRUS.]

DROMO: Hey, Syrus, Ctesipho wants you.

SYRUS [*sufficiently sobered to act promptly, pushes him in again*]: Go away!

DEMEA: What's he saying about Ctesipho?

SYRUS: Nothing.

DEMEA: You brute, is Ctesipho in there?

SYRUS: No, he isn't.

DEMEA: Then why did I hear his name?

SYRUS: It's someone else, a pretty little bit of a boy who hangs around here. [*Nudging him*] Know him?

DEMEA [*grimly, as he strides towards the door*]: I shall soon find out.

SYRUS [*catching at him*]: What's this? Where are you going?

DEMEA: Let me go!

SYRUS: You're not going in there!

DEMEA: Keep your hands off me, you rascal, unless you want me to knock your brains out! [*He dashes into* MICIO's *house.*]

SYRUS: He's gone . . . and a damned unwelcome visitor he'll be, especially to Ctesipho. Now what shall *I* do? Best wait for all this to-do to settle down and find a quiet corner to sleep off this drop I've taken. That's the idea.

[*He staggers off right. Soon afterwards* MICIO *comes out of* SOSTRATA's *house.*]

MICIO: Everything's ready on our side, as I said, Sostrata. When you want. . . . Whoever is that hammering on my door?

[DEMEA *bursts out.*]

DEMEA: Good God, what can I do? How can I deal with this?

Shame and sorrow, what can I say? Heaven and earth, Neptune's ocean!

MICIO: Just look at that; no wonder he's shouting, he's found it all out. We're done for, the battle's on, and I'll have to go to the rescue.

DEMEA: Here he comes! You corrupter of both our sons!

MICIO: Kindly control your temper. Calm yourself, Demea.

DEMEA: I *am* controlled, I *am* calm. I won't say another word. Let's face facts. Wasn't it agreed between us (and it was your suggestion, Micio) that you'd not worry about my boy and I'd not worry about yours? Answer me that.

MICIO: It was, I don't deny it.

DEMEA: Then why is my boy drinking in your house? Why receive him there? Why buy him a mistress? Haven't I a right to expect fair play, Micio? What do you want from me? I'm not worrying about your boy, so you leave mine alone.

MICIO: Now you're not being fair —

DEMEA: What!

MICIO: There's an old proverb that friends have everything in common.

DEMEA: Witty, aren't you. Isn't it rather late in the day for that sort of talk?

MICIO: Just listen to me a minute, Demea, if you've no objection. First of all, if it's the money the boys spend which is bothering you, please try to look at it this way. At one time you were supporting both your sons according to your means, because you thought you would have enough for two, and I suppose at the time you expected me to marry. Very well, keep to your original plan; hoard, scrape, and save to have as much as possible to leave them. You can see merit in that: all right. My money is something they didn't expect, so let them enjoy it. Your capital won't be touched, and anything I add can be counted as pure gain. If only you would be willing to see this in a true light, Demea, you'd save yourself and me and the boys a great deal of trouble.

DEMEA: I'm not talking about money. It's their morals, both of them –

MICIO: Wait. I know, I was coming to that. There are a lot of traits in people from which inferences can be drawn. Two men often do the same thing and you might say that one can safely be allowed to do it while the other might not. The difference is not in the thing done but in the doer. I can see signs in these boys which make me confident they will turn out as we want them. I see good sense, intelligence, deference when required, and mutual affection, and we can be sure they are open and generous in heart and mind. You can call them back to the right path any day you like. You may say you are anxious for them not to be so careless about money, but, my dear Demea, you must realize that in every other respect we grow wiser with increasing years, but the besetting fault of old age is simply this: we all think too much of money. Time will develop this in them well enough.

DEMEA: Be careful, Micio: these fine-sounding arguments and easy-going temperament of yours may destroy us all.

MICIO: No, no, impossible. Come along now, try to listen to me and stop frowning.

DEMEA: As things are I suppose I'll have to. . . . But tomorrow morning at crack of dawn I'm taking my boy away from here to the farm.

MICIO [*humouring him*]: *Before* dawn, I dare say. Only make yourself agreeable for today.

DEMEA: And I'm taking that girl too.

MICIO: That'll do the trick! The best way of tying him down. Only mind you keep her there.

DEMEA: I'll see to that. Once she's there I'll have her cooking and grinding corn till she's covered with ash and grime and flour, and then I'll send her out gleaning in the midday sun and make her black and burnt as a cinder!

MICIO [*ironically*]: Good! Now I find you talking sense. Go on: 'And then I'll force my son whatever he says to sleep with her –'

DEMEA: All right, laugh at me. You're lucky to be in the mood. I have my feelings. . . .

MICIO: Now don't start again –

DEMEA: No, I've done.

MICIO: Come in then, and spend this day with us in the proper way.

[*They go into* MICIO's *house. After a short interval* DEMEA *reappears, much smartened up and perhaps wearing some of* MICIO's *clothes.*]

DEMEA: A plan for life may be well worked out, but a man can still learn something new from circumstances, age and experience. You find you don't know what you thought you did, and things which seemed so important before, you reject in practice. This is what has just happened to me, for I've lived a hard life up to this very moment, and now I'm giving up when my course is almost run. And why? Hard facts have shown me that a man gains most from affability and forbearance. Look at my brother and me if you want to see the truth of this. He has always led a life of leisure, sociable, easy-going, and tolerant, with never a black look for anyone and a smile for all. He's lived for himself and spent on himself, and he's won praise and affection from everyone. I'm the country bumpkin, mannerless and surly, truculent, mean and close-fisted, and when I took a wife what troubles I brought on myself! Two sons were born – more worry. While thinking of them and struggling to make all I could for them, see how I've wasted my youth and my life in money-grubbing! Now I'm old, and what's my reward for all my trouble? They don't like me. It's my brother who enjoys the benefits of fatherhood without having lifted a finger. They love him and avoid me. He has their confidence and their affection, the two of them are always with him and I'm left all alone. They offer prayers for his long life, but you may be sure they're counting the days for me to die. I've toiled and slaved to bring them up, but he has made them his own for next to nothing, so he has all the enjoyment while the trouble's left to me. Very well then, two can play at that game; let's see now whether I can take up his challenge and show myself capable of soft answers and winning ways! *I* could also do with a bit of love and appreciation from my own children. If that comes from being generous and agreeable, I can take the lead all right. The property won't stand it, but that needn't worry me – I'm old enough for it to last *my* time.

[SYRUS *comes out of* MICIO's *house.*]

SYRUS: Please, sir, your brother hopes you're not leaving us.

DEMEA [*genially*]: Who's that? Ah, Syrus, my man, good evening. How are you and how are things going?

SYRUS: All right, sir.

DEMEA: Splendid. [*Aside*] That's three things already which aren't like me, 'my man', 'how are you', and 'how are things going'. [*Aloud*] You may be a slave, but you have your finer points, and I should be glad to do you a good turn.

SYRUS [*incredulous*]: Thank you, sir.

DEMEA: But I mean it, Syrus, as you'll soon see.

[SYRUS *goes back into the house and* GETA *comes out of* SOSTRATA's.]

GETA [*to* SOSTRATA]: I'm just going next door, madam, to see how soon they want the bride. Why, here's Demea. Good evening, sir.

DEMEA: Let me see now, what's your name?

GETA: Geta, sir.

DEMEA: Geta, today has convinced me that you are a most valuable person. Nothing recommends a slave to me so much as his care for his master's interests, such as I have seen in you. For this, if the opportunity arises, I should be glad to do you a good turn. [*Aside*] I think my affability improves with practice.

GETA [*puzzled*]: It's kind of you to think so, sir.

DEMEA [*aside*]: I've made a start, winning over the masses one by one.

[AESCHINUS *and* SYRUS *come out of* MICIO's.]

AESCHINUS: They're killing me with all their fuss over wedding ceremonies! Here's a whole day wasted with preparations.

DEMEA: What's the matter, Aeschinus?

AESCHINUS: Hullo, father, are you there?

DEMEA: Father, yes, in heart and nature, your father who loves you more than his own eyes. But why don't you bring your wife home?

AESCHINUS: That's just what I *want* to do. I'm kept waiting for the flute-player and the choir for the marriage-hymn.

DEMEA: Will you take a word of advice from your old father?

AESCHINUS: What is it?

DEMEA: Scrap the lot – flutes, torches, hymn, and fuss – knock a hole in the garden wall here and now and take her across that way, join the two houses and bring the whole lot of them, mother and all, over to us!

AESCHINUS [*hugging him*]: Father darling, you're splendid!

DEMEA [*aside*]: Bravo, now I'm splendid! Micio'll have to keep open house, with all these people to entertain and no end of expense, but what do I care? I'm splendid and popular! Tell that Croesus[1] to pay out two thousand on the spot! Syrus, what are you waiting for?

SYRUS: What am I to do, sir?

DEMEA: Knock down the wall. Geta, you go and fetch them.

GETA: Heaven bless you, sir, for being so kindly disposed to us all.

DEMEA: It's no more than you deserve. [GETA *and* SYRUS *go in.*] What do you say?

AESCHINUS [*somewhat bewildered*]: I agree.

DEMEA: She's not well yet after having the baby – much better bring her that way than through the street. [*Banging and hammering are heard.*]

AESCHINUS: Nothing could be better, father.

DEMEA [*smugly*]: Ah, it's just my way. . . . But look, here's Micio.

[MICIO *bursts out of his house.*]

MICIO: My brother's orders? Where is he? *Are* these your orders, Demea?

DEMEA [*impressively*]: They are. In this and every other way we should unite with this family to cherish and support it and make it one with ours.

AESCHINUS: Yes, please, father.

MICIO [*reluctantly*]: I suppose I have to agree.

DEMEA: Believe me, it's our duty. And now, to start with, this boy's wife has a mother.

MICIO: I know; what of it?

DEMEA: She is virtuous and discreet.

1. 'Croesus' as a symbol of wealth instead of *Babylo*, only found here; but Donatus implies that a Babylonian was proverbial for extravagance.

MICIO: So I'm told.

DEMEA: Not too young –

MICIO: I know.

DEMEA: But long since past the age to have children, and with no one to look after her. She's alone. . . .

MICIO: What's the point of all this?

DEMEA: The proper thing for you to do is to marry her. Aeschinus, you persuade him.

MICIO: *I* marry?

DEMEA: You.

MICIO: Did you say *I* should marry her?

DEMEA: I did.

MICIO: You're joking.

DEMEA [*to* AESCHINUS]: Talk to him as man to man and he'll do it.

AESCHINUS: Father –

MICIO: You silly ass, must you listen to him?

DEMEA: It's no good, Micio, you'll have to give in.

MICIO: You're crazy.

AESCHINUS: Do it for my sake, father.

MICIO: You're mad, leave me alone.

DEMEA: Come, do as your son asks.

MICIO: You're off your head. I'm sixty-four: should I embark on matrimony at my age with this decrepit old hag for a wife? Is that your idea?

AESCHINUS: Come on: I've promised them.

MICIO: *Promised* them? Kindly restrict your generosity to your own person, my boy.

DEMEA: But he might be asking more of you. . . .

MICIO: There couldn't be anything more.

DEMEA: Do it for him –

AESCHINUS: Don't be difficult –

DEMEA: Come, promise.

MICIO: Leave me alone, can't you!

AESCHINUS: Not until you'll give in.

MICIO: It's sheer coercion!

DEMEA: Now be generous, Micio.

MICIO: This is monstrous, crazy, ludicrous, entirely foreign to my whole way of life . . . but if you are both so set on it . . . all right.[1]

AESCHINUS: Well done! You deserve all my love now.

DEMEA: But – [aside] What else can I say now I've won that point?

MICIO: Now what is it?

DEMEA: There's Hegio, their closest relative, who'll be a connection of ours. He's a poor man, and we ought to do something for him.

MICIO: Well, what?

DEMEA: There's that little bit of property just outside the town which you're always letting out. We can give it to him and he'll make good use of it.

MICIO: Do you call that a 'little bit'?

DEMEA: Big or little, it's what we must do. He has been a father to the girl, he's a good man and one of us, so he ought to have it. After all, I'm only appropriating the sentiment you expressed just now, Micio: 'the besetting fault of us all is that in old age we think too much of money'.[2] Wise words and well put! We must rid ourselves of this defect, and put the truth in this saying into practice.

MICIO [drily]: I'm glad to hear it. Very well. Hegio shall have it when Aeschinus likes.

AESCHINUS: Oh, father!

1. Donatus comments that in Menander's play Micio did not object to the marriage, so this scene is Terence's innovation.

2. In ll. 833–4.

DEMEA: Now you are my true brother, body and soul! [*Aside*] And I've got his own knife at his throat!

[SYRUS *comes out of the house, dusting himself down.*]

SYRUS: Your orders have been carried out, sir.

DEMEA: Good man. And now I should like to propose that this very day Syrus ought to receive his freedom.

MICIO: His freedom? *Him*? Whatever for?

DEMEA: For lots of reasons.

SYRUS [*eagerly*]: Oh, master, you're a fine gentleman, sir, indeed you are. I've looked after both the young masters properly since they were boys, taught them, guided them, always given them the best advice I could. . . .

DEMEA [*drily*]: So I see. And there are other things besides – reliable shopping, procuring a girl, putting on a dinner-party at all hours. It needs no ordinary man to perform services like *these*.

SYRUS: Sir, you're really splendid!

DEMEA: To crown all, it was he who helped us to buy the music-girl; in fact, he arranged it all. He ought to get something for it, and it will have a good effect on the others. . . . And then, Aeschinus wants it.

MICIO: Do you, Aeschinus?

AESCHINUS: Yes, very much.

MICIO: Well, if you really want it – Syrus, come here. [*With a blow*] Take your freedom.

SYRUS [*rubbing himself ruefully*]: You're very kind. I'm grateful to you all, especially you, sir [*to* DEMEA].

DEMEA: My congratulations.

AESCHINUS: And mine.

SYRUS: Thank you. Now there's just one thing to complete my happiness. . . . If only I could see my wife, Phrygia, freed as well!

DEMEA: A very fine woman.

SYRUS: And she was the first, sir, to come forward as wet-nurse for your grandson, the young master's son, this very day –

DEMEA: Ah, that's a serious reason. If she was the first, she certainly ought to have her freedom.

MICIO: Just for that?

DEMEA: Why not? I'll pay you her value to settle it.

SYRUS: Oh, sir, heaven always grant you all your wishes!

MICIO: Well, Syrus, you've done pretty well for yourself to-day.

DEMEA: He has, if you'll carry on with your duty and give him a little something in hand to live on. He'll soon pay you back.

MICIO [snapping his fingers]: That's more than he'll get.

DEMEA: He's a good fellow.

SYRUS: I'll pay it back, sir, I promise you, just give me –

AESCHINUS: Come on, father.

MICIO: I'll think about it.

DEMEA [to AESCHINUS]: He'll do it.

SYRUS: You're wonderful, sir!

AESCHINUS: Father, you're a darling!

MICIO: What *is* all this? Why this sudden change of heart? What's the idea? Why this sudden outburst of generosity?

DEMEA: I'll tell you. I wanted to show you, Micio, that what our boys thought was your good nature and charm didn't come from a way of living which was sincere or from anything right or good, but from your weakness, indulgence and extravagance. Now, Aeschinus, if you and your brother dislike my ways because I won't humour you in all your wishes, right or wrong, I wash my hands of you – you can spend and squander and do whatever you like. On the other hand, being young, you are short-sighted, over-eager and heedless, and you may like a word of advice or reproof from me on occasion, as well as my support at the proper time. Well, I'm here at your service.

AESCHINUS: We'd like that, father. You know best what to do. But what's going to happen to Ctesipho?

DEMEA: I've given my consent; he can keep his girl. But she must be his last.

MICIO: Well done, Demea. [*To the audience*] Now give us your applause!

[*They all go into* MICIO's *house.*]

APPENDIX A
SUETONIUS: ON THE POETS
'The Life of Terence'

PUBLIUS TERENTIUS AFER was born at Carthage and was the slave in Rome of the senator Terentius Lucanus,[1] by whom, on account of his intelligence and good looks, he was given not only a liberal education but soon afterwards his freedom. Some people believe he was a prisoner of war, but Fenestella[2] shows this was quite impossible, since the dates of his birth and death both fall between the end of the Second Punic War and the beginning of the Third. Again, had he been captured by the Numidians or Gaetulians, he could not have come into the possession of a Roman master, as there was no trade between Italy and Africa until after the destruction of Carthage. He lived on intimate terms with many of the nobility, in particular with Scipio Africanus and Gaius Laelius, who, it is thought, were even attracted by his personal beauty; but Fenestella disproves this too, arguing that Terence was older than either of them. Nepos,[3] on the other hand, writes that they were all much the same age, and Porcius[4] rouses suspicion about their relationship in these words:

While he courted the wanton nobility and their feigned admiration, drank in the godlike voice of Africanus with greedy ears, thought it fine to dine out regularly with Philus and Laelius and was often carried off to their Alban property on account of his youthful

1. Not otherwise known.
2. The antiquarian and historian of Rome: ?52 B.C.–?A.D. 19.
3. Cornelius Nepos, the biographer: c. 99–24 B.C.
4. Porcius Licinus, a poet of the later second century B.C.; this attack on Terence is practically all that survives of his literary history of Rome.

charms, later on he was stripped of his possessions and reduced to utter poverty. So he fled from men's sight to a remote part of Greece, and died at Stymphalus, a town in Arcadia. Thus he gained nothing from Scipio, nothing from Laelius and Furius, the three noblemen who were most comfortably off at the time. They did not help him even with a rented house which could at least have been a place for a slave to announce his master's death.

He wrote six comedies. When he offered the aediles the first of these, *The Girl from Andros*, he was told he should first read it aloud to Caecilius.[1] He arrived when Caecilius was at dinner, and because he was shabbily dressed it is said he read the opening lines sitting on a stool by Caecilius's couch. But after a few lines he was invited to take a place at table, and when the meal was over he read the rest of the play, which won Caecilius's warm admiration. Indeed, this and his five other plays were equally pleasing to the people, though Volcacius[2] in listing them has said that 'The sixth, *The Mother-in-Law*, will not be included.' *The Eunuch* was actually staged twice in a day, and won 8,000 sesterces, the highest fee ever paid for a comedy. The sum is accordingly recorded on the title-page.

. . . .[3] for Varro[4] even preferred the beginning of *The Brothers* to the original opening by Menander. It is popularly believed that Terence was helped in his writings by Laelius and

1. Caecilius Statius, Rome's chief comic dramatist after Plautus. Cf. *The Mother-in-Law*. If he died in 168 B.C. as St Jerome says, and *Andria* was first performed in 166, we have to suppose an interval between this interview and the play's production, if the story is to be believed.

2. Volcacius Sedigitus, who lived around 100 B.C., wrote in verse on the 'Ten Best Writers of Comedy'. Caecilius heads the list, Plautus comes second, Terence sixth and Ennius last. See Aulus Gellius, 15.24.

3. The gap in the MSS. here may have included comments on Terence's use of Greek sources.

4. M. Terentius Varro (116–27 B.C.), the librarian and polymath. This probably refers to Terence's introduction of dialogue for monologue.

Scipio, a rumour which he helped to spread himself by never attempting to rebut it except in a half-hearted way, as in the prologue to *The Brothers*:

As to the spiteful accusation that eminent persons assist the author and collaborate closely with him: his accusers may think it a grave imputation, but he takes it as a high compliment if he can win the approval of men who themselves find favour with you all and with the general public, men whose services in war, in peace and in your private affairs are given at the right moment, without ostentation, to be available for each one of you.[1]

He seems to have been half-hearted about defending himself because he knew the rumour pleased Laelius and Scipio; anyway, it gained ground and persisted down to later times. In a speech for his own defence Gaius Memmius[2] says that 'Scipio borrowed a character from Terence and put on the stage in his name what he had amused himself with at home'; and Nepos relates how he heard on good authority that while Laelius was staying in his villa at Puteoli he was asked by his wife to be a little more punctual at dinner one first of March. He begged her not to interrupt him, and finally came late into the dining-room remarking that he had seldom been so pleased with his writing. When asked to produce what he had written, he quoted the lines from *The Self-Tormentor* starting 'Damn Syrus for his impudence, bringing me here with his promises.'[3]

Santra[4] takes the view that if Terence had really needed help with his writing, he would have been unlikely to make

1. ll. 15–21.
2. Praetor in 58 B.C., patron of Catullus and Lucretius. The speech is probably one delivered in 54/3 when he was on trial for electoral corruption.
3. l. 723.
4. A grammarian and literary historian of the later Republic.

use of Scipio and Laelius, who were very young at the time, but of Gaius Sulpicius Gallus, a man of learning at whose consular games Terence had produced his first play,[1] or of Quintus Fabius Labeo and Marcus Popilius,[2] both poets and men of consular rank; and that is why Terence does not refer to those said to have helped him as *young* men, but as 'men whose services in war, in peace and in private affairs' are available to the people.

He was not yet twenty-five[3] when he left Rome after bringing out his comedies, either for pleasure or to get away from the rumour that he was passing off other people's work as his own, or to study the institutions and customs of the Greeks which he felt he had not always represented accurately in his plays. He never returned. Volcacius gives this account of his death:

But when Terence had brought out six comedies he went on a journey to Asia; and from the time he embarked on shipboard he was never seen again. So his life ended.

Quintus Cosconius[4] says that he died at sea on the return voyage from Greece bringing new adaptations of Menander, while the other authorities declare that he died at Stymphalus in Arcadia or on the island of Leucadia, in the consulship of Gnaeus Cornelius Dolabella and Marcus Fulvius Nobilior,[5] after an illness brought on by grief and annoyance at the loss of his luggage which he had sent on by sea, and with it the new plays he had written.

He is described as being of average height, slight build and

1. See the Production Notice to *Andria*.
2. Consuls in 183 and 173, not known to have literary interests.
3. i.e. in 160 B.C..
4. A grammarian and writer on law of the first century A.D.
5. In 156 B.C.

dark complexion. He left a daughter, who subsequently married a Roman knight, and gardens of twenty *jugera* near the Villa of Mars. This makes me all the more surprised that Porcius writes that 'he gained nothing from Scipio, nothing from Laelius and Furius, the three noblemen who were most comfortably off at the time. They did not help him even with a rented house which could at least have been a place for a slave to announce his master's death.' Afranius,[1] in his *Compitalia*, rates him above all other writers of comedy ('As for Terence, you will not find his like'), but Volcacius puts him lower not only than Naevius, Plautus and Caecilius, but even than Licinius and Atilius.

Cicero pays him this tribute in his *Limo*:[2]

You too, Terence, who alone had command of words to put Menander in our midst, translated and set out in the Latin tongue, in your quiet tone; whose speech can charm, whose every word delights

Caesar also says:

You too will take your place on the heights, O half-sized Menander, and rightly, as a lover of natural speech. If only your even measures had been endowed with vigour, so that your gift for comedy could be valued as highly as the Greeks', and you were not despised and neglected on this account! Here is my only deep sorrow, Terence, my grief for what you lacked.

POSTSCRIPT BY AELIUS DONATUS

This is the account by Suetonius Tranquillus. Maecius[3] writes that there were in fact two poets called Terence, Terentius

1. Lucius Afranius, born about 150 B.C., was a prolific composer of the *fabulae togatae* portraying Italian domestic life.
2. i.e. *The Meadow*, a miscellany otherwise unknown.
3. Possibly Sp. Maecius Tarpa, the official licenser of plays, mentioned by Horace in *Satires* 1.10.38. Terentius Libo is virtually unknown.

Libo of Fregellae and the freedman Terence, born an African, to whom we now refer. Vagellius[1] argues in a speech that Scipio was the author of the plays produced by Terence:

The plays which are called yours, Terence, whose are they really? Wasn't it our great lawgiver and highly honoured citizen who wrote them?

Two of the plays are said to have been translated from the comedies of Apollodorus (*Phormio* and *The Mother-in-Law*), and the remaining four from Menander. Of these, *The Eunuch* had great success and won a high fee, while *The Mother-in-Law* was driven off the stage more than once and proved difficult to produce.

1. If this reading is accepted, the reference is to a Neronian poet and friend of Seneca.

APPENDIX B
THE ORDER AND DATES OF THE PLAYS

1. *Andria* performed at the Megalensian Games   166 B.C.
   Hecyra (a failure) at the Megalensian Games   165 B.C.
   (Possible first performance of *Eunuchus*)   ?
2. *Heauton Timorumenos* at the Megalensian Games   163 B.C.
3. *Eunuchus* (?second performance) at the
   Megalensian Games   161 B.C.
4. *Phormio* performed at the Roman Games   161 B.C.
5. *Hecyra* (second failure) at the Funeral Games for
   L. Aemilius Paullus   160 B.C.
6. *Adelphoe* performed at the Funeral Games for
   L. Aemilius Paullus   160 B.C.
   Hecyra performed successfully at the Roman Games 160 B.C.

SELECT BIBLIOGRAPHY

TEXTS AND EDITIONS

S. G. Ashmore, *The Comedies of Terence*², 1908.

T. F. Carney, ed., *P. Terenti Afri Hecyra*, 1963.

B. Kauer and W. M. Lindsay, with addition by O. Skutsch, *P. Terenti Afri Comoediae* (O.C.T.), 1958.

J. Marouzeau, *Térence, texte établi et traduit* (Budé edition), 1947–9.

R. H. Martin, ed., *Phormio*, 1959.

G. P. Shipp, ed., *Andria*², 1960.

A. Sloman, ed., *Adelphi*², 1891.

A. Thierfelder, ed., *P. Terenti Afri Andria*², 1961.

P. Wessner, ed., *Aeli Donati Commentum Terenti*, 1902–5.

GENERAL

J. T. Allardice, *The Syntax of Terence*, 1929.

W. G. Arnott, 'The End of Terence's Adelphi, a postscript', *Greece & Rome* n.s. 10 (1963), 140–47.

'Phormio Parasitus', *Greece & Rome* n.s. 17 (1970), 32–57.

'The Modernity of Menander', *Greece & Rome* n.s. 22 (1975), 140–55.

Menander, Plautus, Terence (Greece & Rome, New Surveys in the Classics No. 9), 1975.

J. W. H. Atkins, *Literary Criticism in Antiquity*, 1934.

W. Beare, *The Roman Stage*³, 1964.

M. Bieber, *The History of the Greek and Roman Theater*², 1961.

R. R. Bolgar, *The Classical Heritage*, 1954.

Mme A. Dacier, *Les Comédies de Térence* (fourth edition, with notes), 1706.

D. Diderot, *Réflexions sur Térence*, 1762.

T. A. Dorey, 'A Note on the Adelphi of Terence', *Greece & Rome* n.s. 9 (1962), 37–9.

G. E. Duckworth, *The Nature of Roman Comedy*, 1951.

D. C. Earl, 'Terence and Roman Politics', *Historia* 11 (1962), 469–85.

E. Fantham, *Comparative Studies in Republican Latin Imagery*, 1972.

T. Frank, *Life and Literature in the Roman Republic*, 1930.

H. Haffter, *Terenz und seine künstlerische Eigenart*, 1953; translated by D. Nardo (*Terenzio e la sua personalità artistica*), 1969.

E. W. Handley, *The Dyskolos of Menander*, 1965.

G. Highet, *The Classical Tradition*, 1949.

W. A. Laidlaw, *The Prosody of Terence*, 1938.

H. W. Lawton, *Térence en France au xvi*e *siècle*, 1926.

R. Levin, 'The Double Plots of Terence', *Classical Journal* 62 (1967), 301–5.

H. Mattingly, 'The Terentian Didascaliae', *Athenaeum*, n.s. 37 (1959), 148–73.

P. McGlynn, *Lexicon Terentianum*, 1963–7.

G. Meredith, *An Essay on Comedy*, 1877.

D. G. Moore, 'The Young Men in Terence', *Proc. African Class. Ass.* 3 (1960), 20–26.

G. Norwood, *The Art of Terence*, 1923.

The Oxford Classical Dictionary², 1970.

L. R. Palmer, *The Latin Language*, 1954.

M. M. Phillips, *The Adages of Erasmus*, 1964.

L. D. Reynolds and N. G. Wilson, *Scribes and Scholars*², 1974.

C. A. Sainte-Beuve, *Les Nouveaux Lundis*, 3 and 10 August, 1863.

W. Y. Sellar, *Roman Poets of the Republic*, 1889.

P. Vellacott, tr., *Menander and Theophrastus* (Penguin Classics), 1967.

E. F. Watling, tr., Plautus, *The Rope and Other Plays* (Penguin Classics), 1964.

Plautus, *The Pot of Gold and Other Plays* (Penguin Classics), 1965.

T. B. L. Webster, *Studies in Menander*, 1949.

An Introduction to Menander, 1974.

H. Marti gives a Bibliography of all articles on Terence between 1909 and 1959 in *Lustrum*, Vol. 6 (1961) and Vol. 8 (1963). Subsequent articles are listed in *L'Année Philologique*. Chapter IX and its Appendix (pp. 292 ff.) in *Fifty Years (and Twelve) of Classical Scholarship* (ed. M. Platnauer, 1968) are on Roman Drama and discuss recent books on Terence.

FOR THE BEST IN PAPERBACKS, LOOK FOR THE 🐧

In every corner of the world, on every subject under the sun, Penguin represents quality and variety – the very best in publishing today.

For complete information about books available from Penguin – including Pelicans, Puffins, Peregrines and Penguin Classics – and how to order them, write to us at the appropriate address below. Please note that for copyright reasons the selection of books varies from country to country.

In the United Kingdom: For a complete list of books available from Penguin in the U.K., please write to *Dept E.P., Penguin Books Ltd, Harmondsworth, Middlesex, UB7 0DA*

In the United States: For a complete list of books available from Penguin in the U.S., please write to *Dept BA, Penguin, 299 Murray Hill Parkway, East Rutherford, New Jersey 07073*

In Canada: For a complete list of books available from Penguin in Canada, please write to *Penguin Books Canada Ltd, 2801 John Street, Markham, Ontario L3R 1B4*

In Australia: For a complete list of books available from Penguin in Australia, please write to the *Marketing Department, Penguin Books Australia Ltd, P.O. Box 257, Ringwood, Victoria 3134*

In New Zealand: For a complete list of books available from Penguin in New Zealand, please write to the *Marketing Department, Penguin Books (NZ) Ltd, Private Bag, Takapuna, Auckland 9*

In India: For a complete list of books available from Penguin, please write to *Penguin Overseas Ltd, 706 Eros Apartments, 56 Nehru Place, New Delhi, 110019*

In Holland: For a complete list of books available from Penguin in Holland, please write to *Penguin Books Nederland B.V., Postbus 195, NL–1380AD Weesp, Netherlands*

In Germany: For a complete list of books available from Penguin, please write to *Penguin Books Ltd, Friedrichstrasse 10 – 12, D–6000 Frankfurt Main 1, Federal Republic of Germany*

In Spain: For a complete list of books available from Penguin in Spain, please write to *Longman Penguin España, Calle San Nicolas 15, E–28013 Madrid, Spain*

FOR THE BEST IN PAPERBACKS, LOOK FOR THE

PENGUIN CLASSICS

A Passage to India   E. M. Forster

Centred on the unresolved mystery in the Marabar Caves, Forster's great work provides the definitive evocation of the British Raj.

The Republic   Plato

The best-known of Plato's dialogues, *The Republic* is also one of the supreme masterpieces of Western philosophy whose influence cannot be overestimated.

The Life of Johnson   James Boswell

Perhaps the finest 'life' ever written, Boswell's *Johnson* captures for all time one of the most colourful and talented figures in English literary history.

Remembrance of Things Past (3 volumes)   Marcel Proust

This revised version by Terence Kilmartin of C. K. Scott Moncrieff's original translation has been universally acclaimed – available for the first time in paperback.

Metamorphoses   Ovid

A golden treasury of myths and legends which has proved a major influence on Western literature.

A Nietzsche Reader   Friedrich Nietzsche

A superb selection from all the major works of one of the greatest thinkers and writers in world literature, translated into clear, modern English.